Newcastle United 1892-93

Season

ZERO

Record of the 1892-93 season which completed the end of the 'Ends' and the beginning of the 'United'.

Kenneth H Scott

Published by KayLynM Publishing
Newcastle upon Tyne, England

Copyright © 2020 Kenneth H Scott
All rights reserved.

Cover design courtesy of PinkTea Vanity

ISBN: 978-0-9934201-6-0

DEDICATION

This book, *as always*, is dedicated to every Newcastle United fan, whoever and wherever you may be.

Together we have experienced the highs and lows of following our beloved Newcastle United and despite the rollercoaster of emotions that is associated with our allegiance we remain proud members of the Toon Army!

A very special thanks must go to my wife and daughters without whose tolerance and support this book would not have been possible. So, to Lynn (*my wife*), Kayleigh, Lynsey and Megan (*our daughters*) a very special thank you.

Table of Contents

the END of the 'Ends' is our Beginning! 7
    The Death Throes of West End   *Farewell to an old friend*.................................8
    The Northern League   *Decisions, decisions*...9
THE SEASON A QUICK GLANCE **13**
    September   *and so it begins* 15
    October   *celebratory blues*...16
    November   *seven(th) heaven*..16
    December   *end of the "Ends"*..17
    January   *5 days, 3 games, 3 wins* 18
    February   *First Tyne-Wear Derby?*..19
    March   *reflection*...20
    April   *and so it ends* 21
Game by Game **23**
September 1892 ....**25**
    Game 1: Saturday September 3, 1892   Newcastle East End vs. Celtic....................25
    Game 2: Wednesday, September 7, 1892   Newcastle East End vs. Sunderland...............28
    Game 3: Saturday, September 10, 1892   Newcastle East End vs. Middlesbrough Ironopolis 30
    Game 4: Saturday, September 17, 1892   Middlesbrough Ironopolis vs Newcastle East End 32
    Game 5: Saturday, September 24, 1892   Sheffield United vs. Newcastle East End 34
October 1892 ....**37**
    Game 6: Saturday, October 1, 1892   Newcastle East End vs. Middlesbrough..................38
    Game 7: Thursday, October 6, 1892   Stockton vs. Newcastle East End 40
    Game 8: Saturday, October 8, 1892   Middlesbrough vs. Newcastle East End 41
    Game 9: Saturday, October 15, 1892   Newcastle East End vs. South of Ayrshire 43
    Game 10: Saturday, October 22, 1892   Newcastle East End vs. Heart of Midlothian........45
    Game 11: Saturday, October 29, 1892   Newcastle East End vs. Mossend Swifts..............48
November 1892 ....**51**
    Game 12: Saturday, November 5, 1892   Newcastle East End vs. Sheffield United 52
    Game 13: Saturday, November 12, 1892   Newcastle East End vs. Darlington 54
    Game 14: Saturday, November 19, 1892   Middlesbrough Ironopolis vs Newcastle East End 56
    Game 15: Saturday, November 26, 1892   Darlington vs Newcastle East End 58
December 1892 ....**61**
    Game 16: Saturday, December 3, 1892   Newcastle East End vs. Stockton.......................62
    Game 17: Saturday, December 10, 1892   Newcastle East End vs. Middlesbrough Ironopolis........64
    Game 18: Saturday, December 17, 1892   Stockton vs. Newcastle East End....................66
    Game 19: Saturday, December 24, 1892   Newcastle United vs. Middlesbrough...............68
    Game 20: Monday, December 26, 1892   The Wednesday vs. Newcastle United 70
    Game 21: Saturday, December 31, 1892   Newcastle United vs. Corinthians....................71
January 1893 ....**75**
    Game 22: Monday, January 2, 1893   Newcastle United vs. Everton 76
    Game 23: Tuesday, January 3, 1893   Newcastle United vs. Glasgow Rangers................78
    Game 24: Saturday, January 7, 1893   Newcastle United vs. Bolton Wanderers..............79
    Game 25: Saturday, January 14, 1893   Newcastle United vs. Sheffield United 81
    Game 26: Saturday, January 21, 1893   Newcastle United vs. Middlesbrough.................84
    Game 27: Saturday, January 28, 1893   Stockton vs. Newcastle United 85
February 1893 ....**89**
    Game 28: Saturday, February 4, 1893   Newcastle United vs. Stockton 90
    Game 29: Saturday, February 11, 1893   Middlesbrough vs. Newcastle United.................91
    Game 30: Saturday, February 18, 1893   Newcastle United vs. Notts County....................95

Table of Contents

Game 31: Saturday, February 25, 1893   Newcastle United vs. Sunderland 97
March 1893 .... **101**
    Game 32: Saturday, March 4, 1893   Newcastle United vs. Stoke 102
    Game 33: Saturday, March 11, 1893   Newcastle United vs. Annbank 103
    Game 34: Saturday, March 18, 1893   Newcastle United vs. Derby County 105
    Game 35: Saturday, March 25, 1893   Newcastle United vs. Nottingham Forest 106
April 1893 .... **109**
    Game 36: Saturday, April 1, 1893   Newcastle United vs. London Casuals 110
    Game 37: Monday, April 3, 1893   Stockton vs. Newcastle United 111
    Game 38: Saturday, April 8, 1893   Newcastle United vs. Liverpool 114
    Game 39: Wednesday, April 12, 1893   Newcastle East End vs. Sunderland 115
    Game 40: Saturday, April 15, 1893   Newcastle United vs. West Bromwich Albion 117
    Game 41: Monday, April 17, 1893   Everton vs. Newcastle United 118
    Game 42: Saturday, April 22, 1893   Newcastle United vs. Accrington 120
    Game 43: Wednesday, April 26, 1893   Newcastle United vs. Middlesbrough Ironopolis ... 121
    Game 44: Saturday, April 29, 1893   Newcastle United vs. Preston North End 123
TABLES & STATISTICS **125**
PLAYER PROFILES **129**
    Barker, John 131
    Collins, James "Jimmy" 131
    Coupar, William 132
    Crate, Thomas "Tom" 132
    Creilly, Robert "Bobby" 132
    Dixon, Henry 133
    Graham, William "Willie" 133
    Jeffrey, Harry 133
    Kirkland, J. 134
    McCabe, Frank 134
    McIntosh, James 134
    McKane, Joseph "Joe" 135
    Miller, James 135
    Pattinson, J 136
    Quinn, Charles "Charlie" 136
    Reay, Harry 136
    Rodgers, Thomas "Tom" 137
    Ryder, Joseph "Joe" 137
    Sorley, John "Jock" 138
    Thompson, William Pringle "Willie" 138
    Wallace, Joseph "Joe" 139
    Watson, Peter 139
    Whitton, David "Dave" 140
THE END BITS… **141**
    Game Changer 1: Friday, December 9, 1892   *arise Newcastle United* 142
    Game Changer 2: Friday, December 23, 1892   *Newcastle United begins…* 143
    The Conundrum   *when was Newcastle United's first game?* 144
    The End   *close of the season* 144
About the Author **145**
Bibliography **147**

Preface

the END of the 'Ends' is our Beginning!

With all the hopes and aspirations of the teams, management, players and fans -so it all begins…

On our journey through the 1892-93 season we must start at the annual meeting of the Football League, held on Saturday, August 14, at Sunderland, with Mr J. J. Bentley of Bolton Wanderers presiding, in the absence of the indisposed Mr McGregor. For it was there that the matter of the composition of the Football League, and the formation of a new second tier, was to be decided. This was of great significance to Newcastle East End as they, along with Small Heath, the two Sheffield clubs (Sheffield United and The Wednesday), Burton Swifts, Newton Heath, Nottingham Forest, and the two Teesside clubs (Middlesbrough and Middlesbrough Ironopolis), had made submissions to join the Football League's top tier, and their applications were to be considered. There was another application, from Liverpool, but this was "*not entertained*". Representatives from both Stoke and Darwen were present at the meeting.

It was ratified at this meeting that the current Football League would become known respectively as "**Football League Division 1**" and "**Football League Division 2**" and that Division 1 would be increased from the current 14 teams to 16 teams. With regards to Division 2 there had already been much discussion, *and some hot debate*, at a previous meeting. Some members had wanted 16 teams, this to match Division 1, others, expressed great worries about maintaining the highest standard of football, and had wanted the division to have only 12 clubs and it was they who won that particular debate.

Football League 1891-92 – Final Standings							
	Pld	W	L	D	F	A	Pts
Sunderland	26	21	5	0	93	36	42
Preston North End	26	18	7	1	61	31	37
Bolton Wanderers	26	17	7	2	51	37	36
Aston Villa	26	15	11	0	89	56	30
Everton	26	12	10	4	49	49	28
Wolverhampton Wanderers	26	11	11	4	59	46	26
Burnley	26	11	11	4	49	45	26
Notts County	26	11	11	4	55	51	26
Blackburn Rovers	26	10	10	6	58	65	26
Derby County	26	10	12	4	46	52	24
Accrington	26	8	14	4	40	78	20
West Bromwich Albion	26	6	14	6	51	58	18
Stoke	26	5	17	4	38	61	14
Darwen	26	4	19	3	38	112	11

As per the rules of the Football League the bottom four clubs from last season would have to apply for re-election, and this would be to Division 1. The four clubs were: Accrington (11th), West Bromwich Albion (12th), Stoke (13th) and Darwen (14th and bottom).

West Bromwich Albion were automatically re-elected, given that they were the current holders of the English Cup, this meant there were only five places to be filled. Resulting from the votes Accrington, with 7 votes, and Stoke, with 6 votes, were re-elected, whilst Newton Heath (6 votes), Nottingham Forest (9 votes) and The Wednesday (10 votes) gained admission to Division 1. So, the composition of the division would therefore be:

Composition of the Football League Division 1 [1892-93]		
Accrington	Everton	The Wednesday (*now Sheffield Wednesday*)
Aston Villa	Newton Heath (*now Manchester United*)	Stoke
Blackburn Rovers	Nottingham Forest	Sunderland
Bolton Wanderers	Notts County	West Bromwich Albion
Burnley	Preston North End	Wolverhampton Wanderers
Debry County		

~ 7 ~

So, the vote did not go well for the North-East sides, all failing in their applications. East End, Middlesbrough and Middlesbrough Ironopolis were subsequently offered places in the new Division 2, which, *perhaps in a fit of pique*, they all refused. Consequently, they all were to re-join the Northern League. In what may be a bit of football history Darwen were given a place in the new Division 2. This potentially making them, *at least arguably*, the very first team to be 'relegated' from the Football League Division 1. Burton Swifts and Sheffield United both accepted places in the new division, following their failed applications to Division 1, and the rest of the teams would come from the Football Alliance, *which would cease to exist*. This 'new' division was therefore comprised of the following teams:

Football Alliance 1891-92 – Final Standings							
	Pld	W	L	D	F	A	Pts
Nottingham Forest	22	14	3	5	59	22	33
Newton Heath	22	12	3	7	69	33	31
Small Heath	22	12	5	5	53	36	29
The Wednesday	22	12	6	4	65	35	28
Burton Swifts	22	12	8	2	54	52	26
Bootle	22	8	12	2	42	64	26
Crewe Alexandria	22	7	11	4	44	49	18
Ardwick	22	6	10	6	39	51	18
Lincoln City	22	6	11	5	37	65	17
Grimsby Town*	22	6	10	6	40	39	16
Walsall Town Swifts	22	6	13	3	33	59	15
Birmingham St George's*	22	5	14	3	34	64	11

Both teams deducted two points for fielding ineligible players.

Composition of the Football League Division 2 [1892-93]

Ardwick (*now Manchester City*)	Darwen	Burslem Port Vale (*now Port Vale*)
Bootle	Grimsby Town	Sheffield United
Burton Swifts	Lincoln City	Small Heath (*now Birmingham City*)
Crewe Alexandria	Northwich Victoria	Walsall

The Death Throes of West End   *Farewell to an old friend*

Before we continue our journey let us temporarily jump back to the week beginning May 2nd, for it was within that week it became official that Messrs William Neasham and J. Black, who controlled the affairs of Newcastle West End, announced that their association with the club would end, this after having done everything in their powers to bring success to the club. In a spirit of sportsmanship, they had made their intentions known to the executive of the East End club. The main reason this was of interest to East End of course was the fact that the leasehold on St James's Park was in the name of Mr Neasham, with some twelve years left to run, this was offered to the East End directorate. In effect these two events would represent the 'end' of West End.

How It Was Reported

"East End F.C. – We understand that it has been definitely settled that East End will occupy St James's Park, Leazes, on which West End played for several years previously."
The Newcastle Daily Chronicle. Tuesday, May 10, 1892.

A NEWCASTLE CLUB DEFUNCT
"The Newcastle West End club has ceased to exist, and on invitation of Messrs W. Neasham and J. Black, the executive of the East End club will become the occupiers of St James's Park."
Sunderland Daily Echo. Tuesday, May 10, 1892.

END OF A FOOTBALL CLUB
"The Newcastle West End Association Football Club has ceased to exit, and their ground at St James's Park will be occupied by Newcastle East End."
The Northern Daily Telegraph, Wednesday May 11, 1892.

"It is reported that the Newcastle West End Club has disbanded and that the East End club are likely to figure on St James's Park next season."
The North-Eastern Daily Gazette. Thursday, May 12, 1892.

We now forward ourselves a week to Monday 9th May, when two meetings were held, one in London, the other in Jesmond, Newcastle upon Tyne.

Preface

The London meeting was that of the council of the Football League. At this meeting they ordered Newcastle West End to pay Burslem Port Vale the sum of £10, this for the non-fulfilment of their fixture set for April 16th. Another *"nail in the coffin"* for West End? Or was this to be an academic exercise? For the important meeting was that which was to take place in Jesmond. It was at this meeting, at the home of Joseph Bell, that West End's fate was finally sealed, or the rumours 'rubber stamped' depending upon one's point of view.

The offer of occupancy of St James's Park was accepted by the directorate of Newcastle East End, agreeing to take over the costs of the remainder of the lease, the registration of those players remaining at West End, become responsible for the rent and other matters arising, but without any undertaking to meet all the remaining liabilities of West End. The demise of West End was therefore complete. The following day, May 10th, it was officially announced that the Newcastle West End Association Football Club ceased to exist. *We can now resume our journey…*

The Northern League   *Decisions, decisions*

On May 16th the Northern League held their annual meeting at the Queen's Hotel in Stockton. Presiding was Mr George H Watson of Stockton. At this meeting it was confirmed that Newcastle West End, along with Sunderland Albion, *both now being defunct*, were no longer members, and therefore dropped from the league. Bishop Auckland, represented by Mr Bowes, and Darlington St Augustine's, represented by Mr Holland, both personally urged that their club's applications for admission to the league be looked upon favourably, this especially in light of the fact that the league, which comprised of nine clubs last season, would now, with the demise of West End and Sunderland Albion, be reduced to seven.

Northern League 1891-92 – Final Standings						
	Pld	W	L	D	F	A	Pts
Middlesbrough Ironopolis	16	14	1	1	48	12	29
Middlesbrough	16	13	3	0	32	13	26
Sheffield United	16	10	4	2	48	21	22
Newcastle East End	16	9	5	2	37	18	20
Stockton	16	6	8	2	30	36	14
Sunderland Albion	16	5	11	0	37	38	10
Newcastle West End	16	4	12	0	21	56	8
South Bank	16	3	11	2	21	50	8
Darlington	16	2	11	3	19	48	7

After due consideration these were refused, and it was decided that Darlington (*not to be confused with Darlington St Augustine's*) who finished bottom of the league last season would be re-elected. The composition of the league would therefore be only of seven teams, these being:

Composition of the Northern League [1892-93]

Darlington	Newcastle East End	South Bank
Middlesbrough	Sheffield United (*also in Division 2*)	Stockton
Middlesbrough Ironopolis		

The secretary of the league, Mr A. Walker, made a report to the effect that whilst he had written to several firms for tenders for the proposed trophy for the coming season's winners he had, to-date, not yet received any 'full' designs that could be put forward for consideration. It was decided that a sub-committee would be formed to select appropriate designs, as and when received, and submit their selections to the full League committee for a final decision. Mr Walker also read out a letter which had been received by the League. This letter was from Mr Beardshaw, of Sheffield United. The purpose of the letter being to encourage the committee, and the individual clubs, to arrange the fixtures in such a manner so as not to visit Sheffield before any 'Football League' fixtures were played. [*Sheffield United were also represented in the new Football League Division 2.*] This, of course, was given full consideration. After due deliberations the fixture list for the 1892-93 season was arranged and published in the July. It was as follows.

SEPTEMBER	
01-Sep	Sheffield United v. Middlesbrough Ironopolis
03-Sep	Middlesbrough v. South Bank
10-Sep	Middlesbrough v. Darlington
17-Sep	Darlington v. South Bank
24-Sep	Sheffield United v. Newcastle East End
24-Sep	South Bank v. Middlesbrough Ironopolis

OCTOBER	
01-Oct	Stockton v. Darlington
01-Oct	Newcastle East End v. South Bank
08-Oct	South Bank v. Darlington
15-Oct	Middlesbrough v. Middlesbrough Ironopolis
22-Oct	South Bank v. Newcastle East End
22-Oct	Middlesbrough Ironopolis v. Stockton
29-Oct	Middlesbrough Ironopolis v. Sheffield United

NOVEMBER	
05-Nov	Newcastle East End v. Middlesbrough
05-Nov	Darlington v. Middlesbrough Ironopolis
05-Nov	South Bank v. Sheffield United
12-Nov	Newcastle East End v. Darlington
12-Nov	Stockton v. Middlesbrough Ironopolis
19-Nov	Middlesbrough Ironopolis v. Newcastle East End
26-Nov	Stockton v. Middlesbrough
26-Nov	Darlington v. Newcastle East End

DECEMBER	
03-Dec	Middlesbrough Ironopolis v. Middlesbrough
03-Dec	Newcastle East End v. Stockton
10-Dec	Newcastle East End v. Middlesbrough Ironopolis
17-Dec	Stockton v. Newcastle East End
24-Dec	Sheffield United v. Darlington
31-Dec	Middlesbrough v. Sheffield United

JANUARY	
02-Jan	Stockton v. Sheffield United
07-Jan	Darlington v. Stockton
07-Jan	Middlesbrough Ironopolis v. South Bank
14-Jan	Newcastle East End v. Sheffield United
28-Jan	South Bank v. Middlesbrough
28-Jan	Middlesbrough Ironopolis v. Darlington
30-Jan	Sheffield United v. Stockton

FEBRUARY	
04-Feb	Stockton v. South Bank
11-Feb	Middlesbrough v. Newcastle East End
11-Feb	Sheffield United v. South Bank
14-Feb	Sheffield United v. Middlesbrough
18-Feb	Middlesbrough v. Stockton

MARCH	
04-Mar	South Bank v. Stockton

APRIL	
03-Apr	Darlington v. Sheffield United
04-Apr	Darlington v. Middlesbrough

Football being football, *even in these early days*, there had to be scandal or controversy, and before the new season had even begun it had its share of that!

Both Middlesbrough and Stockton had earned the enmity of several Football League teams and were to be boycotted. This may have serious financial implications for them as the lost gate receipts from fixtures with the "big boys" in the football world, over the course of the season, will undoubtedly be heavy. Stockton's offence was that they tempted, or attempted to entice, players from Football League clubs, (*so 'poaching' is certainly nothing new*), in the main this centres around their purchase of Townley from Blackburn Rovers, whom they adamantly claim they secured in a "fair and honourable dealing". The offence of Middlesbrough was a little more trifling. They had a "little difference" with West Bromwich

Albion some time ago and the seemingly petty revenge continues. As the season develops, we may also discover the true effects of these situations and see how the boycott holds or progresses.

Stockton also had a further problem, owing to an error they are not included in the list of clubs entered for the Football Association Challenge Cup. It transpired that the club management omitted to send in their entry request on time and were desperately trying to remedy the situation. All hoped of course that this situation would be resolved but it is fairly assumed that someone at the club will, undoubtedly, be in very hot water indeed!

So, the picture is now set, all the pieces are in place, now let us explore the season that saw the end of the 'Ends' and the beginning of the 'United', the season that placed the foundations of the club we all adore, **Newcastle United**.

Howay the Lads *(and Lasses)*...

The Season

A Quick Glance

September — and so it begins

"and so, it begins…"

Newcastle East End have made a brave and bold move across the city from their base in Heaton, in not unsurprisingly the East of the city, to their new ground of St James's Park in the West of the city. However not only is St James's Park on the opposite side of the city, it was also the home ground to their fierce city rivals Newcastle West End, *now defunct of course*.

To do this, to leave one's home, is undoubtedly hard enough, but to move from one end of the city to the other and to move into the ground that was held by your city rivals is no mean feat to undertake by any stretch of the imagination.

Whilst the whole idea of moving may have made perfectly good sense it was an idea that was fraught with danger. There is the danger that you alienate your own fans, this simply by moving let alone into "opposition" ground, there is the almost certainty that the die-hard West End fans will be against you taking over 'their turf' even if their team is now defunct.

However, there can be no doubt that the executive of the East End club was totally committed to making a success of this venture. To that end they had engaged the very well renowned Glasgow club, Celtic, to be East End's first opponents at St James's Park, with the current champions of the Football League, and already fierce local rivals, Sunderland, were to be the second! Both severe tests for East End. They also were to face current Northern League champions, Middlesbrough Ironopolis, twice!

In relation to the Northern League September would also see East End opening their account, and it was to prove to be a sharp "wake up call" from the "friendly" games they had been prior involved in.

Games Played in September 1892

V	Date	F	A	R	Opposition	Competition
H	03/09/1892	0	1	L	Celtic	Friendly
H	07/09/1892	2	2	D	Sunderland	Friendly
H	10/09/1892	4	1	W	Middlesbrough Ironopolis	Friendly
A	17/09/1892	2	1	W	Middlesbrough Ironopolis	Friendly
A	24/09/1892	1	5	L	Sheffield United	Northern League

Appearance & Goalscoring Record for September 1892

Name	Total Apps	Total Goals	League Apps	League Goals	Friendly Apps	Friendly Goals
Collins, James	5	2	1		4	2
Crate, Thomas "Tom"	5	1	1		4	1
Creilly, Robert "Bobby"	5		1		4	
Graham, William "Willie"	5		1		4	
Jeffrey, Harry	5		1		4	
McKane, Joseph "Joe"	5		1		4	
Miller, James	4		1		3	
Reay, Harry	1		0		1	
Sorley, John "Jock"	4	2	1	1	3	1
Thompson, Willie	5	2	1		4	2
Wallace, Joseph "Joe"	5	1	1		4	1
Watson, Peter	1		0		1	
Whitton, David "Dave"	5		1		4	

October   *celebratory blues*

"Charter Day Blues"

But for the acceptance of celebrating "Charter Day" with Stockton the month of October would have been a perfect month for East End. They played six games and won every one except the Charter Day celebratory match. Taking the Stockton game out of the equation they had scored no fewer than seventeen goals and had conceded only two. Included in their wins was a thrashing of Mossend Swifts by seven goals to one goal. Yes, East End had an *almost* perfect October!

Games Played in October 1892						
V	Date	F	A	R	Opposition	Competition
H	01/10/1892	3	1	W	Middlesbrough	Northern League
A	06/10/1892	1	3	L	Stockton	Friendly
A	08/10/1892	1	0	W	Middlesbrough	Friendly
H	15/10/1892	7	0	W	South of Ayrshire	Friendly
H	22/10/1892	2	0	W	Heart of Midlothian	Friendly
H	29/10/1892	4	1	W	Mossend Swifts	Friendly

Appearances & Goals ~ October 1892

	Total		League		Friendly	
Name	Apps	Goals	Apps	Goals	Apps	Goals
Barker, John	1		1		0	
Collins, James	5	4	1		4	4
Coupar, William	1		0		1	
Crate, Thomas "Tom"	6	2	1		5	2
Creilly, Robert "Bobby"	4	1	0		4	1
Dixon, Henry	2	1	0		2	1
Graham, William "Willie"	6		1		5	
Jeffrey, Harry	6		1		5	
Kirkland, J.	1				1	
McKane, Joseph "Joe"	6		1		5	
Miller, James	5		1		4	
Reay, Harry	5	1	1		4	1
Sorley, John "Jock"	3	4	0		3	4
Thompson, Willie	3	1	1	1	2	
Wallace, Joseph "Joe"	5	2	1	2	4	
Watson, Peter	1		0		1	
Whitton, David "Dave"	6		1		5	

November   *seven(th) heaven*

seven(th) heaven...

What a great month November was for Newcastle's forwards, sharing no fewer than sixteen goals between them. Seven of those, *well six plus an 'own goal'*, coming in a seven-nil mauling of fellow Northern League side, Darlington, and to make things worse for Darlington the game was played at Feethams! What a great month it was for their Newcastle's defence too, keeping two clean sheets out of four, conceding only five times in total and three of those being in the same game which was against the reigning Northern League champions, current runaway leaders of the Northern League, and not to mentioned unbeaten, Middlesbrough Ironopolis.

Games Played in November 1892

V	Date	F	A	R	Opposition	Competition
H	05/11/1892	2	2	D	Sheffield United	Friendly
H	12/11/1892	5	0	W	Darlington	Northern League
A	19/11/1892	2	3	L	Middlesbrough Ironopolis	Northern League
A	26/11/1892	7	0	W	Darlington	Northern League

Appearances & Goals ~ November 1892

	Total		League		Friendly	
Name	Apps	Goals	Apps	Goals	Apps	Goals
Collins, James	4	1	3	1	1	
Crate, Thomas "Tom"	4		3		1	
Creilly, Robert "Bobby"	4		3		1	
Graham, William "Willie"	4	1	3	1	1	
Jeffrey, Harry	2	1	1		1	
McKane, Joseph "Joe"	3		2		1	
Miller, James	4		3		1	
Reay, Harry	4	2	3	1	1	1
Sorley, John "Jock"	4	4	3	3	1	1
Thompson, Willie	3	4	3	4	0	
Wallace, Joseph "Joe"	2	3	1	3	1	
Watson, Peter	2	2	2		0	
Whitton, David "Dave"	4		3		1	

December

end of the "Ends"

"end of the Ends"

Undoubtedly the most important event of the month was one which happened off the field of play. It was of course the momentous decision to change the name of Newcastle East End to Newcastle United. So now the "Ends" have now definitely 'ended', West End are no more and have not been since the decision to fold the club, East End are now no more as is popularly demanded by fans and executive alike, now it is the time of the "United" the phoenix of East and West to rise!

As it turned out however the very first game under the new name was not a one to cause much celebration as it was a defeat, at St James's Park, by the odd goal in three at the hands of the current Northern League champions Middlesbrough Ironopolis. *Or was it*? Dependent upon one's point of view was it the emphatic 8-1 victory over the famous amateurs the Corinthians?

Games Played in December 1892

V	Date	F	A	R	Opposition	Competition
H	03/12/1892	5	1	W	Stockton	Northern League
H	10/12/1892	1	2	L	Middlesbrough Ironopolis	Northern League
A	17/12/1892	5	2	W	Stockton	Northern League
H	24/12/1892	2	1	W	Middlesbrough	Friendly
A	26/12/1892	0	1	L	The Wednesday	Friendly
H	31/12/1892	8	1	W	Corinthians	Friendly

Newcastle United 1892-93: Season Zero

Appearances & Goals ~ December 1892

Name	Total Apps	Total Goals	League Apps	League Goals	Friendly Apps	Friendly Goals
Collins, James	6		3		3	
Crate, Thomas "Tom"	3	2	3	2	0	
Creilly, Robert "Bobby"	6	1	3	1	3	
Graham, William "Willie"	6	1	3	1	3	
Jeffrey, Harry	5		2		3	
McIntosh, James	2	2	0		2	2
McKane, Joseph "Joe"	5	1	2		3	1
Miller, James	6		3		3	
Reay, Harry	6	5	3	2	3	3
Sorley, John "Jock"	6	4	3	3	3	1
Thompson, Willie	4	4	1	1	3	3
Wallace, Joseph "Joe"	4	1	3	1	1	
Watson, Peter	1		1		0	
Whitton, David "Dave"	6		3		6	

January — 5 days, 3 games, 3 wins

five days, three games, three wins

Happy New Year to one and all, and what a hectic start to the new year for Newcastle United, get used to that new moniker folks – Newcastle United!

January saw three games within a five-day period, this resulted in the winning of all three games and the scoring of eleven goals whilst only conceding three goals. Whilst they may only have been "friendly" games, they were against top-class opposition. Two of the opposition coming from Football League Division One, the other being former champions of the Scottish Football League. Formidable opposition indeed. It was quite unfortunate that the month did not end as well as it had begun. The penultimate game of the month being an early exit from the FA Cup, indeed at the very first hurdle, and the final game of the month being a particularly poor "friendly" fixture against Stockton, perhaps there being an element of apathy following the cup exit?

Sandwiched in between the excellent start and the abysmal finish was a reasonably credible draw in the league against Sheffield United, given that they had demolished Newcastle by five goals to one goal at the beginning of the season. Incidentally this game representing the very last Northern League fixture Newcastle United would play at St James's Park, *perhaps another one for you to keep up your sleeve for your next Pub-Quiz night.*

Games Played in January 1893

V	Date	F	A	R	Opposition	Competition
H	02/01/1893	4	2	W	Everton	Friendly
H	03/01/1893	4	0	W	Glasgow Rangers	Friendly
H	07/01/1893	3	1	W	Bolton Wanderers	Friendly
H	14/01/1893	1	1	D	Sheffield United	Northern League
H	21/01/1893	2	3	L	Middlesbrough	FA Cup [Round 1]
A	28/01/1893	2	3	L	Stockton	Friendly

The Season: Quick Glance

Appearances & Goals ~ January 1893

Name	Total Apps	Total Goals	League Apps	League Goals	FA Cup Apps	FA Cup Goals	Friendly Apps	Friendly Goals
Collins, James	5		1		1		3	
Crate, Thomas "Tom"	2		1				1	
Creilly, Robert "Bobby"	6	1	1		1		4	1
Graham, William "Willie"	6		1		1		4	
Jeffrey, Harry	5		1		1		3	
McKane, Joseph "Joe"	6		1		1		4	
Miller, James	6		1		1		4	
Reay, Harry	6	5	1		1	1	4	4
Sorley, John "Jock"	6	4	1		1		4	4
Thompson, Willie	5	5	0		1	1	4	4
Wallace, Joseph "Joe"	6		1		1		4	
Watson, Peter	1		0				1	
Whitton, David "Dave"	6		1		1		4	

February   *First Tyne-Wear Derby?*

Tyne-Wear Derby No.1?

Here is another one of those infuriating "facts" that can have so many different answers that it cannot be classified as a "fact". Now that is confusing to write, let alone read, so if you're confused then read on my friend, please read on. The Tyne-Wear Derby is the fixture played between Newcastle United and their close neighbours, *and fiercest of rivals*, Sunderland. So, we have in February the first meeting between Newcastle United and Sunderland. All the other times Sunderland have played a "Newcastle" it was either Newcastle East End or Newcastle West End, so given the Tyne-Wear Derby is Newcastle United vs. Sunderland none of those other meetings can be counted. So, the February meeting is Tyne-Wear Derby No.1 – *dependent upon one's point of view*.

This particular Tyne-Wear Derby was a "friendly fixture" between the two sides, as being such the vast majority of people do not count this fixture as being the first, absolutely understandable of course, that honour being held over until the 1898-99 season and the Division One fixture at Roker Park on 24/12/1898. As to whether that is a "Wear-Tyne Derby" given that it's at Sunderland, believe me it just doesn't work like that, *sorry*, it is **always** called the Tyne-Wear Derby irrespective of the ground it is played at. So, there is another Pub-Quiz teaser for you to hold up your sleeve and smugly question as to when the first Tyne-Wear Derby took place, 25/02/1892 or 25/12/1898. The choice is yours.

February also saw Newcastle United say farewell to the Northern League as they played out their last fixture in the competition and a disaster that was to prove. A heavy defeat jeopardising Newcastle's second place in the table, both Middlesbrough and Sheffield United now able to take that spot from them meaning they could finish as low as fourth in a league of only six teams! However, there were mitigating circumstances as they arrived at Middlesbrough with only ten men!

Games Played in February 1893

V	Date	F	A	R	Opposition	Competition
H	04/02/1893	3	1	W	Stockton	Friendly
A	11/02/1893	0	4	L	Middlesbrough	Northern League
H	18/02/1893	3	2	W	Notts County	Friendly
H	25/02/1893	1	6	L	Sunderland	Friendly

Appearances & Goals ~ February 1893

Name	Total Apps	Total Goals	League Apps	League Goals	Friendly Apps	Friendly Goals
Collins, James	4		1		3	
Crate, Thomas "Tom"	4	1	1		3	1
Creilly, Robert "Bobby"	4		1		3	
Graham, William "Willie"	4		1		3	
Jeffrey, Harry	3		1		2	
McKane, Joseph "Joe"	1		0		1	
Miller, James	4		1		3	
Reay, Harry	4	1	1		3	1
Rodgers, Thomas "Tom"	1		0		1	
Sorley, John "Jock"	3	2	0		3	2
Thompson, Willie	4	1	1		3	1
Wallace, Joseph "Joe"	3	1	1		2	1
Whitton, David "Dave"	4		1		3	

March — reflection

time for reflection

A very quiet month indeed for Newcastle, this with their league season being over, finishing in second place to the reigning champions, Middlesbrough Ironopolis, of course, and their exit from the FA Cup. Despite this however they were able to attract three high profile teams from the top league in the land, Stoke, Derby and Forest, and an 'old friend' from Scotland, Annbank, to St James's Park. These games rewarded Newcastle with no fewer than sixteen goals being registered in their 'plus' column, half of these coming from Harry Reay. Indeed, he got five of his eight goals in the one game, *read on to find out which*, and was a player whom Newcastle were to lose within a matter of weeks, but of course neither he nor the team were aware of this fact, or were they? You never really can tell when a transfer process really begins.

The defence of Newcastle were to prove meagre as well. With the exception of the seven goal thriller against Stoke they conceded only a single goal per game, unfortunate not to keep a clean sheet, but conceding only once when you've got the best forward quintet in the Northern League and are actually facing Division One opponents is, again, no mean feat indeed.

So, March, overall, was a rewarding month for Newcastle, it was certainly a time for reflection, a time for planning. Their place in the structure of English football needed to be decided. The Northern League had quite outlived its purpose. The league matches had been too few and too far between to maintain a steady interest from the football attending public. They most certainly would not, and going forward could not, generate the sort of income the Newcastle executive felt they would need to fulfil their aspirations for the club.

Games Played in March 1893

V	Date	F	A	R	Opposition	Competition
H	04/03/1893	3	4	L	Stoke	Friendly
H	11/03/1893	6	1	W	Annbank	Friendly
H	18/03/1893	3	1	W	Derby County	Friendly
H	25/03/1893	4	1	W	Nottingham Forest	Friendly

The Season: Quick Glance

Appearances & Goals ~ March 1893

Name	Total		League		Friendly	
	Apps	Goals	Apps	Goals	Apps	Goals
Collins, James	4	1	0		4	1
Crate, Thomas "Tom"	4		0		4	
Creilly, Robert "Bobby"	3		0		3	
Graham, William "Willie"	3	2	0		3	2
Jeffrey, Harry	4		0		4	
McCabe, Frank	2		0		2	
McKane, Joseph "Joe"	4		0		4	
Miller, James	4		0		4	
Reay, Harry	3	8	0		3	8
Ryder, Joseph "Joe"	1		0		1	
Sorley, John "Jock"	4	1	0		4	1
Thompson, Willie	3	2	0		3	2
Wallace, Joseph "Joe"	4	1	0		4	1
Whitton, David "Dave"	1		0		1	

April   and so it ends

and so, it ends...

So, that is it, the season is over. A season which started with Newcastle East End moving across the city to take up home in the ground of their old rivals, Newcastle West End. A season which then saw Newcastle East End become Newcastle United! All legends, myths, heroes and villains regarding Newcastle United and/or St James's Park begin at this season, as of course do all the triumphs and disasters. It, season 1892-93 of the Northern League, is without doubt the most important season in the entire history of Newcastle United.

As a parting farewell, and a promise of the future to come, the Newcastle United executive had arranged a massive programme of football for St James's Park and the team. There were no fewer than nine games played in this month. Seven of those nine being played at home, reinforcing the fact that this ground, St James's Park, now belonged to Newcastle United, not East End, nor West End but UNITED!

Yes, April was a hectic month indeed, and one that was to prove somewhat of a rollercoaster of emotions for followers of Newcastle United. The month started with a 5-0 victory, and it ended with a 5-0 victory, and in between it saw the high of a 7-2 victory against Division One opposition and the utter low of defeat in the second "Tyne-Wear Derby", with the same stipulations on that as mentioned before, *i.e. it was a friendly encounter so doesn't 'really' count*, not officially anyway, it is just another "Pub-Quiz" banker for you. Then, there was also the very strange case of the game that never was...

Games Played in April 1893

V	Date	F	A	R	Opposition	Competition
H	01/04/1893	5	0	W	London Casuals	Friendly
A	04/04/1893	3	3	D	Stockton	Friendly
H	08/04/1893	0	0	D	Liverpool	Friendly
H	12/04/1893	0	4	L	Sunderland	Friendly
H	15/04/1893	7	2	W	West Bromwich Albion	Friendly
A	17/04/1893	2	5	L	Everton	Friendly
H	22/04/1893	5	0	W	Accrington	Friendly
H	26/04/1893	1	0	W	Middlesbrough Ironopolis	Friendly
H	29/04/1893	5	0	W	Preston North End	Friendly

Appearances & Goals ~ April 1893

Name	Total		Friendly	
	Apps	Goals	Apps	Goals
Collins, James	9	9	9	9
Crate, Thomas "Tom"	9	5	9	5
Creilly, Robert "Bobby"	9		9	
Graham, William "Willie"	8	1	8	1
Jeffrey, Harry	9		9	
McCabe, Frank	1		1	
McKane, Joseph "Joe"	9		9	
Miller, James	9		9	
Pattinson, J	3	2	3	2
Quinn, Charles "Charlie"	1		1	
Reay, Harry	6	1	6	1
Sorley, John "Jock"	5	7	5	7
Thompson, Willie	6		6	
Wallace, Joseph "Joe"	7	1	7	1
Whitton, David "Dave"	8		8	

Game by Game

September 1892

Games Played in September 1892						
V	Date	F	A	R	Opposition	Competition
H	03/09/1892	0	1	L	Celtic	Friendly
H	07/09/1892	2	2	D	Sunderland	Friendly
H	10/09/1892	4	1	W	Middlesbrough Ironopolis	Friendly
A	17/09/1892	2	1	W	Middlesbrough Ironopolis	Friendly
A	24/09/1892	1	5	L	Sheffield United	Northern League

Appearance & Goalscoring Record for September 1892

	Total		League		Friendly	
Name	Apps	Goals	Apps	Goals	Apps	Goals
Collins, James	5	2	1		4	2
Crate, Thomas "Tom"	5	1	1		4	1
Creilly, Robert "Bobby"	5		1		4	
Graham, William "Willie"	5		1		4	
Jeffrey, Harry	5		1		4	
McKane, Joseph "Joe"	5		1		4	
Miller, James	4		1		3	
Reay, Harry	1		0		1	
Sorley, John "Jock"	4	2	1	1	3	1
Thompson, Willie	5	2	1		4	2
Wallace, Joseph "Joe"	5	1	1		4	1
Watson, Peter	1		0		1	
Whitton, David "Dave"	5		1		4	

Game 1: Saturday September 3, 1892   **Newcastle East End vs. Celtic**

Competition: Friendly   Venue: St James's Park   Gate: 6,000

Newcastle East End   0 - 1   Celtic

Scorer(s): none

Goal, Dave Whitton; *backs*, Harry Jeffrey and James Miller; *half-backs*, Bobby Creilly, Willie Graham and Joe McKane; *forwards*, James Collins, Tom Crate, Willie Thompson, Jock Sorley, Joe Wallace

Referee: Mr Robert Campbell (Sunderland)

Scorer(s): McMahon (30 mins)

Goal, Joe Cullen; *backs*, Daniel Doyle and Tom Dunbar; *half-backs*, Willie Maley, James Kelly and Jake Madden; *forwards*, Michael Murray, John Campbell, Alex McMahon, William McCann, James Blessington

Kick-Off: 4.00 PM

The football season was opened at St James's Park with East End suffering defeat by the narrowest of margins, Alex McMahon with the only goal of the game, securing the victory for Celtic.

As this was the very first game Newcastle East End would be playing at their new home of St James's Park, and with that being Newcastle West End's old home the East End executive knew that in order to "heal the wounds" of as many West End supporters as they could they needed to open with a "spectacular". The fact that Celtic were the current Scottish Cup holders, and already a very well renown side, they seemed to fit the bill perfectly as that 'spectacular' opening. It certainly seemed to work as since its announcement this match had been very eagerly anticipated.

Befitting to the occasion, and the opposition, there was a large gathering of around six thousand spectators. This was indeed a healthy attendance as in the wide-open space of St James's Park there was no hiding place from the quite miserable and showery September weather.

In anticipation of the healthy attendance the gates to the St James's Park enclosure were opened at 2:30pm, for an advertised 3:30pm kick-off. All public entrances were confined to the Leazes whilst season ticket holders had two special entrances, one at the Leazes and another in Strawberry Lane. In what was a grand gesture by the East End executive, Ladies were admitted free of charge and were instructed that entry was to be at the gates reserved for ticket holders.

The homesters appeared soon on the field, and were received by hearty cheers, but the Celts were a long time in arriving, and when they did the crowd made their displeasure at this fact known, but also greeted them heartily. Because of Celtic's late arrival on the pitch, the kick-off was delayed and made about twenty-five minutes after the advertised time – around four o'clock.

The visitors won the toss, setting East End to play up the incline. Thompson started, sending the ball straight into the Celtic quarters, but Kelly returned, with the ball going to Jeffrey, who gave to Creilly and the latter passed back up the field to Collins who sent behind. From the goal kick, the ball was worked down to midfield, and a fine kick in was excellently saved by Whitton, and Graham put in some good balls directly afterwards. Some midfield play followed, then the ball was shot over the home byline by Blessington. After the goal kick Celtic regained possession and worked their way smartly down on the left, but the ball was again sent behind.

Wallace cleverly tackled Murray, and ran up the wing, but he was dispossessed by Dunbar, and then Graham showed some good play taking the ball past the Celtic forwards. The ball was then kept in the visitor's quarters for some time, and a foul against Kelly gave East End a chance, but when the ball was sent in McMahon ran it out of danger. Wallace then made a grand run up, but he was too easily dispossessed of the ball which was sent behind the line.

Jeffrey came to the rescue when the Celtic left wing was looking dangerous, as did Miller soon afterwards.

Thompson ran up in the centre but when he passed to the right the ball was lost. It was soon, however, taken to midfield but went into touch. Collins and Madden had a tussle, to the disadvantage of the home man, the ball again sent into touch by Kelly. From the throw-in the home team worked their way into the visitor's quarters but Maley intercepted and the danger was passed.

The East End again ran up, and Cullen had to save a good shot from Crate, but subsequent pressure was cleared by Doyle for a while. The homesters were soon in returning however, and, after some very good combination play, Crate was severely unlucky when he just missed with a beautiful shot at the Celtic goal. Sorley directly afterwards sent in a hard shot, which, but for the utility of Cullen, would have scored, the Celtic custodian saving brilliantly.

Some further play in the centre of the field took place until the home forwards exhibited some nice skill. The visitors, however, then gained an advantage and ran down as a body, and McMahon shot severely. Whitton saved in a marvellous fashion at the expense a corner, but Murray sent behind the line. Celtic pressed again and, after Miller had made a good intervention, Whitton fisted out when everyone thought the ball had gone through the posts.

The Glaswegians continued to press but eventually Dunbar sent the ball over the byline. They, however, won a corner off Miller but this was nullified by the leather being once again shot over the bar. Play was confined to the backs, until Kelly sent in a splendid shot to the home goal, but Jeffrey saved by heading behind. The corner was of no avail. Some further nice play was witnessed, and Jeffrey saved in good fashion when Celtic were becoming dangerous.

The visitors, however, came down on the left wing, and McMahon scored the first goal for the Celts half-an-hour after the start.

Celtic were very lucky in having this point allowed as it should not legitimately have been, this as Whitton was charged before he had played the ball. The referee, although appealed to at the time, allowed the goal to stand but afterwards admitted that he had done so in error, having overlooked the new rule regarding the charging of a goalkeeper.

From the restart following the goal, *and unsuccessful appeals*, the home team worked the ball up the field. Graham showed up well, as did Creilly, who took the ball off Campbell in excellent form, though there was no tangible result. Regaining possession Celtic besieged the home goal, but Miller relieved the pressure very cleverly. The home forwards rushed the ball up the field, but Dunbar dispossessed them, and with a very 'no-nonsense' approach to defending he sent the ball well into home territory. The home defence was however equally of a very proficient description, and the danger was cleared by Graham. The home vanguard made another grand run up, and pressed smartly, but Wallace sent over the byline, as did Crate after some more good play on the part of the home forwards. Play ruled in mid-field until half-time and with no further scoring the interval was reached with the score at Celtic, one goal, East End, nil.

On restarting the home team had the best of matters, but Crate could not capitalise, sending the ball behind. Continuing to dominate play the East End forwards rushed to the Celtic goal and Thompson sent the ball through, but the point was disallowed on the ground of an off-side.

A free-kick for East End was cleared by Doyle, and then play was very slow for a while. It was Doyle again who saved another attack of the home team. The East End again pressed, and Graham sent in a lightning shot, but Cullen saved in good fashion. Wallace soon after had a good chance but his shot was always rising and ended up going high over the bar. From the goal-kick Sorley returned in magnificent style and his shot was only just saved by Cullen, at the expense of a corner. Though the corner was well delivered the danger from it was initially cleared by Celtic, but it was quickly returned and ultimately Jeffrey sent over the byline.

Thompson showed some clever play in midfield, and passing back to Miller, who delivered a great ball towards the goal and a charge by the home forwards was saved in marvellous fashion by Cullen. Jeffrey bothered the Celtic forwards, and the ball going across the field, Wallace showed up well, taking the ball well down, when he was tackled by Dunbar. Collins, however, got possession, and sent in a swift shot, but Cullen fisted out splendidly. Dunbar kicked out a shot by Crate, and the ball was then sent behind by one of the home vanguards. The home team pressed and a free-kick against Kelly let the home team in, the subsequent corner being followed by a similar concession. This second East End corner was not to pose any danger and the ball was cleared. Play became very poor for some time until Wallace had a chance, but he failed to take advantage of his opportunity. East End pressed, and had hard lines, and then the Celtic worked their way up only to be deprived of the ball by Graham.

The defence of the Celtic was superb, and numerous attacks on the part of East End were unavailing, until Crate shot in and the homesters won a corner which was unfruitful. Graham put in some good work. and then Celtic made a run up, but McKane gave a long kick down the field. From another East End corner Miller sent in a splendid shot, but the ball was got away.

It was pretty much immediately after this that time was called, bringing the game to a close. Whilst of course there is no point in hiding the fact that this was a defeat for East End against such established and well-respected opposition it was a very creditable defeat it must be said.

Newcastle East End ....None.
Celtic........................1 goal.

The gate receipt for this game reached £147, this was quoted as being *"not bad for a start"*. This especially given that St James's Park did not have any stands at the time, East End were not allowed to erect any by the owners of the ground, Newcastle Corporation, so yes, I would say that the return was not bad at all. As stated in the Scottish Referee (by T.T.Mac):

"the Celts received £80 guarantee but it would be highly unlikely for the East End committee to agree such a figure again as when the engagement was made it was understood that Celtic would only visit Newcastle and not make a tour of it as they had done."

Perhaps in some small compensation for this 'oversight/misunderstanding' the Celtic committee heaped praise upon the play of East End and said, *"they had no idea we had such an excellent club in the district"*.

Newcastle Daily Chronicle (03/09/1892) p7d.
Athletic News (05/09/1892) p7e.
Glasgow Herald (05/09/1892) p10d.
Newcastle Evening Chronicle (05/09/1892) p2d.
Newcastle Daily Chronicle (05/09/1892) pp6f-7a.
The Scottish Referee (05/09/1892) p4b.

Game 2: Wednesday, September 7, 1892 — Newcastle East End vs. Sunderland

Competition: Friendly   Venue: St James's Park   Gate: 3,000

Newcastle East End   2 - 2   **Sunderland**

Scorer(s): Crate (5 mins); Wallace (30 mins)

Goal, Dave Whitton; *backs*, Harry Jeffrey and James Miller; *half-backs*, Bobby Creilly, Willie Graham and Joe McKane; *forwards*, James Collins, Tom Crate, Willie Thompson, Jock Sorley, Joe Wallace

Referee: Mr F. Hardisty (Middlesbrough)

Scorer(s): D. Hannah (23 mins); Gillespie (35 mins)

Goal, Ned Doig; *backs*, Tom Porteous and Robert Smellie; *half-backs*, James Dalton, John Auld and William Gibson; *forwards*, James Gillespie, David Hannah, W Brand, Jimmy Millar, Jimmy Hannah

Kick-Off: 5:55 PM

The current Football League Champions, and of course our closest neighbours in relation to 'top-class' football, Sunderland, came visiting St James's Park today. Last season, when East End were still at Heaton, they played Sunderland no fewer than four times, the first being exactly a year ago today, September 07, 1891, and they became the first team to beat them that season, this by a score of two goals to nil. The Wearsiders, not being satisfied with that, arranged a return game at their Newcastle-road ground, 26/09/1891, and were victorious by the same score, two goals to nil. The third meeting was on 09/01/1892, and it was played in a veritable snowstorm. Sunderland won by six goals to four, this after it looked impossible for East End to lose at half time. No '*best out of three*' for these two sides as they organised yet another fixture, at Heaton on 11/04/1892, and Sunderland again took the honours, this time by four goals to one.

It was not surprising then that once the Wearsiders were confirmed as East End's second opponents at St James's Park there was great interest shown. Even in these early days the history of this fixture was growing. An attendance of circa 3,000 spectators, for a Wednesday evening game, bore testament to that fact.

Unfortunately, for Sunderland they had notable absentees from their side for this encounter, John Scott their popular outside-left suffered a dislocated shoulder following a heavy charge in the game against Celtic on Monday night. Hugh Wilson required medical attention during the interval of the same game, and Johnny Campbell was also injured during its course. Several other players were also stated to be suffering by the "rough treatment" they received. Scott, Campbell and Wilson were replaced by James Dalton, W. Brand (*of the second team*), and James Gillespie, the latter of whom was making his Sunderland debut.

The Sunderland team left Wearside for the short journey to Tyneside by special train at four o'clock accompanied by a large cohort of their fans and were followed somewhat later by an even larger number of their supporters. By the time kick-off was upon us there were fairly 3,000 spectators gathered, amongst them were several soldiers adding colour to the scene. The weather had been fine and bright, with a cold wind blowing down the field but owing to the now failing light it was agreed to confine the game to two periods of thirty-five minutes each.

The Wearsiders, dressed in white, were the first to enter the field, Porteous leading the way. East End quickly followed, resplendent in their becoming scarlet and white uniforms.

Having won the toss, the visitors selected the upper end of the field, which gave them the advantage of the slope, the wind, and the sun.

At precisely 5.55 p.m. the East End captain, Thompson set the ball in motion, and, after a rapid run into the Sunderland half a chance was taken by Sorley but it went by.

From the goal kick (J.) Hannah and Millar were able to break away and play was shifted to East End ground, where the ball was shot over by Gillespie. The goal-kick by Whitton did not, unfortunately, go very far and Sunderland regained possession in a dangerous place resulting in a demon of a shot by Millar which luckily for East End struck one of his own team and went out of play. Soon after (J.) Hannah gained the first corner of the game, which he placed well in front of the East End goal. The ball was coming away when Gibson secured it, but he lost a splendid chance in sending the ball wide. 'Hands' was given against the visitors enabling the home forwards to make a charge up the field. In evading the Sunderland defence Thompson came through and gave smartly to Crate, he eluded Smellie in fine style and with a splendid shot the first goal was secured for the East End, amidst loud applause. This being after barely five minutes had elapsed.

The game now became exceedingly fast, both sides doing their utmost, and for a time East End had the best of matters, and the visitors' defence was severely taxed, Crate having another opportunity but this time sending the ball wide. East End then secured a corner which was well placed for Collins, but his shot was cleverly intercepted and cleared by Porteous.

Directly after this a mis-kick by Miller sent the ball almost through his own goal, but Whitton managed to fist it away. Unfortunately, the ball fell to (D.) Hannah who sent it straight back, and straight through, giving the home custodian not a chance. The point was received by the East End supporters in significant silence.

From the kick-off a return was made by Sunderland, but their forwards were halted by the intervention of Graham. Then 'hands' against the Wearsiders further relieved the pressure for East End. A rush was then put on the Sunderland citadel and Sorley just failed to score, sending the ball outside the sticks at a fast pace. Creilly and Graham were putting in a goodly amount of work, as was Porteous, who sent out of bounds at a critical time.

A big return by (D.) Hannah was well repulsed by Jeffrey, and some lively scenes were enacted at the top end, the visiting backs being kept active in defence. Miller, the East End back, repulsed a lunge from the Wearside right wing and Porteous at the other end was again kept busy with both head and feet until the ball was centred to Brand, who took it into the East End half, his style of play in doing so being commendable. From a free-kick to the home team Jeffrey shot the ball right into the Sunderland goal mouth, Smellie, however, was equal to the emergency, and as soon as he had cleared Gillespie took up the running, only to drive outside the posts.

Nice play by the whole of the visiting forward quintet was well backed up by Auld, whose second kick sent the ball across the East End goal mouth and out wide. Play from the goal-kick by Whitton went into the Sunderland half again, and another free-kick was won by East End.

McKane sent in a fine shot that Doig managed to fist out but it only went as far as Wallace who returned it in equally splendid style straight into the goal amidst wild cheers, the Novocastrians obtaining their second goal at the end of about half an hour.

The visitors once more retaliated, gaining a corner which was put in by Gillespie, struggle after struggle followed at the lower end, Whitton spoiling a grand shot by Porteous, which brought down the house. However, Gillespie at length found an opening, and sent through, half-time being almost at once called, with the score tied at two goals apiece.

There was only a short interval, barely five minutes, and at 6.35pm Brand resumed for the Wearsiders who now faced having the hill to play against. This seemed not to perturb them as straight from the restart Sunderland made a rally up to the home goal but were stopped in their tracks by Miller. They however continued to press and from a good opening Porteous sent his shot wide and over the byline. Breaking up another Sunderland press Thompson, Sorley and Wallace ran down and a slip by Smellie almost let them in but a handball decision against Thompson halted any danger there was to Sunderland. The homesters pressed again but Collins put his effort over the crossbar and then another good run down was ended when Wallace sent in a poor shot which Doig easily claimed.

From a long kick by Jeffrey an opportunity arose for Thompson but Porteous managed to intercept his effort at the expense of a corner from which Thompson sent over the byline when close in at the post. Play became fast paced and varied, the ball being almost as much in the visitors' quarters as at the home quarters. 'Hands' against McKane once again let in the Wearsiders but Wallace cleared the danger. Collins put in a clever cross-field ball for Wallace, but he just could not reach it in time. Yet another free-kick for 'hands', this time against Jeffrey, was awarded to Sunderland which they could not turn to their advantage. A fast drive by Collins went close, dropping just over the bar. Gillespie thereupon took the ball along to East End territory and crossed it to Brand who's shot went close indeed. Going even closer was an effort by Thompson, a splendid piece of play from Collins saw him deliver a cross to the head of Thompson and the ball missed by a matter of inches.

The East End forwards continued to pressure their opponents' goal and a corner was won but a handball decision against Thompson allowed Sunderland to clear their citadel. A foul by Jeffrey then gave them a fine chance and Whitton had to fist out an effort from Gillespie in magnificent style.

Over the next five minutes or so East End had by far the best of matters during which the ball was taken by Collins right through to Doig who ran out and saved at the cost of a corner, which was headed behind. Play then settled down in midfield for a few minutes. From here Gillespie executed several good runs, but to no avail. Wallace secured a throw-in, and had he been able to screw from one corner he might just have scored, instead he sent the ball wide. Nothing further of a noteworthy character ensued, the visitors' defence proved equal to all the attacks levelled at it, *and there were many of them indeed*, and the game thus ended in a draw.

Newcastle East End..................2 goals.

Sunderland ....2 goals.

Newcastle Daily Chronicle (08/09/1892) p7e.
Sportsman (08/09/1892) p4e.
Sunderland Daily Echo (08/09/1892) p4e.

Game 3: Saturday, September 10, 1892   Newcastle East End vs. Middlesbrough Ironopolis

Competition: Friendly   Venue: St James's Park   Gate: 4,000

| Newcastle East End | 4 - 1 | Middlesbrough Ironopolis |

Scorer(s): Thompson (3 mins, sh); Collins (5 mins); OG [Oliver] (sh)

Scorer(s): Gordon (sh)

Goal, Dave Whitton; *backs*, Harry Jeffrey and Peter Watson; *half-backs*, Bobby Creilly, Willie Graham and Joe McKane; *forwards*, Tom Crate, Harry Reay, Willie Thompson, James Collins, Joe Wallace

Goal, Charles Watts; *backs*, James Elliott and John Oliver; *half-backs*, Thomas Seymour, Robert Chatt and R. Nicholson; *forwards*, Jack Hill, Archibald Hughes, Bob Gordon, Peter Coupar, Wallace McReddie

Referee: Mr Coleman (West Hartlepool)

Kick-Off: 3:45 PM

After having secured a very creditable draw against the champions of the Football League, Sunderland, it was the champions of the Northern League who were the opposition for East End today, and what an impressive display they provided. Making a quick-fire start East End saw themselves two goals to the good within the first five minutes, adding a further two whilst conceding only the once, they therefore ran out winners by four goals to one.

Kick-off, which was scheduled for 3:15pm, had to be delayed by some half-an-hour due to the late arrival of the visitors so the game commenced at 3:45pm. The weather was bright and warm, rather too warm for the physical exertions which lay ahead for the players perhaps, but for the spectators, of which there were at least 4,000, it was beautifully fine, and the delay was not really passed comment upon by them.

Ironopolis started the game at the top of the hill, and rapidly worked their way downfield but McKane was alert to any danger and defended well. This then allowed East End to advance and getting up via good work from the defence through the midfield to the forwards they got the ball into a dangerous area and Elliot was forced to concede a corner. When it was delivered in it was well placed but eventually saved. East End quickly repossessed from the goal-kick and the ball was again driven upwards. From a defensive clearance Reay centred the ball back into the Ironopolis area and Thompson scored the first goal for East End three minutes from the start.

With East End continuing to press hard barely another two minutes had elapsed before they doubled their lead. Watts had come away from his goal to closedown Reay and in the ensuing tackle the ball span free to Collins who had the very simple task of guiding the rebound into a now unguarded net.

Two goals up against the current Northern League champions, within the first five minutes!

This was surely almost too good to be true.

Ironopolis, *as true champions do*, showed that this setback would not deter their efforts and attacked, trying to pass through the home backs, and Coupar was able to get a ground shot away which was gathered up and thrown out by Whitton. They then had a glorious opportunity as they were awarded a free kick for 'hands' right in front of the home goal. Unfortunately for them McReddie ultimately sent it over.

Collins and Crate dodged their way up, showing some good footwork, this was equalled by Chatt who was in evidence, and stopped their advance.

Another free-kick placed the East End goal in jeopardy, this one awarded against Creilly, but the ball was sent through without touching anyone, and that was the chance was gone. East End were playing much the better game, Wallace and Collins doing tricky work. A pass from the left wing let East End in again, but Reay, with a rather wretched effort, failed from in the goal mouth.

Ironopolis did not show up as well as they usually did, but in fairness to the homesters this was because they did not let them. The East End half backs spoiling what little combination there was from them.

Crate had hard lines in not scoring with a shot from distance which went just over the bar. Both Hill and Hughes improved matters for Ironopolis at length but Whitton was in no mood to be beaten. Wallace with a really good sprint got himself well up into the 'Nops area but his own speed was his downfall as he outpaced his other forwards and had to try to hold up play for too long and Chatt relieved the danger.

There followed a corner for East End which was easily got rid of, and when the 'Nops had a series of attacks they were guilty of the most woeful shooting, the ball going absolutely anywhere and everywhere apart from into the goal. Play then slowed considerably for a period, both goals being visited, but neither custodian having much to do.

Hughes, with a long shot, went closest to scoring, indeed he was not far away at all, and any threat to East End was always coming down that Ironopolis right wing, with the other wing forwards not getting much joy. Reay and Crate had the best of a tussle with Oliver, a corner being the result, but this was cleared without difficulty. Play was in midfield when halftime was called, the score being East End two goals, Ironopolis, none.

After a short interval. the game was again set in motion, East End, now having the advantage of the slope, at once attacked the bottom goal. Some exciting scrimmages took place in front of the Ironopolis goal, but for some time their defence managed to hold off the danger. That was until a grand centre by Wallace, from out on the wing, went through off the unfortunate Oliver making a third goal for East End.

Ironopolis then threatened as Coupar and McReddie beat Jeffrey and looked like getting away but Graham came to the rescue and turning defence into attack Oliver was again called to kick away. A free-kick a few yards off the goal line gave the 'Nops a grand chance, but the fates were evidently against them, the kick being dealt with easily and indeed sending Wallace racing away down the field. Thompson and Crate both had an attempt to score but both shot weakly. The visitor's goal was severely bombarded, Oliver and Watts playing strongly.

A visit was paid to the top goal, but Whitton was not called upon. Watson returning to Wallace dodged Chatt and shot strongly all along the ground, Oliver stopped the ball, but Thompson returned it immediately scoring No. 4 for the home team, amid great cheering from the crowd.

Now the Ironopolis were completely outmatched, and rarely crossed the centreline, Oliver being their only man who showed anything like first-class status.

Holding such a substantial lead, East End were now able to reduce their exertions, whilst still ensuring that play ruled in their opponent's half. Wallace had a fair opening but sent his shot way too high and over the bar amid rather ironical laughter from the crowd. Watson sent a long shot down which was blocked, and Collins headed the rebound beautifully, but just over the bar. Crate then shot the ball through, but for some infringement of the rules it was not allowed, though many people did not understand why. Watts then cleared another stinger from the same player. Then, to the astonishment of all, Ironopolis broke away and Gordon scored an easy goal. Immediately on the ball being set down for the restart the whistle declared the game at an end.

Newcastle East End..................4 goals.

Middlesbrough Ironopolis........1 goal.

THE NORTHERN LEAGUE

Middlesbrough vs. Darlington:
The new season of the Northern League was opened today with a fixture between Middlesbrough and Darlington on the Linthorpe Road ground, home of the former of the two. It was the homesters, Middlesbrough, who were to prove victorious, and quite handsomely by three goals to nil. Their opening goal was a penalty and was scored by Roberts, this after about ten minutes of play. The penalty was awarded for a rather cruel and cynical foul on Cronshaw.

Not long after Middlesbrough doubled their lead. This second goal resulted from a corner being well delivered in by Black and was received by Bach who played it on, and it was ultimately headed home by Lewis.

Darlington were reduced to ten-men just before half-time as Fleming, who had been playing a clinking game at inside-right, had the misfortune to twist his knee. There was no more scoring in the first half. The injury to Fleming was serious enough to prevent him making an appearance for the second half so again Darlington were numerically disadvantaged. Despite this they performed admirably but could do nothing about the third goal which came following a melee in the Darlington goal and was scored by Cronshaw.

Middlesbrough ....3 goals.

Darlington ....None.

Middlesbrough: *Goal*, H. Mackay; *backs*, R. Crone and J. Bell; *half-backs*, R. Roberts, J. Stott and T. Bach; *forwards*, T. Cronshaw, B. Lewis, J. McKnight, J. Abraham and D. Black.

Darlington: *Goal*, Auld; *backs*, Coleman and Norris; *half-backs*, Campbell, McDonald and McLean; *forwards*, McPherson, Fleming, Hutchinson, McFarlane and Keay.

Referee: Mr J. Potts (Stockton)

The Referee (11/09/1892) p6c.
Athletic News (12/09/1892) p7f.
Newcastle Daily Chronicle (12/09/1892) p6f.
Northern Echo (12/09/1892) p4d.
Sporting Life (12/09/1892) p4a.

THE NORTHERN LEAGUE
RESULTS TO SATURDAY, SEPTEMBER 10 [INCLUSIVE]

Pos	Team	Pld	W	D	L	Goals F	Goals A	Avg.	Pts
1	Middlesbrough	1	1	0	0	3	0	3.0000	2
2	Middlesbrough Ironopolis	0	0	0	0	0	0	0.0000	0
3	Newcastle East End	0	0	0	0	0	0	0.0000	0
4	Sheffield United	0	0	0	0	0	0	0.0000	0
5	Stockton	0	0	0	0	0	0	0.0000	0
6	Darlington	1	0	0	1	0	3	0.0000	0

Game 4: Saturday, September 17, 1892   **Middlesbrough Ironopolis vs Newcastle East End**

Competition: Friendly   Venue: Paradise Ground   Gate: 5,000

Middlesbrough Ironopolis   1 - 2   Newcastle East End

Scorer(s): Chatt (sh)

Goal, Charles Watts; *backs*, James Elliott and John Oliver; *half-backs*, Duncan McNair, Robert Chatt and R. Nicholson; *forwards*, Jack Hill, Archibald Hughes, William McArthur, Peter Coupar, Wallace McReddie

Referee: Mr Coleman (West Hartlepool)

Scorer(s): Sorley (fh); Collins (sh)

Goal, Dave Whitton; *backs*, Harry Jeffrey and James Miller; *half-backs*, Bobby Creilly, Willie Graham and Joe McKane; *forwards*, James Collins, Tom Crate, Willie Thompson, Jock Sorley, Joe Wallace

Kick-Off: 3:45 PM

The return friendly fixture between East End and Ironopolis drew great interest given that the East Enders had beaten the Northern League champions so handsomely last week. The 'Nops certainly had revenge on their minds, much like last season in their league fixtures.

East End had won at Heaton by the same score as they did at St James's Park last week, four goals to one, whilst Ironopolis won the fixture at Middlesbrough by three goals to one. Indeed, a similar turning of the tables was eagerly looked forward to by Ironopolis, whilst just as eagerly East End were anxious to *"do the double"* over the champions. So, it was in fine weather, and before some five thousand spectators, that battle was commenced.

East End won the toss and with a powerful sun, and a rather strong wind, behind them pressed hard for the first twenty minutes or so, however they were unable to register a point during this period. Oliver, Elliott, McNair and Chatt were proving to be an impenetrable defence against the East End forwards.

The homesters had a few 'break-away' sorties but were never in reality posing much of a threat. Their best effort coming via McReddie who gained possession on the left wing and drove forward with a good run, finishing with a splendid shot, but Whitton fisted away. East End followed this with a grand charge and Collins sent in a hot shot which Watts saved in very fine style.

The next ten minutes or so saw the 'Nops kept pushed back and totally on the defensive as East End pressed hard for the opener. Hughes relieved the pressure temporarily when he dashed down the right wing and gave to McArthur, who was well placed, but with a very timely interception Miller put in a tackle and East End were soon back in front of the Ironopolis goal.

Then it seemed the breakthrough had arrived. From a free kick, awarded for a foul, Jeffrey sent in a fine looping ball which Sorley managed to get on the end of and headed through in equally fine style.

The East End jubilation was abruptly cut short when the goal was disallowed for an offside decision being awarded. The efficacy of the decision is hard to determine as it was variously described as *"narrow"* and *"unlucky"*.

Two minutes later East End had a glorious opportunity to finally open the scoring when they were awarded a penalty, Sorley unfortunately sent his spot-kick just a little too high, and over the bar it went, a desperate disappointment.

East End were somewhat piqued at their seemingly bad luck and made some desperate charges on the Ironoplis goal. During one Sorley sent in a cracker of a shot which Watts caught, but inexplicably dropped immediately, and the ball rolled over his goal line and through. Truly a most bizarre opening goal indeed.

Almost directly after this Thompson very nearly doubled East End's lead when he hit a clinking shot that went a mere inch or two over the bar. In another East End attack Watts was forced to leave his goal and running out he got the ball away, but badly, as it went straight to East End but when the ball was sent towards the now unguarded goal it went harmlessly wide, much to the relief of Watts no doubt.

McNair then had to concede a corner, but East End could not make any advantage from it. Ironopolis then had a breakaway but they were also unable to profit from it and it was during this that the half time whistle was sounded.

Following the short interval East End resumed their pressing but the ball was soon returned, and Nicholson managed to get a beauty of a shot away, but Whitton fisted it out. The 'Nops then won a corner, thanks to the persistence of McReddie, which proved fruitless and McNair then followed with another splendid shot, but this time Whitton caught the ball.

Immediately after this Hughes shot straight into the hands of Whitton who got it away and East End were back on the attack. The game was being played at a fast pace, and was terrifically exciting, the action going from end-to-end keeping the crowd thoroughly entertained. Undoubtedly though it was East End who were having the better of the play, on balance, and they certainly looked the more dangerous when attacking, which they did at every opportunity afforded them.

As had seemed to be increasingly inevitable East End were soon to get their second goal and it was from a hot scrimmage in front of the Ironopolis goal. With the ball zipping around the area Collins was able to get a decent purchase on it and shot it through splendidly.

Having already made two serious errors, one leading to the first, the other giving East End an open goal to shoot for, Watts made a third 'unforced' error. East End where pressing in yet another attack and the ball was shot in, but straight at Watts. He dithered and dallied for what seemed like an age and the East End forwards rushed him and the ball was got away more by good luck than good management. Not long after East End launched another attack at the Ironopolis goal, but this was to no avail.

Ironopolis then earned some respite as their left wing broke away and the ball was passed inside to McArthur who hit a splendid shot that brought about an equally splendid save from Whitton. Another grand run from the 'Nops left wing resulted in another save from Whitton.

Immediately after this, from a free-kick, Chatt sent in a high shot which had Whitton beaten and the arrears were halved, the champions at last beginning to show some form.

Another attack on the East End citadel saw Hill desperately unlucky as he saw his shot going just past the post. The game was then halted for a few minutes as Collins was hurt. On resuming the 'Nops played much better, and made several attempts at securing the equaliser, but the East End defence proved too strong and the game ended without further scoring. The result therefore being:

Middlesbrough Ironopolis.......1 goal.

Newcastle East End.................2 goals.

Newcastle Daily Chronicle (17/09/1892) p7e.
North-Eastern Daily Gazette (19/09/1892) p3e.
Northern Daily Telegraph (19/09/1892) p3f.
Newcastle Daily Chronicle (19/09/1892) p6f.
Yorkshire Herald (19/09/1892) p7e.

Game 5: Saturday, September 24, 1892 — Sheffield United vs. Newcastle East End

Competition: Northern League Venue: Bramall Lane Gate: 5,000

Sheffield United   5 - 1   Newcastle East End

Scorer(s): Drummond (51 mins); Scott (55 mins); Wallace (60 mins); Hammond (64 mins); Dobson (87 mins)

Goal, Harry Lilley; *backs*, Michael Whitham and Bob Cain; *half-backs*, Rab Howell, Billy Hendry and Ernest Needham; *forwards*, Alexander Wallace, Sammy Dobson, Jack Scott, Harry Hammond, Jack Drummond

Referee: J. Potts (Stockton)

Scorer(s): Sorley (38 mins)

Goal, Dave Whitton; *backs*, Harry Jeffrey and James Miller; *half-backs*, Bobby Creilly, Willie Graham and Joe McKane; *forwards*, James Collins, Tom Crate, Willie Thompson, Jock Sorley, Joe Wallace

Kick-Off: 3:00 PM

The opening game of the Northern League campaign for both Sheffield United and Newcastle East End, was an eagerly anticipated affair, especially with Sheffield United also having representation in the new Division Two of the Football League, *an opportunity that had been turned down by East End*. The performances of East End prior to this match had been of the most brilliant character, and consequently it was generally expected of them to play well against Sheffield United. In their Northern League meetings last season, the Sheffielders proved too strong for the Novocastrians and they won both fixtures, the first by two goals to one, the second by three goals to nil, however Newcastle were now a far stronger team than they were last year.

Both clubs played their full-strength elevens and as kick-off approached the weather was dry and bright and some 5,000 spectators had gathered around the ropes. Winning the toss East End elected to kick towards the Shoreham-street end thus taking advantage of a strong wind and having the bright sun in their favour.

Sheffield were the first to show to any advantage, indeed immediately attacking with vigour. Wallace, *of the Sheffield variety*, was the first to have an effort on target when he whipped in a shot from the extreme right, but Whitton made the save. Minutes later Hendry was unlucky to see a fast effort he put in go just wide of the post. East End then pressed and Sorley saw two opportunities go begging. The first was an effort he put wide but the second moments later was a clinker of a shot that brought out an excellent save from Lilley as he just managed to push it over the bar and concede a corner. Whilst the corner was to no avail East End kept up the pressure and a hot shot from Collins cannoned off a defender and a similar effort from Crate not long after seeing the ball going only inches wide.

With a smart passing move Sheffield made progress up the field and looked like scoring but

Jeffrey cleared the danger. Collins then sped away once more, and the ball was back in the home quarters and Crate again missed by mere inches. Aided by the wind and the sun East End were having the best of matters, but the Sheffielders defended resolutely. Then their forwards, ever and anon, came away racing up the field together, only however to be driven back. East End appeared to have the advantage of the physique and they went mainly in for long crossing whilst the United front rank on the other hand adopted mainly a short passing style. Play was for the most part during this period in the home half.

Hendry and his companions were forced to work tirelessly in defence and Lilley was called upon to make two or three very smart saves, one of these being a puzzler from Collins. Next Sorley sent a shot only narrowly high. Despite good work from Cain and Whitham they could not prevent East End getting near and they sent in a succession of shots, all which Lilley stopped, except one, but to the dismay of East End the point was disallowed for offside decision. At this point East End must have been wondering what they had to do to score.

The East End continued to press and attacked mercilessly and with great vigour then on 38 minutes they finally made the breakthrough, Sorley, being left in possession in the left channel scored with a fantastic screw-shot that gave Lilley absolutely no chance whatsoever. A very well-deserved lead for East End.

Funnily the goal seemed to invigorate the Sheffielders more than the Novocastrians as it was the homesters who now 'took up the baton' as it were. Making a rush on the East End goal they were awarded a foul in a promising position but when they delivered in the free-kick Jeffrey intervened just in the nick of time and sent the ball well out. Play was then transferred to the United lines and the backs had all their work cut out to relieve. Dobson, from the return, dashed away and with the East End goal at his mercy he put in a great shot, but Whitton beat it back and from the second return he made the most marvellous of saves. With the homesters a goal behind, but in the ascendancy, half time was called.

Upon resumption Sheffield went straight on the attack and within the first minute had a corner, it was however to be fruitless. Returning to the attack Wallace, *for Sheffield*, had a fine opening but his effort went over the bar. Again, Hendry got the United going away down the right and the ball was put into the East End centre where Miller, with an unfortunate mis-kick, scooped the ball into the air and Drummond pounced on it to head it home and the homesters were level.

Within a matter of minutes, they were then in the lead!

Scott worked his way down, passing and repassing, until he was near enough for a shot, his effort however was beaten out by Whitton, but only to Dobson. He passed it once again to Scott and this time his shot was true, and Whitton could do nothing about it.

With the wind and sun now behind them, and a lead of one goal, the United were now unstoppable and they attacked almost continuously. Wallace added a third for them, following a great pass by Hammond.

Still attacking Whitton was forced into making a great save and then four minutes after being the provider for Wallace's goal Hammond was the scorer as he got an opening and scored with a capital shot.

Shortly after the fourth goal East End had their first real attack of the second half and Creilly gave Lilley a long shot to deal with. A corner for East End came to nothing, as did a one for the United. Play dropped off quite dramatically as with a lead of four goals to one in favour of the homesters the result was in no doubt and there was little interest shown by either side. Sheffield kept up the pressure, in a manner, and Whitton had a few saves to make but all were relatively easy. East End only had the one serious effort, that coming from a fine shot by Crate which Lilley saved, on all other occasions when they got forward, they showed hesitancy, which allowed the United defence to prevail.

In an unfortunate incident during a United attack Creilly and Hammond collided, dashing their heads together, whilst going for the ball. Both players were stunned, and the game was stopped for several minutes. Creilly, in addition to being stunned, was bleeding quite badly from a scalp wound. Ultimately, he was forced to leave the field of play and could take no further part in proceedings. Shortly after this Collins was seriously winded and the game was once again stopped. With East End now down to ten-men they were kept almost camped in the top third of the pitch and whilst the Sheffield forwards were not exerting themselves there were several 'half attempts' on the East End goal. It was from one of these, and a mere three minutes before time was due to be called, that Dobson managed to put through and secure a fifth goal for the Sheffielders.

Sheffield United...................5 goals.

Newcastle East End ....1 goal.

Sheffield and Rotherham Independent (24/09/1892) p11c.
Newcastle Daily Chronicle (26/09/1892) p6f.
The Northern Echo (26/09/1892) p4d.
Sheffield Daily Telegraph (26/09/1892) p7d.

THE NORTHERN LEAGUE RESULTS TO SATURDAY, SEPTEMBER 24 [INCLUSIVE]							Goals		
Pos	Team	Pld	W	D	L	F	A	Avg.	Pts
1	Sheffield United	1	1	0	0	5	1	5.0000	2
2	Middlesbrough	1	1	0	0	3	0	3.0000	2
3	Newcastle East End	1	0	0	1	1	5	0.2000	0
4	Middlesbrough Ironopolis	0	0	0	0	0	0	0.0000	0
5	Stockton	0	0	0	0	0	0	0.0000	0
6	Darlington	1	0	0	1	0	3	0.0000	0

In other news...

Whilst pre- "Tyne-Wear Derby" days, do we have within the pages of The Athletic News, the beginnings of the rivalry between the Tynesiders and the Wearsiders? Also, do we have the evidence to suggest that this rivalry was started, *and supported,* by the press! Here is an exchange between two correspondents for said newspaper for you to make up your own mind. First, this snippet from Monday, September 5th:

"*Having sent the Celts home to Glasgow in a sufficiently humiliated mood, the Wanderers will cross over to Newcastle on Wednesday, and take out some of the colossal bumptious and bounce with which East End seems to be afflicted.*"   TOM TIDDLER.

Now the retort which appeared in the edition printed a week later, Monday, September 12th:

BUMPTIOUSNES AND BOUNCE

"*I would like to ask your Wearside savant what price the above as regards East End, who took his remarks of last week as a sort of sneer. Knowledge of football is certainly not confined to Sunderland, and the ability to play football is also spread over other parts of the country to some extent. Knowing well these facts I don't feel hurt myself, but I can assure you many bitter things were said on Wednesday as the outcome of the indiscreet – chaff it may have been – words of the gentleman on Wearside.*"   TOWN MOOR

As to the "A's"...

Date	Home	Score	Away	
September 3, 1892	Gateshead NER	3 - 1	Newcastle East End A	*Northern Alliance*
Gateshead NER:	*Goal,* J. Bewley; *backs,* Duncan and Redpath; *half-backs,* Atkinson, Manners (captain) and Jefferson; *forwards,* Hulse, Noble, W. Bewley, Dean and Minns.			
Newcastle East End A:	*Goal,* Scott; *backs,* Crichton and Rodgers; *half-backs,* Wilde, Kirkland and Fitzgerald; *forwards,* Simm, Grierson, Cattell and Dixon.			
Referee: Mr D. Petch (Sunderland). NB: East End arrived a man short therefore played the game with only 10 men				
September 10, 1892	Seaham Harbour	1 - 1	Newcastle East End A	*Northern Alliance*
Newcastle East End A:	*Goal,* Scott; *backs,* Crichton and Rodgers; *half-backs,* Fitzgerald, Wilde and Queen; *forwards,* Grierson, Dixon Donaldson, Simm and Barker.			
Referee: Mr J. Taylor				
September 17, 1892	Newcastle East End A	7 - 2	Ashington	*Northern Alliance*
Newcastle East End A:	*Goal,* Ward; *backs,* Rodgers and Crichton; *half-backs,* Cattell, Wilde and Fitzgerald; *forwards,* Coupar, Dixon, Donaldson, Dodds and Grierson.			
Ashington:	*Goal,* Hind; *backs,* Milburn and Milligan; *half-backs,* Bates, Atkinson and Williams; *forwards,* Lettsome, Wetherstone, Dean, Cowen and Boutland.			
Referee: Mr G.B. McQuillen (Newcastle)				
September 24, 1892	Newcastle East End A	3 - 0	Newcastle Albion	*Friendly*
Newcastle East End A	*Goal,* Ward; *backs,* Rodgers and Crichton; *half-backs,* Fitzgerald, Wilde and Atteridge; *forwards,* Dixon, Simm, Donaldson, Dodds and Grierson.			
Newcastle Albion	*Goal,* Ryder; *backs,* Knight and Neal; *half-backs,* Thompson, Donald and Anderson; *forwards,* Murray, Rennolds, Halliday, Kirkpatrick and Ridley.			
NB: Game played to fill a vacant date for East End.				

October 1892

Games Played in October 1892						
V	Date	F	A	R	Opposition	Competition
H	01/10/1892	3	1	W	Middlesbrough	Northern League
A	06/10/1892	1	3	L	Stockton	Friendly
A	08/10/1892	1	0	W	Middlesbrough	Friendly
H	15/10/1892	7	0	W	South of Ayrshire	Friendly
H	22/10/1892	2	0	W	Heart of Midlothian	Friendly
H	29/10/1892	4	1	W	Mossend Swifts	Friendly

Appearances & Goals ~ October 1892

	Total		League		Friendly	
Name	Apps	Goals	Apps	Goals	Apps	Goals
Barker, John	1		1		0	
Collins, James	5	4	1		4	4
Coupar, William	1		0		1	
Crate, Thomas "Tom"	6	2	1		5	2
Creilly, Robert "Bobby"	4	1	0		4	1
Dixon, Henry	2	1	0		2	1
Graham, William "Willie"	6		1		5	
Jeffrey, Harry	6		1		5	
Kirkland, J.	1				1	
McKane, Joseph "Joe"	6		1		5	
Miller, James	5		1		4	
Reay, Harry	5	1	1		4	1
Sorley, John "Jock"	3	4	0		3	4
Thompson, Willie	3	1	1	1	2	
Wallace, Joseph "Joe"	5	2	1	2	4	
Watson, Peter	2		0		2	
Whitton, David "Dave"	6		1		5	

Season to Date (03/09/1892 - 29/10/1892 inclusive)

	Total		League		Friendly	
Name	Apps	Goals	Apps	Goals	Apps	Goals
Barker, John	1		1		0	
Collins, James	10	6	2		8	6
Coupar, William	1		0		1	
Crate, Thomas "Tom"	11	3	2		9	3
Creilly, Robert "Bobby"	9	1	1		8	1
Dixon, Henry	2	1	0		2	1
Graham, William "Willie"	11		2		9	
Jeffrey, Harry	11		2		9	
Kirkland, J.	1				1	
McKane, Joseph "Joe"	11		2		9	
Miller, James	9		2		7	
Reay, Harry	6	1	1		5	1
Sorley, John "Jock"	7	6	1	1	6	5
Thompson, Willie	8	3	2	1	6	2
Wallace, Joseph "Joe"	10	3	2	2	8	1
Watson, Peter	2		0		2	
Whitton, David "Dave"	11		2		9	

Game 6: Saturday, October 1, 1892　　　　　　　　　Newcastle East End vs. Middlesbrough

Competition: Northern League　　　Venue: St James's Park　　　　　　　Gate: 4,000

Newcastle East End　　3 - 1　　Middlesbrough

Scorer(s): Wallace (fh, fh); Thompson (sh)

Goal, Dave Whitton; *backs*, Harry Jeffrey and James Miller; *half-backs*, Tom Crate, Willie Graham and Joe McKane; *forwards*, Harry Reay, James Collins, Willie Thompson, John Barker, Joe Wallace

Referee: W. H. Stacey (Sheffield)

Scorer(s): Abraham (sh)

Goal, J.W. Fall; *backs*, T. Bach and Bob Crone; *half-backs*, J. McManus, Bob Roberts and J. Stott; *forwards*, Abraham, W. McCabe, J. McKnight, Ben Lewis, D. Black

Kick-Off: 3:45 PM

Newcastle East End welcomed Middlesbrough to St James's Park for the first time to play out their Northern League fixture. A historic occasion indeed as whilst the games played previously this season were all 'friendlies' this match represented East End's very first 'official' fixture at their new home. Befitting of such an occasion there were fully 4,000 spectators in attendance.

The homesters were a slightly weakened team as both Sorley and Creilly had picked up injuries in the game against Sheffield United at Bramall Lane last week and were not sufficiently recovered enough to be in the team. Middlesbrough won the toss and elected to play 'downhill'.

Thompson kicked off and an excursion was made to the top goal, but Roberts intervened with a smart tackle and sent the ball back down. A good run up, and pass, by Barker was nullified by offside against Wallace. Black then ran down and gave to Abraham who had the goal at his mercy but failed with his shot. The East End goal was again hotly besieged, but the Middlesbrough forwards were in very poor shooting form, Roberts, from the half-back position, also making some weak attempts. A free-kick for 'hands' almost let East End in with a chance to open the scoring but Graham very narrowly missed the target with the custodian, Fall, well beaten. Running up the left-wing Wallace put a grand cross in and from this Collins put in a good effort, but McManus was able to kick away.

East End once again took up the play and put the Middlesbrough defence under extreme pressure, Crone being forced to play a saving kick out. His clearance however only went as far as Wallace, who, with a fantastic and acrobatic overhead kick, sent it through at the top corner, amidst tremendous applause from the crowd.

This reverse brought the expected reaction from the Middlesbrough and they made a concerted effort to bring about the equaliser. Though making quite a lot of headway they were to find that Miller was in no mood to be beaten in the heart of the East End defence. Crone almost fell victim to one of Miller's long clearing punts, as his attempted return was sliced and almost went into his own goal. Luckily for him the only damage was conceding a corner which was well placed, but ultimately dealt with.

Starting another East End attack Crate played the ball through for Collins who dribbled his way quite beautifully past McManus and crossed at the opportune moment to Wallace, who, from quite close quarters, fired a shot past Fall. There were loud appeals for an 'offside' against Wallace from the Middlesbrough players, and their supporters, but these were dismissed and waved away by the referee, Mr Stacey.

Though now two goals to the good East End kept up the pressure and both Collins and Wallace, now looking for his hat-trick, had hard lines. Black played well on the Middlesbrough left-wing but found Jeffrey always ready and alert to any danger. Miller, with a quite spectacular shot from the half-way line, was unlucky to see his effort go barely a yard wide. Then a slight scare for East End as a rare mis-kick from Miller fell to McCabe and his effort went only narrowly over the bar. A huge let-off for East End, and a saving of any embarrassment for Miller!

The visitors, to a man, carried more weight than East End and were solid in the tackle which hampered the progress of East End to a fair degree, though in counter-balance they were the swifter of the two sides and were having the greater percentage of possession.

Lewis ran down and almost reached the byline but McKane got across to put in a successful tackle, managing to get the ball to Barker in the process. He and Wallace raced down the left-wing exchanging passes and delivered the ball into Thompson who unfortunately sent the ball wide of the post. As half-time was called the ball was being played harmlessly in midfield.

With McKnight striding into the centre and starting the ball rolling for Middlesbrough the second half was set underway. East End though soon gained possession and took the play to their opponents' goal, and some pressure was put on the Middlesbrough defence. Crone managed to clear the danger and a race was on towards the other end. Miller, as in the first half, provided a stout obstacle to the attack and finally Stott kicked at goal and his shot just grazed the top of the bar as it went over and out of play. The game then, for little apparent reason, sank into a one of poor play indeed concentrated mainly around the midfield.

A free-kick awarded to East End broke the monotony as it was launched into the area and from it a corner was won. The ball was well placed in and Collins made a fine shot which just missed the post and went out. The Middlesbrough right-wing broke away but once again Miller was there, and he sent the ball back up the field and East End won another free-kick in a promising position but no advantage to them was gained. Indeed, the Teesiders were the ones to benefit most and foraged forward, making up a lot of ground. They managed to get a shot away from which Whitton had to concede a corner in making his save. The delivery from the corner was comfortably dealt with and Thompson ran the ball out of danger.

Collins had a beauty of a shot gathered and threw out by Fall, after which a shot, from a long distance, was thundered in by McKane but Fall easily managed to save that one with his feet, kicking it well out. Soon pressure was put on the home goal which Collins was called upon to deal with. On the ascendancy Middlesbrough continued to probe for an opening and Whitton was called upon to do some work but did all that was asked of him.

A rush was then made by the home forwards and from this Reay, on the end of a grand cross from McKane, was unlucky to see his headed effort go just outside. Play was now beginning to speed up again and each goal was visited in turn, but on each occasion the defences were found to be superb. After one rather concerted attack on the East End goal Whitton was called upon to make a fine save and the ball was cleared momentarily. The visitors returned in greater force and overwhelmed the home defence and with a clever shot from in the middle of the area Abraham scored smartly for the Teesiders.

This rather irked the homesters and their forwards pressed high up the field and Crone had to defend a shot from Collins. Whitton was then given more work to do as the visitor's forwards were buoyed by their success as much as the East End defence were irked. They forced a corner but could not capitalise and the danger was passed. Continuing the 'to-and-fro' nature of the game East End once again forced play but were weak in front of goal. Collins though did get away a good shot which missed by a matter of inches. This was immediately followed up by an effort from Reay which went equally close. Fall then fisted out a shot by Wallace and the ball fell directly to Collins who sent in a swift shot which struck the bar and rebounded into play.

A run up by the Middlesbrough left wing led to a corner from which the ball was taken away by Thompson and pressure was resumed on the Middlesbrough goal. East End won a couple of corners which were ineffectual, and then their forwards once again awoke to their task. McKane worked his way up and passed through to Thompson who put on Newcastle's third goal with a grand flying shot. That third goal for East End in effect killed off the game as a spectacle and it petered out with play of a pretty poor standard from both sides. A disappointing end to what had been a quite entertaining game.

Newcastle East End .... 3 goals.
Middlesbrough .... 1 goal.

STOCKTON VS DARLINGTON

A good crowd, of around 6,000 spectators, gathered at the Victoria Ground Stockton to witness this encounter in rather resplendent weather. Darlington won the toss and decided to play with a gentle breeze in their favour from the Oxbridge-road end. The first half produced a rather uncharacteristic performance from the homesters as they showed decidedly poor form. Despite this they managed to score twice but conceded thrice! The goals, as they arrived, were from Hutchinson, putting the visitors in front and then Baillie bringing up the first equaliser. Then Hutchinson and McLean each scored for Darlington but and before the break Townley pulled one back for Stockton. The second half saw the Stocktonians deliver a far better performance and they dominated proceedings and ultimately McLean equalised once more for them. Try as each side might neither could go on to find a winning and a quite thrilling match ended with probably the fairest of results.

Stockton .... 3 goals.

Darlington .... 3 goal.

Stockton: *Goal*, Ramsay; *backs*, Lindsay and McDermid; *half-backs*, Shaw, Baillie and Graham; *forwards*, Crawford, McClung, Thompson, Jones and Townley.

Darlington: *Goal*, Auld; *backs*, Coleman and Denman; *half backs*, McDonald, Waites and Campbell; *forwards*, McPherson, McLean, Hutchinson, McFarlane and Keay.

Newcastle Daily Chronicle (01/10/1892) p7e.
Evening Press (03/10/1892) p4g.
Newcastle Daily Chronicle (03/10/1892) p5e.
The Northern Echo (03/10/1892) p4e.
Sporting Life (03/10/1892) p4d.

THE NORTHERN LEAGUE
RESULTS TO SATURDAY, OCTOBER 1 [INCLUSIVE]

Pos	Team	Pld	W	D	L	F	A	Avg.	Pts
1	Sheffield United	1	1	0	0	5	1	5.0000	2
2	Middlesbrough	2	1	0	1	4	3	1.3333	2
3	Newcastle East End	2	1	0	1	4	6	0.6667	2
4	Stockton	1	0	1	0	3	3	1.0000	1
5	Darlington	2	0	1	1	3	6	0.5000	1
6	Middlesbrough Ironopolis	0	0	0	0	0	0	0.0000	0

Game 7: Thursday, October 6, 1892 — Stockton vs. Newcastle East End

Competition: Friendly Venue: Victoria Ground Gate: 4,000

Stockton 3 - 1 Newcastle East End

Scorer(s): McClung (sh, sh); Townley (sh)

Goal, Charlie Ramsay; *backs*, Bob Shaw and Robert McDermid; *half-backs*, Willie Willocks, James Graham and J. Baillie; *forwards*, Bill Crawford, D.C. Atkin, Jack Jones, Robert McClung, Billy Townley

Referee: Mr Kellcher (South Bank)

Scorer(s): Collins (sh)

Goal, Dave Whitton; *backs*, Harry Jeffrey and James Miller; *half-backs*, Willie Graham, J. Kirkland and Joe McKane; *forwards*, James Collins, Tom Crate, Willie Thompson, Jock Sorley, Joe Wallace

Sheffield United were supposed to play a friendly fixture against Stockton today in celebration of "Charter Day" but when they disappointed Stockton by withdrawing from the game Newcastle East End accepted an invitation to play in their stead. Charter Day being a local holiday which was declared in honour of the incorporation of the new borough of Thornaby-on-Tees.

There was a good attendance at the game and Stockton were giving a start to their new half-back, Willocks, who had arrived from Arbroath, and were giving a trial to an amateur, Atkin, at outside-right. Atkin it was noted seemed to make the greater impression of the two with his dashing play and the confidence in which he delivered balls into the centre. His accuracy and timing were also noted by local reporters. For East End Peter Watson and Harry Reay travelled with the team as the reserve players.

The first half of the game was a very tightly fought affair, each side having opportunities but neither side scoring. However, Stockton did have the ball in the East End goal on two occasions. The first was disallowed for an offside decision against Crawford, whilst the second saw a free-kick being sent into the goal but as no one had touched the ball in its passage it too was disallowed. For the latter period of the half Stockton were reduced to ten men as new boy Willocks had to retire due to an injury. On balance East End did have the better of things, being quicker on the ball and playing more precise and accurate football, but the work rate of Stockton and their closing down of the East End forwards nullified any benefit of the superior football displayed by East End.

In the second half numerical equality was restored as Willocks returned to the Stockton line-up. Despite this it was East End, via Collins, who opened the scoring. There was a splendid combined rush by the East End forward quintet and Collins finished the move with a rattling good shot which gave Ramsay no chance of saving.

This certainly livened up the play and Stockton went heavily for the equaliser which they justly got through McClung. Stockton had made a good move down and Townley sent in a magnificent shot which Whitton as finely repulsed. They were not to be denied though as Atkin put in a beautiful centre for McClung to bring about the equaliser, amidst much, and loud, cheering. This seemed to act like an inspiration for the Stocktonians as within less than a minute of the equaliser their right wing again got down and

Atkin passed to Crawford who lofted the ball to McClung who headed home the second goal amid an ovation. It was not lost on anyone that both these goals were excellently set up by Atkin.

Further joy was to come to the homesters as they pressed East End heavily and getting possession Townley, with a grand effort, scored with a beauty of a shot that gave Whitton absolutely no chance of saving. With Stockton now comfortably, *if somewhat surprisingly*, in the lead, there was no chance of them relinquishing it. Try as they might, East End, with all their superior brand of football, were not breaking down the resolute Stockton defence. Conversely, Stockton were not too interested in pushing for a fourth goal. So, with Stockton defending stoutly and East End attacking ineffectually there was no further scoring and the game ended with a win for the Charter Day celebrators.

Stockton .... 3 goals.
Newcastle East End .... 1 goal.

Newcastle Daily Chronicle (07/10/1892) p7e.
Northern Echo (07/10/1892) p2f.
Northern Daily Telegraph (07/10/1892) p7e.

Game 8: Saturday, October 8, 1892   Middlesbrough vs. Newcastle East End

Competition: Friendly   Venue: Linthorpe Road   Gate: 3,000

Middlesbrough   0 - 1   Newcastle East End

Scorer(s): *none*

Goal, J.W. Fall; *backs*, T. Bach and J. McManus; *half-backs*, Bob Crone, J. Stott and Bob Roberts; *forwards*, Cronshaw, W. McCabe, J. McKnight, Ben Lewis, D. Black

Referee: A. Grundy (Whitburn)

Scorer(s): Collins (fh)

Goal, Dave Whitton; *backs*, Harry Jeffrey and James Miller; *half-backs*, Bobby Creilly, Willie Graham and Joe McKane; *forwards*, Harry Reay, Tom Crate, Henry Dixon, James Collins, William Coupar

Kick Off: 3:45 PM

Following their defeat last week, in a Northern League fixture at St James's Park, this was an early opportunity for Middlesbrough to recoup some pride, if not points, in this friendly fixture. This was East End's second visit to Teesside, the other being to oppose Northern League champions Ironopolis, which East End duly won. So, in more than one way this was quite an eagerly anticipated encounter by both sides.

An excursion train left Newcastle Central Station at 13:15 and the players travelled on a saloon car attached to the train thus ensuring anyone travelling on said train would be on time

for kick-off. East End travelled without Sorley and Thompson, both of whom had picked up injuries in the game against Stockton on Thursday, Henry Dixon and William Coupar being called up from the reserves to replace them. Wallace, who was reported as being *"very unwell"* did not travel either. The weather was most beautiful for the time of year with the only drawback being the state of the ground, it was soft underfoot and cut up easily, not very conducive to accurate football.

Play opened in favour of East End and McManus in the heart of the Middlesbrough defence was called upon three times to clear the danger. Each time he did so the visitors just once again pressured until finally this pressure was relieved as Crate sent a shot by. From the goal-kick the ball travelled quickly, and for a period the game went from end-to-end in a most exciting manner. Both defences were admirable, with Graham for East End particularly distinguishing himself. In one Middlesbrough attack McManus found himself well up the pitch and passed to Cronshaw who ran away from all pursuers and delivered a hard shot which beat Whitton but unfortunately for him, and luckily for East End, smacked the upright. Whitton got to the rebound but in doing so conceded a corner. This was well delivered, and McKnight should have done better but missed a capital opportunity.

The homesters were then severely pressed. McManus and Crone were both called into action, making desperate clearances, and Fall had to save brilliantly from an effort by Crate. The Middlesbrough defence was becoming seriously, and increasingly, taxed and eventually conceded a corner from which East End earned no advantage. With East End not letting up and sustaining the pressure they were placing on the Middlesbrough goal, it looked as if their defence was finally broken when Collins played the ball to Crate and he sent through with relative ease. Any excitement was however short-lived as the point was ruled out for offside. The relief was tangible amongst the home team, and supporters, and with renewed vigour they began to exert some pressure of their own, unfortunately for them though the combinations of their forward line was anything but good and the East End defence easily frustrated their efforts.

After Fall had cleared some grand shots a little midfield play followed before East End once again surged forward and in a great passing move Reay gave to Dixon who in turn sent to Collins who scored with a smart shot. Even, and exciting, play was the order up to the interval and with no further addition to the scoring East End were deserved of their lead.

On resumption, following the break, East End worked their way into the Middlesbrough quarters but were well driven back. A free-kick for Middlesbrough allowed them to make great territorial advantage and with the ball well forward McKnight sent his shot wide. Middlesbrough were now working very hard and were having the best of matters, but again their forward combination was ineffectual and comfortably dealt with by the East End defence. Whenever that defence was breached Whitton was there to deal with anything, and everything, with relative ease.

East End then once more took up the running and Bach distinguished himself on several occasions with his timely interventions and smart tackling. Even work then became the order of play once more and towards the close Middlesbrough pressed. On one occasion the excitement rose in the crowd as Lewis had a grand shot, but Whitton was there and saved equally grandly. Struggle as hard as they might the homesters could not bring about the equaliser and the game ended with the first half goal from Collins being the only one scored. The result was therefore:

Middlesbrough..........................None.

Newcastle East End ....1 goal.

Northern League

Sheffield United vs. Middlesbrough Ironopolis
This match was brought off at Bramall Lane, Sheffield before some 3,000 spectators. The weather was fine, dry and bright, perfect conditions for the eagerly anticipated encounter between the United of Sheffield, also represented in the 'new' Division Two, and the current champions of the Northern League, Middlesbrough Ironopolis. The United won the toss and took the slight advantage of having the wind and sun in their favour. McArthur kicked off towards the Bramall Lane end for the 'Nops but during a finely, and closely, contested first half, it was indeed the homesters who had the better of things but try as they might they could not break through a very resolute Ironopolis defence who proved to be impenetrable. When the interval arrived, there had been no scoring.

The second half was again a stubbornly contested affair with neither side able to conquer the other. The home side, having only the slightly better of the play. Try as they might however, they could not find a way through and the game ended in a goalless draw.

Sheffield United ....None.

Middlesbrough Ironopolis ....None.

Game by Game ~ October 1892

Sheffield United: *Goal*, Lilley; *backs*, Cain and Whittam; *half-backs*, Howell, Hendry and Needham; *forwards*, Drummond; Hammond, Dobson, Watson and Scott.

Middlesbrough Ironopolis: *Goal*, Watts; *backs*, Elliott and Langley; *half-backs*, McNair, Chatt and Oliver; *forwards*, McReddie; Seymour, Hughes, Hill and McArthur.

Referee: Mr W.H. Jope (Wolverhampton).

Newcastle Daily Chronicle (08/10/1892) p7e.
Athletic News (10/10/1892) p6d.
Evening Press (10/10/1892) p4g.
Newcastle Daily Chronicle (10/10/1892) p6e.
Sheffield and Rotherham Independent (10/10/1892) p7c.
Sporting Life (10/10/1892) p4e.

THE NORTHERN LEAGUE
RESULTS TO SATURDAY, OCTOBER 8 [INCLUSIVE]

Pos	Team	Pld	W	D	L	F	A	Avg.	Pts
1	Sheffield United	2	1	1	0	5	1	5.0000	3
2	Middlesbrough	2	1	0	1	4	3	1.3333	2
3	Newcastle East End	2	1	0	1	4	6	0.6667	2
4	Stockton	1	0	1	0	3	3	1.0000	1
5	Darlington	2	0	1	1	3	6	0.5000	1
6	Middlesbrough Ironopolis	1	0	1	0	0	0	0.0000	1

Game 9: Saturday, October 15, 1892   Newcastle East End vs. South of Ayrshire

Competition: Friendly   Venue: St James's Park

Newcastle East End   7 - 0   South of Ayrshire

Scorer(s): Reay (fh); Creilly (fh); Collins (fh, sh); Crate (fh, sh); Dixon (sh)

Scorer(s): *none*

Goal, Dave Whitton; *backs*, Harry Jeffrey and Peter Watson; *half-backs*, Bobby Creilly, Willie Graham and Joe McKane; *forwards*, Harry Reay, Tom Crate, Henry Dixon, James Collins and Joe Wallace.

Goal, A. Stark; *backs*, R. Laffardy and Mason; *half-backs*, Baird, Heslop and J. Walker; *forwards*, Currock, McLane, W. Graham, J. Watson and J. Bunyton.

Referee: Mr Coleman (Gateshead)

Kick-Off: 3:15 PM

Annbank, who created a very favourable impression here last season, were to have been the visitors to St James's Park today but this fixture clashed with their cup tie, which of course took priority. A 'scratch' team was procured in their stead by J. Graham, late of Preston North End. The weather was beautifully fine, but the attendance was only small, this perhaps reflecting the enforced change of opposition,

South of Ayrshire kicked-off but it was not long before East End were in front of their goal. Whilst there was quite a rally nothing of importance was gained by East End and the danger was cleared. It was not long however before East End were again looking dangerous as Jeffrey put a great return into the visitor's goal, giving their custodian, Stark, some difficulty in making the save. Crate then sent an effort behind. A rush up the field by the Ayrshire vanguard was brought to a finish by Jeffrey, and then some midfield play ruled for a while. This period came to a splendid end as East End launched a rather marvellous passing and advancing movement which culminated in Reay scoring quite easily.

Ayrshire then made a rally, but the East End defence was solid, and the ball was soon returned into their quarters. The game then dropped considerably in quality, though rose in excitement, as the ball went from end-to-end. Then a fine rush by the East End forwards was desperately intercepted by Mason, and just in the nick of time too. Stark then was called upon to make a fine save from Collins. The East End players seemed to be very comfortable and there was no evidence of them having to exert themselves. Winning a corner, they unfortunately sent the ball over the line and out for a goal-kick.

A free-kick temporarily cleared some of the pressure on the visitor's goal but Collins gained possession and returned the ball in, and just grazed the outside of one of the posts. Stark had to cleverly save a fine shot from Graham and then an effort from Wallace went narrowly over the bar. The Ayrshire defence was being severely taxed, but the backs cleared cleverly, and Graham sent the ball wide. Crate then missed when he was well placed. East End got a corner and Stark saved cleverly, though luckily. East End then got a free-kick for 'hands' near the goal. Taking the free-kick Creilly placed it in nicely and the ball took a terrible ricochet off Currock and, unfortunately for him went through after having wrong-footed his own keeper. Directly after, from a grand centre from Wallace, a third goal for East End was registered by Collins, but the homesters weren't finished quite yet.

Barely two minutes after knocking in their third goal there was another dash down by the East End forwards, this ended with Crate shooting through a fine fourth goal. Not long later half time was called with East End having a grand lead, four goals scored, and none conceded, the home fans were in buoyant mood indeed.

Dixon, after a somewhat lengthy interval, got the game restarted, with East End now kicking up-the-hill. A corner was soon forced but the delivery was not of the best quality and Baird had little difficulty in clearing. Currock and McLane ran well down and Watson had to concede a corner. When this was sent in Jeffrey cleared but at the expense of another corner. This second corner placed the home goal in imminent danger, but nothing resulted. Reay then took the ball up the other end and his cross, meant for Wallace, was headed over the bar by Mason, the subsequent corner being of no avail. Graham, (*of Ayrshire*), dribbled grandly downfield and Watson intervened, passing the ball back to Whitton who had to dodge the advance of Bunyton before he could clear the ball away. The visiting forwards then had another charge and advanced to just in front of the East End goal where Graham, (*of Ayrshire*), had an excellent shot that went wide by barely a foot. Wallace then executed a rather dashing run up the left but ran the ball out behind under the pressure of both Laffardy and Baird. Reay then started another attack down the opposite wing and timing his pass to perfection he sent the ball to Collins who got his way through the remainder of the opposition and scored with a great shot that he put beyond the reach of Stark.

The game continued at a great pace with neither side showing any signs of flagging in the least, but it was quite plain that the East End had the full measure of their opponents and Whitton was not often called upon. On one occasion when Ayrshire did break away, through Currock, the attack was halted by Jeffrey and any danger was dealt with. Stark on the other hand was kept busy and showed up in good form as even though five had already been sent past him he was not at fault for any of them. Nor was he to be at fault for numbers six and seven.

The sixth came courtesy of Crate, from a grand centre by Collins. The seventh again featured Collins but this time he was the provider as he played the ball to Dixon who beat Stark with a fine shot. Not long after that time was called, and the game ended:

Newcastle East End..................7 goals.

South of Ayrshire......................None.

The visiting team and entourage were put up at Mr W. Liddle's Clock Restaurant, Clayton Street, Newcastle.

NORTHERN LEAGUE

Middlesbrough vs. Middlesbrough Ironopolis

The first league meeting of the two Middlesbrough clubs for this season took place on the "old club's" ground at Linthorpe Road. Unfortunately, the ground was in a frightful condition, this owing to the heavy rainfalls that had been almost continuous from Thursday night until Saturday morning. Several parts of the pitch, and the adjoining fields, had been flooded and whilst most of the surface water had drained away there remained some pools of water, and some quite "slushy" places for the players to negotiate during the game. Therefore, any thoughts of attractive and fast flowing football were completely redundant. This was a war of attrition and the strongest were the ones who were going to take the "Derby glory" not the most skilful.

Despite this, with the rivalry between these two sides already very intense, there were around 4,000 spectators ready and awaiting the kick-off. Just prior to the kick-off it was noted that objections had been lodged by both teams as to whether the game should continue to be classified as a Northern League fixture or whether it should be 'downgraded' to a club match and be replayed at some later date. [*History was to show the objections were overruled.*]

However, as it happened the game turned out to be very competitive, as expected but was also quite skilful with both goals being visited frequently. Thrown into the mix were moments of merriment as the players had to leap over, around, or through, the pools of water and frequently coming to grief. In the end the two 'town rivals' were separated by a goal in either half from Seymour of Ironopolis. It was thought midway through the first half that Hill had opened the scoring for Ironopolis but his effort from a well delivered free-kick, taken in midfield and centred by McReddie, was ruled out for offside.

Hill was involved in the opener soon after however as he took possession of a corner and dropped the ball perfectly for Seymour to put through from very close range. Strangely it was the Middlesbrough who had the better of things up to the break, but their shooting was described as "*ludicrously wide*" at times.

At the beginning of the second half Bach, who had suffered an injury in a collision with an opposing player in the first half did not take up his position so Ironopolis were reduced to ten men.

Middlesbrough though could not take advantage of their numerical supremacy and about fifteen minutes into the half Bach made his return to the fray and numerical equilibrium was restored.

The game followed a pattern like that of the first half with both goals being visited regularly and both custodians saving magnificently. Indeed, it was from a save that Seymour sent the leather through for the second goal this after Fall had fisted out an effort from the same player, Seymour, he simply lifting his return over the head of the stricken Fall. With what little remained of the game Middlesbrough tried strenuously but to no avail.

Middlesbrough..........................None.
Middlesbrough Ironopolis.....2 goals.

Middlesbrough: *Goal*, Fall; *backs*, Crone and McManus; *half-backs*, Bach, Bell and Stott; *forwards*, Cronshaw; Lewis, McKnight, Abraham and Black.

Middlesbrough Ironopolis: *Goal*, Watts; *backs*, Elliott and Langley; *half-backs*, McNair, Chatt and Oliver; *forwards*, Hill, Hughes, McArthur, Seymour and McReddie.

Referee: Mr Tomlinson (Sheffield).

Newcastle Daily Chronicle (15/10/1892) p7e.
The Referee (16/10/1892) p6c.
Newcastle Daily Chronicle (17/10/1892) p6e.
Scottish Referee (17/10/1892) p4b.
Sporting Life (17/10/1892) p4e.
York Herald (17/10/1892) p8e.

		THE NORTHERN LEAGUE RESULTS TO SATURDAY, OCTOBER 15 [INCLUSIVE]								
								Goals		
Pos	Team		Pld	W	D	L	F	A	Avg.	Pts
1	Sheffield United		2	1	1	0	5	1	5.0000	3
2	Middlesbrough Ironopolis		2	1	1	0	2	0	2.0000	3
3	Middlesbrough		3	1	0	2	4	5	0.8000	2
4	Newcastle East End		2	1	0	1	4	6	0.6667	2
5	Stockton		1	0	1	0	3	3	1.0000	1
6	Darlington		2	0	1	1	3	6	0.5000	1

Game 10: Saturday, October 22, 1892   **Newcastle East End vs. Heart of Midlothian**

Competition: Friendly   Venue: St James's Park   Gate: 3,000

Newcastle East End   2 - 0   Heart of Midlothian

Scorer(s): Harry Reay (10 mins, sh)

Goal, Dave Whitton; *backs*, Harry Jeffrey and James Miller; *half-backs*, Bobby Creilly, Willie Graham and Joe McKane; *forwards*, Harry Reay, Tom Crate, Jock Sorley, James Collins, Joe Wallace

Referee: Robert Campbell (Sunderland)

Scorer(s): none

Goal, Jock Fairbairn; *backs*, W. Anderson (Leith) and McCartney (Leith); *half-backs*, George Hogg, David Ellis and John Waterson; *forwards*, Willie Taylor, John Cunningham, James L. Morrison, George Scott, H. McQueen (Leith)

Kick-Off: 3:15 PM

Edinburgh side, and current Scottish League leaders, Heart of Midlothian, were the visitors to St James's Park today. Unfortunately, due to an annual 'inter-city' match between the East of Scotland and Glasgow Associations they were not a fully representative side, indeed only five 'first-team regulars' had travelled with them. The team that did travel were supplemented by three players "loaned" to them by Leith Athletic, these being McCartney, W. Anderson and H. McQueen. Adding further to the woes of Hearts was that Goodfellow had to "cry off" resulting in David Ellis, one of their forwards, being played at half-back. Ellis himself was just recovering from an injury to his left leg, sustained in the game against Renton at Tynecastle, and was really in need of an extra week's recovery but had to be called into action. Despite this they still represented a reasonably strong team and there was still a large gathering to witness the event.

With the reserves having only just vacated the pitch it must be remarked that the areas around the goals was not of the highest quality, indeed they resembled nothing more than mud pools. Perhaps having two games in succession, given the prevailing weather conditions, was not the best of ideas.

Sorley, the East End captain, kicked off facing up the hill, and immediately they set about a rush into the visitor's territory. The East End pressure was temporarily relieved by the boot of Anderson, but the homesters were soon back applying the pressure. In a notable passage of play Sorley made some excellent progress and passed the ball to Reay but his final cross intended for the goalmouth area was, unfortunately, placed badly.

In the next passage of play the Hearts right wing ran the ball all the way down and their forwards amassed around the East End goal where Whitton had to perform almost miracles to keep the ball out of his charge. It was only a foul for 'hands' that allowed East End to clear the danger that had been put upon their citadel.

The ball was worked up the field by Wallace and Collins who came very close to opening the scoring but in a desperate rush by several of the Hearts backs he was dispossessed. The ball however broke for Graham who sent in a beauty of a shot, but Fairbairn was just about equal to it and managed to scramble it away. East End kept up the pressure, the ball not leaving the visitors half, and Sorley once again started a great move and with a delightful pass he gave to Reay who shot splendidly and his effort struck the crossbar and bounded through, one-nil to the East End after ten minutes!

The game progressed through the half with East End in the ascendancy but from a set-piece their left wing ran up and losing possession were left exposed and some pressure was applied to their goal and they were thankful to see Cunningham put the ball behind.

The game continued at some pace, with the play being from end-to-end, and exciting. Waterson, for the visitors, put in some good work and a free-kick for 'hands' against Sorley gave them an excellent chance to equalise but when the ball came in Miller was there to kick it out. Hearts regained possession and then Ellis had a shot which he sent behind. Next up was a shot for Collins, which he missed, and it was back up the other end and Sorley gave away another free-kick for a foul but Hearts could make nothing of this one either.

Play then slowed considerably and became quite poor until another free-kick for 'hands' gave the visitors a very good chance close to the home goal. Yet again the visitors failed to capitalise on the situation and Crate got the ball away. This started a rush by the East End forwards which was brought to an abrupt halt by the timely intervention of McCartney. Hearts had another good chance directly afterwards, but McQueen made a very bad shot indeed. Hearts kept up the pressure though and the East End goal was severely taxed, but the defence, and custodian, were equal to the onslaught. Even though they were in front East End were the more relieved side when half time was called.

The second half was gotten underway by Morrison for Hearts but immediately East End gained possession and rushed to their opponents' goal and Fairbairn failed to save a fine shot from Reay. Unfortunately, the point was disallowed for an offside. Putting that disappointment behind them East End were very soon on the attack again and a splendid shot from Collins was kicked out by Fairbairn when a goal looked by far the most likely outcome.

There then followed a period where the play was confined to the midfield but then the visitors besieged the home goal and Scott got a shot away but to no effect. Directly afterwards Sorley had a great opportunity but narrowly missed and then East End won a corner. The danger was cleared for a while but the East End pressure was soon reasserted and some of the forwards congregated around the Hearts goal where a clever little pass from Wallace to Reay saw him smartly put the ball into the goal for his, and East End's, second goal.

Hearts were undeterred by this second setback and immediately set about trying to reduce the arrears and forced a great save out of Whitton, which he made at the expense of a corner. East End managed to clear the danger and ran up to win a corner of their own, which was equally dealt with. Nothing of importance occurred for the next few minutes and the light was becoming bad.

East End continued to press and won a free-kick for 'hands' near to the Hearts goal but Wallace sent it behind, they however were bizarrely awarded a corner. When the ball was swung in Reay made good connection, but his shot was well saved by Fairbairn. The Hearts forwards then showed some smart play and the game moved into the midfield and became a tad rough, with the visitors having the best of it for a while. A break from East End saw Wallace having another effort that went wide of the mark. Just before time Hearts made a concerted effort but failed to capitalise and with that the game was brought to a close and East End continued their good start to the new season by registering a third straight win.

Newcastle East End.................2 goals.

Heart of Midlothian..................None.

This was indeed a 'very curious' experience for Hearts. Upon their arrival at St James's Park they were to find that the changing room was already occupied by the reserve elevens, who had just finished their game, so the unfortunate Hearts had to get ready in the press box of all places!

Also, and this was as if it were adding "*insult to injury*" once the game was over, the poor Hearts players had to avail themselves of a neighbouring public bath to wash in!

NORTHERN LEAGUE

Middlesbrough Ironopolis vs. Stockton: Great interest taken in this game, with some 8,000 spectators turning up at the Paradise Ground, to witness this encounter between the champions, Ironopolis and their local rivals Stockton.

The assembled crowd were not to be disappointed either as they saw a clinker of a game that had not only five goals and superb non-stop and end-to-end action. Ironopolis managed to get themselves a two-goal lead during the first half, the first arriving from a rather splendid effort by Seymour and the second being from a combined rush by the Ironopolis forward line and the ball was bundled through. However, Stockton, were not too disheartened and no doubt spurred on by their sizable portion of the crowd managed to reduce the arrears as a long shot by Atkin went through.

In what turned out to be an equally exciting second half Ironopolis restored their two-goal cushion as that man Seymour once again scored for the homesters. It looked as if that would be the sum of the scoring for today and to an extent Ironopolis eased up a little towards the end of the game. They did this at their peril as once again the Stocktonians came back at them and in a period of play where they were totally dominant, they got their just reward as Townley scored a fine goal. Perhaps it was just a little too late as 'time' was called not long afterwards. In an event, if truth were to be told, one always suspected that Ironopolis had enough "left in reserve" to take hold of the game again should they have so needed.

Middlesbrough Ironopolis.....3 goals.

Stockton..................................2 goals.

Middlesbrough Ironopolis: *Goal*, Watts; *backs*, Elliott and Langley; *half-backs*, McNair, Chatt and Oliver; *forwards*, Hill, Hughes, McArthur, Seymour and McReddie.

Stockton: *Goal*, Ramsay; *backs*, Shaw and McDermid; *half-backs*, Graham, Baillie and Willocks; *forwards*, Crawford, Atkin, Thompson, Jones and Townley.

Referee: Mr Tomlinson (Sheffield).

Edinburgh Evening News (22/10/1892) p4f.
Newcastle Daily Chronicle (22/10/1892) p7e.
Edinburgh Evening News (24/10/1892) p4e.
Newcastle Daily Chronicle (24/10/1892) p6d.
Scottish Referee (24/10/1892) p4a.

Newcastle United 1892-93: Season Zero

THE NORTHERN LEAGUE RESULTS TO SATURDAY, OCTOBER 22 [INCLUSIVE]								Goals		
Pos	Team	Pld	W	D	L	F	A	Avg.	Pts
1	Middlesbrough Ironopolis	3	2	1	0	5	2	2.5000	5
2	Sheffield United	2	1	1	0	5	1	5.0000	3
3	Middlesbrough	3	1	0	2	4	5	0.8000	2
4	Newcastle East End	2	1	0	1	4	6	0.6667	2
5	Stockton	2	0	1	1	5	6	0.8333	1
6	Darlington	2	0	1	1	3	6	0.5000	1

Game 11: Saturday, October 29, 1892   **Newcastle East End vs. Mossend Swifts**

Competition: Friendly   Venue: St James's Park   Gate: 1,500

Newcastle East End   4 - 1   Mossend Swifts

Scorer(s): Sorley (fh, fh, fh, sh)

Goal, Dave Whitton; *backs,* Harry Jeffrey and James Miller; *half-backs,* Bobby Creilly, Willie Graham and Joe McKane; *forwards,* Harry Reay, Tom Crate, Jock Sorley, Willie Thompson, Joe Wallace

Referee: Mr Coleman (Gateshead)

Scorer(s): J. Fairley (fh)

Goal, R. Russell; *backs,* A. Ellis and A. Rankine; *half-backs,* T. McKenna, R. Howieson and C. Brown; *forwards,* R. Sneddon, J. Fairley, W. Robb, A. Watson, J. Boyce

Kick-Off: 3:00 PM

The East End executive were somewhat disappointed today owing to the scheduled fixture against Queen of the South Wanderers being cancelled due to them having to replay a cup tie. It was therefore a rather hurried arrangement that brought West Lothian outfit Mossend Swifts to St James's Park this afternoon. The Swifts were of course no strangers to Newcastle East End as when they were at their old enclosure in Heaton, they were the visitors on no less than three occasions, and on each they left victorious. It must be said though that the Newcastle East End of today were a stronger team now than at those past meetings and both they and their supporters were quietly confident that East End could reverse that trend at St James's Park today.

For the time of year, the pitch was in fair condition, if a little soft, but considering the conditions last week it was much improved. The dull and damp weather cleared towards the afternoon, but the crowd was kept moderate, around 1,500 spectators being in attendance. Given the quality of the opposition, and the anticipated quality of game, this was a little surprising. When kick-off approached the sides were represented as advertised with one change on each. For East End it was Thompson replacing Collins who had fallen unwell, and for the Swifts McKenna replaced Davidson.

East End won the toss, the Swifts started, but were quickly dispossessed by Creilly. Then Sorley, Wallace and Thompson ran nicely down but the latter sent the ball past. A corner was got by the homesters, but the danger was 'swiftly' dealt with and this allowed Mossend to break smartly up the field via their right-wing. Miller relieved the pressure and play was once again taken to the Mossend quarters. The visitors doing some sterling work to keep out the homesters.

Miller sent in a long and rather splendid shot but Russell, the Mossend custodian, fisted it away quite cleverly. East End kept up the pressure on the Mossend goal until Wallace eventually sent over the byline. The game remained in the Mossend third, Graham working well and Miller also, who came very smartly to the rescue when the Mossend left-wing were becoming dangerous. The visitors however managed to get to the home goal, albeit briefly, as Wallace gained possession and ran the ball down the field and East End won a corner. This led to some interesting play and the Mossend goal was bombarded but this was ended when 'hands' was awarded against Graham and the pressure was relieved.

Making their way down the other end another free-kick for 'hands' this time gave the Swifts an opportunity to open the scoring, but Jeffrey bravely cleared. Immediately after the ball was back in the Swifts quarters and Wallace sent a beauty to Reay who made a very decent shot, but it went just a little high. The pressure was resumed by East End for a while but eventually the Swifts broke out, working the ball well and making good progress, but they proved weak in front of goal as Robb sent the ball past the post.

Play became fast and a rush down was made by the home forwards and several ineffectual shots were made but the visitors defence performed admirably. Wallace sent in a beauty, but Ellis kicked out, then Reay just missed with a grand effort. From the goal kick the Mossend forwards worked well and ran the leather up to the top and after some more finessing Robb shot. Whitton managed to fist this effort away, but the ball fell to Fairley who smartly drove it in with Whitton now stranded. An unexpected opening goal indeed, and totally against the 'run of play'.

The jubilation of the Mossend was short-lived however as within a minute East End brought about the equaliser. As smart as the Mossend forward line had been for their goal the East End forward line were clever alike. After working their way well up Crate passed to Sorley who scored with an impressive shot. The game was barely a couple of minutes older when there was an almighty melee in front of the Swifts goal, the ball was ping-ponging all over, the tackles were going in hard and heavy and from this commotion the ball was rushed home by Sorley. Two goals in not more than the same number of minutes, East End, and Sorley, had turned this game right around.

Even though they were now in the lead East End did not rest, they kept the pressure on the Mossend defence and 'hands' was given against Ellis but McKane sent the free-kick outside. An unexpected rush was made by the visitors' forwards but Jeffrey cleverly dispossessed Boyce and sent the ball long back up the field. Reay missed an excellent chance and when the ball came back to him, he laid on a great ball for Thompson who was desperately unlucky to see his effort just fail. However, Crate was soon to make amends for that misfortune as with an excellent pass to Sorley, he was enabled to shoot through, to bring about East End's third goal, and of course his hat-trick!

No more than another minute had elapsed when Creilly very narrowly missed with a fine effort. Miller rained in several shots, but each was from distance and Russell had little difficulty in dealing with each of them. The Swifts goal was now subject to an almost constant onslaught, but their defence held up magnificently. This continued right up until half time was called.

Owing to the failing light the interval was but a short one and the game was once again soon underway with East End setting the ball in motion. East End basically picked up from where they had left off and were immediately pressurising the Mossend goal. Miller sent in a long ball from midfield and who else but Sorley, managed to put the leather through with a grand header. Four goals for East End, and four goals for Sorley!

Still East End continued to press, Thompson sending well in thrice but each time the backs managed to return it. Mossend were then awarded a free-kick for 'hands' relieving the pressure, albeit temporarily. This as they only managed to clear to the halfway line and Miller was there to put a huge punt back into their third. The Swifts at length got down but Jeffrey was there to stop them.

A long shot from Graham almost brought about East End's fifth but Russell managed to fist it out strongly. Sorley sent in a low shot and Russell was fortunate in getting down to scoop it out. Before Russell could get back up Crate pounced on the loose ball and put through, the goal however being disallowed for offside against Reay, which had been previously claimed and subsequently allowed. There was a mini rally from the Mossend right wing but McKane stopped the advance and East End were on the attack again with Wallace and Sorley involved in some tricky play. Reay had a fine opening but sent over the bar. Russell then had great difficulty in dealing with an effort but eventually got the ball away nicely. Good play between Crate and Reay provided Sorley with another opportunity but Russell, dodging a heavy charge from Thompson, coolly threw the ball out. Mossend at last got down but their efforts were wasted as a long shot was sent in but went bye.

East End had another goal, this time by Thompson who shot well though, disallowed for offside. Wallace then hit the post but for some reason a corner was allowed but it was delivered to no effect. The Mossend goal was under continuous siege and Thompson was once again to be disappointed as courtesy of a neat pass by Sorley he again put the ball through, but again an offside was ruled. Reay then had a turn and was only marginally high. A charge from the goal-kick lead to Whitton, a lonely figure in this second half, then having his first kick.

In effect the visitors were 'played out' towards the latter stages of the game and such was the superiority of East End that they were virtually teasing their heavy opponents and indulged in a lot of 'gallery play'. This was much to the delight of the majority of those assembled. East End never distressed themselves, Wallace and Sorley in particular, being far too tricky for the Swifts. Play was confined almost exclusively in the Mossend half and the East End forwards were happy to spend the remainder of the game indulging in tricks and attempting long shots and were never too concerned that their tally wasn't added to.

Newcastle East End................4 goals.

Mossend Swifts........................1 goal.

The visitors arrived in Newcastle at around noon and availed themselves of the facilities of Mr W. Liddle's, Clock Restaurant, Clayton Street, as their headquarters during their short stay.

NORTHERN LEAGUE

Middlesbrough Ironopolis vs. Sheffield United: These teams met at the Paradise Ground, Middlesbrough, and a capital game was witnessed by the 5,000 spectators. Great credit however should go to the Sheffielders as they had to play the whole of the second half with only ten men - and a defender in goal!

There was little to separate the sides, and in an exciting end-to-end first half the only goal of the game was scored, this by McReddie, with a fine header from a cross by Hill, late in the first half. Just after this goal the 'Nops pressed again and the Sheffield goalkeeper, Lilley, in an endeavour to save came to grief during a scrimmage. The game was stopped for a couple of minutes and he bravely carried on, though was visibly lame. It was of little surprise that he did not turn out for the second half and Hendry, one of their half-backs, took his place between the posts.

Middlesbrough Ironopolis.......1 goal.

Sheffield United ....None.

Middlesbrough Ironopolis: *Goal*, Watts; *backs*, Elliott and Langley; *half-backs*, McNair, Chatt and Oliver; *forwards*, Hill, Hughes, McArthur, Seymour and McReddie.

Sheffield United: *Goal*, Lilley; *backs*, Cain and Lilley; *half-backs*, Howell, Hendry and Needham; *forwards*, Wallace, Dobson, Scott, Hammond and Drummond.

Referee: Mr G. Hay.

Newcastle Daily Chronicle (29/10/1892) p7e.
The Referee (30/10/1892) p6c.
Athletic News (31/10/1892) p7d.
Newcastle Daily Chronicle (31/10/1892) p6e.
Scottish Referee (31/10/1892) p4a.
Sheffield and Rotherham Independent (31/10/1892) p7d.

THE NORTHERN LEAGUE
RESULTS TO SATURDAY, OCTOBER 29 [INCLUSIVE]

Pos	Team	Pld	W	D	L	F	A	Avg.	Pts
1	Middlesbrough Ironopolis	4	3	1	0	6	2	3.0000	7
2	Sheffield United	3	1	1	1	5	2	2.5000	3
3	Middlesbrough	3	1	0	2	4	5	0.8000	2
4	Newcastle East End	2	1	0	1	4	6	0.6667	2
5	Stockton	2	0	1	1	5	6	0.8333	1
6	Darlington	2	0	1	1	3	6	0.5000	1

As to the "A's"...

NEWCASTLE EAST END 'A' RESULTS OCTOBER 1892

Date	Home	Score	Away	
October 1, 1892.	Shankhouse	2 - 1	Newcastle East End A	Northern Alliance
October 8, 1892.	Newcastle East End A	4 - 2	Seaham Harbour	Northern Alliance
October 15, 1892.	Bill Quay	1 - 5	Newcastle East End A	Friendly
October 22, 1892.	Newcastle East End A	4 - 1	Sunderland A	Northern Alliance
October 29, 1892.	Berwick Rangers	1 - 5	Newcastle East End A	Friendly

November 1892

Games Played in November 1892

V	Date	F	A	R	Opposition	Competition
H	05/11/1892	2	2	D	Sheffield United	Friendly
H	12/11/1892	5	0	W	Darlington	Northern League
A	19/11/1892	2	3	L	Middlesbrough Ironopolis	Northern League
A	26/11/1892	7	0	W	Darlington	Northern League

Appearances & Goals ~ November 1892

Name	Total Apps	Total Goals	League Apps	League Goals	Friendly Apps	Friendly Goals
Collins, James	4	1	3	1	1	
Crate, Thomas "Tom"	4		3		1	
Creilly, Robert "Bobby"	4		3		1	
Graham, William "Willie"	4	1	3	1	1	
Jeffrey, Harry	2		1		1	
McKane, Joseph "Joe"	3		2		1	
Miller, James	4		3		1	
Reay, Harry	4	2	3	1	1	1
Sorley, John "Jock"	4	4	3	3	1	1
Thompson, Willie	3	4	3	4	0	
Wallace, Joseph "Joe"	2	3	1	3	1	
Watson, Peter	2		2		0	
Whitton, David "Dave"	4		3		1	

Season to Date (03/09/1892 - 26/11/1892 inclusive)

Name	Total Apps	Total Goals	League Apps	League Goals	Friendly Apps	Friendly Goals
Barker, John	1		1		0	
Collins, James	14	7	5	1	9	6
Coupar, William	1		0		1	
Crate, Thomas "Tom"	15	3	5		10	3
Creilly, Robert "Bobby"	13	1	4		9	1
Dixon, Henry	2	1	0		2	1
Graham, William "Willie"	15	1	5	1	10	
Jeffrey, Harry	13		3		10	
Kirkland, J.	1				1	
McKane, Joseph "Joe"	14		4		10	
Miller, James	13		5		8	
Reay, Harry	10	3	4	1	6	2
Sorley, John "Jock"	11	10	4	4	7	6
Thompson, Willie	11	7	5	5	6	2
Wallace, Joseph "Joe"	12	6	3	5	9	1
Watson, Peter	4		2		2	
Whitton, David "Dave"	15		5		10	

Game 12: Saturday, November 5, 1892   Newcastle East End vs. Sheffield United

Competition: Friendly   Venue: St James's Park   Gate: 4,000

Newcastle East End   2 - 2   Sheffield United

Scorer(s): Sorley (fh); Reay (sh)

Goal, Dave Whitton; *backs*, Harry Jeffrey and James Miller; *half-backs*, Bobby Creilly, Willie Graham and Joe McKane; *forwards*, Harry Reay, Tom Crate, Jock Sorley, James Collins, Joe Wallace

Referee: J. Potts (Stockton)

Scorer(s): Howell (10 mins); Hammond (fh)

Goal, Charlie Howlett; *backs*, Bob Cain and Billy Mellor; *half-backs*, Rab Howell, Billy Hendry and Ernest Needham; *forwards*, Fred Davies, Alexander Wallace, Jack Scott, Harry Hammond, Arthur Watson

Kick-Off: 2:45 PM

Sheffield United were scheduled to be playing a league fixture against South Bank this afternoon, however, with the withdrawal of the Teesside outfit from the Northern League this left a gap in the Sheffield fixtures, which was filled by this visit to St James's Park.

It should not be forgotten that only a matter of a few weeks ago Newcastle East End had been the visitors to Bramall Lane for a Northern League fixture and were incisively beaten by the Sheffielders. Revenge was most certainly on the minds of the Tynesiders today, even if just for the pride rather than the points!

Sheffield were unable to muster their strongest side for today's clash, they were lamenting quite a heavy injury list, which included Lille, their first-choice custodian, Whittam was an absentee at the back, and both Drummond and Dobson were missing from their front ranks.

Despite this the interest in the game was still very high and a good crowd of around 3,000 to 4,000 were gathered in the St James's Park enclosure to witness the start of the match, in what was the most beautiful weather for a November.

East End won the toss and elected to play 'uphill' with the mild breeze in their faces, so it fell to Scott of Sheffield to set the game in motion. In doing so he launched an immediate attack, demonstrating no doubt the intents of the Sheffielders, and the East End goal was under pressure from the off. Davies missed with an opportunity, sending the ball bye. From the goal-kick Wallace and Collins managed to get the ball up to the Sheffield goal but the latter missed with his shot by a good yard. A free-kick, against Jeffrey, almost let the Sheffielders in but Scott kicked no more than a foot wide. Another free kick against East End again placed the home goal in danger. Howell took the free-kick, sending it swiftly along the ground, and the ball rebounded off player and through the posts, and a fortuitous opening goal was scored, after some ten minutes of play.

Following this setback east End played up hard, taking the ball regularly to the top goal and keeping the Sheffield backs very busy indeed in their endeavours to clear their charge. Unfortunately for East End they accomplished their task with aplomb. Then came an almost inevitable quick break from Sheffield which saw Davies and Wallace racing down the right before delivering a fine cross in for Hammond to score their second goal.

On re-starting, one of the visitors was severely winded and had to retire for a few minutes. The homesters now held their own. Collins ran nicely up, but Crate made a pretty poor attempt when in front of goal. 'Hands' against Sheffield almost enabled Graham to score but he was desperately unlucky.

Then with a grand centre by Collins was headed back by Reay and sent through by Sorely, amidst the most enthusiastic of cheering. Collins was again conspicuous with a good run and delivering an equally good shot. A corner, well taken by Wallace, was headed just past the post by Reay. This was followed up with a good combination from Sheffield which saw them within shooting distance of Whitton, but the final effort was poor and went harmlessly bye. Again, the East End goal was visited, but a fine centre by Wallace was not taken advantage of, and a good opportunity was lost. There was little doubt that Sheffield were most in evidence leading up to half time, but the home backs did well to prevent any further scoring.

On the resumption of play following the interval East End pressed and worked their way up, and a foul was given against Needham, but the danger from the resulting free-kick was cleared by Mellor. This clearance was returned immediately by Miller towards the Sheffield goal but ultimately the leather went behind. Play continued to be kept near the United goal, until Wallace sent over the line from a throw in from touch. Play became rather rough and Graham only just missed with a good long shot, and then sally by the visitors culminated in some merry work in midfield, with strong kicking being the order of the day.

A great rush by the visitors down the left was halted unfairly but Graham cleared the danger from the free-kick. Sheffield returned the ball into the danger zone, but Scott was way too high with the final shot. Reay then ran swiftly down and passing to Crate who made a flying shot which was blocked at the expense of a corner which was unfortunately fruitless. The East End vanguard made another assault which was quickly turned around and now Sheffield were bearing down on the home goal. However, this was a fruitless as East End's corner had been thanks to the efforts of Miller who cleared cleverly. The ball eventually going 'bye' from Watson.

East End once again assumed the role of aggressors and Reay made attempt, but missed, as did Crate with a good shot. Miller put in some good work and Wallace was very unlucky as his effort only just missed the target. Sheffield then succeeded in working the ball up the field, but Hammond made a poor shot. Reay then missed at the other end. Never giving up East End put these disappointments behind them and got their just reward as following some good play they made a combined effort, and Reay rushed an equalising point through from a cross by Collins.

The excitement became great at this stage and the home eleven worked hard. There was a tremendous scrimmage taking place in the United goal, but the defence was equal to a heavy attack, the ball eventually going behind. East End got a corner, but it was to no avail. A Sheffield attack was broken up when Miller dispossessed their forwards and Collins ran down. Crossing to Reay, he received a return ball from him and rushed the ball through to put East End in front, or so he thought, as groans from all around the ground signalled that he had been ruled offside and the goal would not stand.

Disappointed, but resilient, East End resumed the attack and a corner was won, but from it Wallace sent the ball behind. Sheffield were then given a free-kick after a run up on the right was halted and from it a corner was won but it was easily cleared by the defence. Going up to the other end Reay put in a decent shot but Howell saved smartly. Towards the close of play Jeffrey got high up the pitch and narrowly missed with a good effort which was in effect the final noteworthy item.

Newcastle East End..................2 goals.

Sheffield United......................2 goals.

The Sheffielders arrived in Newcastle at around about noon and made their headquarters at Mr W. Liddle's, Clock Restaurant, Clayton Street.

Northern League

Darlington vs. Middlesbrough Ironopolis: There was a large contingent of supporters from Middlesbrough swelling the crowd at Feethams to around 4,000. After a bright start by both teams, perhaps more notably the visitors, a goal was registered by a glorious solo effort from McReddie who ran from almost his own goal line, up the left, getting past McLane and the home backs and having a clear shot at the goal. Auld made a good effort to save the ball, getting to it with his fingertips but being unable to keep it out.

This was the only goal of an otherwise even and exciting first half.

The second half was quite a different story and Ironopolis registered a further three goals without conceding. These coming from Hughes, putting through from a centre when almost on the line himself, Hill with an easy goal when fed from an attack up the centre and McArthur with a well-timed shot beating Auld after another attack up the centre.

Both sides had second half 'goals' ruled out for offside, Hutchinson for Ironopolis then Hill for the homesters, both when the score was 2-0 to Ironopolis.

Darlington..............................0 goal.

Middlesbrough Ironopolis.....4 goals.

Newcastle United 1892-93: Season Zero

Darlington: *Goal*, Auld; *backs*, Coleman and Norris; *half-backs*, McLaine, McDonald and Campbell; *forwards*, McPherson, Fleming, Hutchinson, McFarlane and Keay.

Middlesbrough Ironopolis: *Goal*, Watts; *backs*, Elliott and Langley; *half-backs*, McNair, Chatt and Oliver; *forwards*, Hill, Hughes, McArthur, Seymour and McReddie.

Referee: Mr Tomlinson (Sheffield).

Newcastle Daily Chronicle (05/11/1892) p7d.
Athletic News (07/11/1892) p5e.
Newcastle Daily Chronicle (07/11/1892) p6d.
Sheffield and Rotherham Independent (07/11/1892) p7g.
Sporting Life (07/11/1892) p4a.

		THE NORTHERN LEAGUE RESULTS TO SATURDAY, NOVEMBER 5 [INCLUSIVE]								
							Goals			
Pos		Team	Pld	W	D	L	F	A	Avg.	Pts
1		Middlesbrough Ironopolis	5	4	1	0	10	2	5.0000	9
2		Sheffield United	3	1	1	1	5	2	2.5000	3
3		Middlesbrough	3	1	0	2	4	5	0.8000	2
4		Newcastle East End	2	1	0	1	4	6	0.6667	2
5		Stockton	2	0	1	1	5	6	0.8333	1
6		Darlington	3	0	1	2	3	10	0.3000	1

Game 13: Saturday, November 12, 1892   Newcastle East End vs. Darlington

Competition: Northern League   Venue: St James's Park   Gate: 2,000

Newcastle East End   5 - 0   Darlington

Scorer(s): Graham (fh); Thompson (fh); Sorley (fh, sh); Collins (sh)

Scorer(s): *none*

Goal, Dave Whitton; *backs*, Harry Jeffrey and James Miller; *half-backs*, Bobby Creilly, Willie Graham and Joe McKane; *forwards*, Harry Reay, Tom Crate, Willie Thompson, Jock Sorley, James Collins

Goal, Edward Auld; *backs*, Sanders and Coleman; *half-backs*, McDonald, Tommy Waites and McLaine; *forwards*, McPherson, Billy Fleming, Tom Hutchinson, McFarlane, Walter Keay

Referee: Samuel "Sam" Kemp (Redcar)

Kick-Off: 2:30 PM

After a series of five 'friendly' games East End returned to league duty for their encounter with Darlington at St James's Park. Though this was their twelfth match it was only their third in the league, having recorded a defeat against Sheffield at Bramall Lane and a victory over Middlesbrough here at Newcastle. Despite the fine weather the attendance was relatively small, circa 1,500 to 2,000 spectators being present.

Darlington won the toss and elected to play 'uphill' with the slight wind to their advantage, Sorley, East End's captain for today, therefore set the game in motion.

Each team attacked in turn, but undoubtedly the best of the exchanges was in East End's favour. Twice Auld was called upon to save his charge. East End continued to press and from an attack down the right Crate was put in, but his effort was sent behind. A series of throw-ins enabled Darlington to work their way up the pitch and when close up Keay sent his shot wide. Keay and Hutchinson were then involved in a strong attack with the latter forcing a corner off Miller, but ultimately it was unproductive. Another corner followed, and though it was well taken by McPherson, Fleming managed to head it out.

Taking up the mantle once more East End progressed upfield only for Coleman to return the ball at a critical moment, but again East End came and this time secured a corner, which unfortunately proved abortive. 'Hands' off Waites gave the homesters another good chance, and they did all but score, keeping the Darlington defence extremely busy for a minute or two. McPherson was next to have a try, but failed; and the Novocastrians forced another corner, from which they again nearly scored. Within the next minute Reay put in a clinker of a shot, which Auld saved beautifully. At this point McDonald, who had been hurt at the game's commencement, had to leave the field of play.

Graham fouled McFarlane quite badly, and then Reay put in a long shot which only just missed. The loss of McDonald was severely felt, and with that advantage of a man to the good East End pressed hard, Auld having to makes saves on one or two very nasty shots indeed.

Darlington broke away with McDonald having returned to restore numerical parity, Fleming made a good attempt, but sent the ball-went wide. Next it was Collins who had a beautiful chance when close in on goal, but he somehow missed and then Auld repelled another effort. Darlington had a brief sortie into the home area, but East End were soon on the attack again. Crate had a glorious opportunity but contrived to sky the ball over when it looked easier to score! They kept up the pressure and the deadlock was finally broken in the most unfortunate of circumstances for Darlington as Coleman got himself in front of Auld, completely un-sighting him, and a shot from Graham was in the back of his goal before he even knew about it.

In the next minute Sorley put across a very fine centre indeed, but Crate made a complete mess of his effort. Thompson then headed a ball beyond the post but was quick to redeem himself as within another minute he received the ball from the right and drove a fast, low shot through. Fleming and McPherson got away down the right in a now rare Darlington attack, but this was broken up and East End were on the attack again. Two or three smart shots were foiled by the defence and custodian, but Sorley finally added a third goal for East End before the break.

Upon the resumption following the interval Darlington presented only ten men as McDonald was unable to shake off the injury which he had obtained in the first half and did not appear. So, three goals down, and now a man down, the omens were not favourable for the men of Darlington. It was surprising then that for quite a period neither side could show to advantage, Darlington were understandably cautious and reticent to commit too much to the attack for fear of opening up an avalanche at the back and because of this East End were puzzled as to how to break them down further. It was again a touch of misfortune for Darlington that saw East End's fourth goal. Collins, getting a chance on the left, put in a strong shot which Auld seemed to catch but it somehow spun through his hands and into his goal.

The game was now basically over as a contest and East End continued to have far the best of matters and Sorley registered their fifth goal with a magnificent shot from an extreme left position. East End eased off a bit and Hutchinson forced a corner which came to nothing and soon after a second corner had the same ineffectual result. Darlington then had two rather excellent chances at scoring but missed on both occasions. This spurred East End to up their game a touch and they took control of affairs through to the final whistle.

Newcastle East End..................5 goals.

Darlington ....None.

The Darlington entourage arrived in Newcastle around about noon and used the facilities of Mr W. Liddle's, Clock Restaurant, Clayton Street, as their headquarters for their brief stay in Newcastle.

STOCKTON VS. MIDDLESBROUGH IRONOPOLIS

This was the third meeting of these elevens already this season, the first, a friendly on September 3rd here at the Victoria Ground saw Stockton taking the honours with a 2-0 victory, the second, on September 22nd, was the corresponding league fixture at the Paradise Ground whereupon Ironopolis were the victors with a 3-2 scoreline.

This was therefore an eagerly anticipated encounter and testament to that there was an enormous gathering of around 7,000 spectators packed into the Victoria Ground.

The game that ensued was a hard, and scientific, struggle right from its commencement. In the first half-an-hour the game could have swung either way, both teams fighting terrifically and both goals being under severe pressure. After that initial period the visitors grew in dominance and following a lively tussle in front of Ramsey, the 'Nops' centre, McArthur, got his head to the ball from Hill, and the big man in the home goal was fairly beaten. This was the only goal scored in the first half.

On crossing over play once again returned to a hard-fought, but even, pattern. Eventually, after continuous pressure, a fortuitous goal was scored by Ironopolis to double their lead. In making a clearance Shaw smashed the ball out only for it to hit Hill and rebound through. This instigated a change for Stockton as McClung went into the centre with Townley moving to the outside-left and Jones moving inside.

The change seemed to work well as the Stockton forwards now put in some grand work, but the visitors packed their goal strongly, and a way through could not be found. Still, from this point up to closing time the home men were mostly the aggressors but could not land a goal, and at the termination of this hard-fought match the result was:

Stockton ....None.
Middlesbrough Ironopolis .....2 goals.

Stockton: *Goal*, Ramsay; *backs*, Shaw and McDermid; *half-backs*, Graham, Baillie and Hutton; *forwards*, Atkin, Crawford, Townley, McClung and Jones.

Middlesbrough Ironopolis: *Goal*, Watts; *backs*, Elliott and Langley; *half-backs*, McNair, Chatt and Oliver; *forwards*, Hill, Hughes, McArthur, Seymour and McReddie.

Referee: Mr Tomlinson (Sheffield).

Newcastle Daily Chronicle (12/11/1892) p7d.
Athletic News (14/11/1892) p6d.
Newcastle Daily Chronicle (14/11/1892) p6d.
Northern Echo (14/11/1892) p4d.
York Herald (14/11/1892) p7e.

THE NORTHERN LEAGUE
RESULTS TO SATURDAY, NOVEMBER 12 [INCLUSIVE]

Pos	Team	Pld	W	D	L	F	A	Goals Avg.	Pts
1	Middlesbrough Ironopolis	6	5	1	0	12	2	6.0000	11
2	Newcastle East End	3	2	0	1	9	6	1.5000	4
3	Sheffield United	3	1	1	1	5	2	2.5000	3
4	Middlesbrough	3	1	0	2	4	5	0.8000	2
5	Stockton	3	0	1	2	5	8	0.6250	1
6	Darlington	4	0	1	3	3	15	0.2000	1

Game 14: Saturday, November 19, 1892   Middlesbrough Ironopolis vs Newcastle East End

Competition: Northern League   Venue: Paradise Ground   Gate: 5,000

Middlesbrough Ironopolis   3 - 2   Newcastle East End

Scorer(s): Seymour (4 mins); Hughes (sh, sh)

Goal, Charles Watts; *backs*, James Elliott and Ambrose Langley; *half-backs*, Donald McNair, Robert Chatt and John Oliver; *forwards*, Jack Hill, Archibald Hughes, William McArthur, Thomas Seymour, Wallace McReddie.

Referee: W. H. Stacey (Sheffield)

Scorer(s): Thompson (14 mins, sh)

Goal, Dave Whitton; *backs*, Peter Watson and James Miller; *half-backs*, Bobby Creilly, Willie Graham and Joe McKane; *forwards*, Harry Reay, Tom Crate, Willie Thompson, Jock Sorley, James Collins

Kick-Off: 2:45 PM

A tough test awaited East End at the Paradise Ground as they visited the reigning Northern League champions. These teams had already met twice this season in 'friendly' fixtures, with East End winning both encounters. However, playing Ironopolis in friendly matches and playing them in league matches was *"a horse of another colour"* indeed, as their status as 'runaway' leaders of the league demonstrated. Great interest was shown in this encounter and in weather that was decidedly dull and ominous looking there were between 4,000 and 5,000 spectators amassed in the enclosure, a good percentage of these being travelling Newcastle fans as they took advantage of a special excursion train which had been laid on by the N.E.R. Company. They were treated to a game of the highest standard, and no doubts arguments would continue for many a month as to whether the Ironopolis victory was deserved or not.

McArthur got the game underway for Ironopolis, kicking towards the Linthorpe-road end. They immediately assumed the aggressor role and pinned East End back in an explosive and intense start. Gradually they were driven back, and for a minute or two it was the visitors who attacked strongly. To relieve the pressure Langley sent a huge punt up the field which was ran onto by Hill and he passed to the left. The ball was then fizzed back across to the right and Miller intercepted but in doing so conceded a corner. Hill placed the ball well from the kick, but Miller again intercepted, heading it away, but it returned to Hill who put the ball across to Seymour who banged a great shot through the uprights – and there was barely four minutes on the clock!

The play that followed was of a strong and fast type by both sides, the 'Nops being buoyed by the goal and the Novocastrians being equally irked by it. Neither side could dominate the other and try as they might neither forward quintet could break down their opposing defences, though both custodians were called upon at times.

The next goal was of vital importance to the outcome of this game, and after about ten minutes of this even play that second goal arrived.

For some strange and unknown reason Ironopolis seemed to 'go to pieces', they simply lost their composure under intense East End pressure and falling on the back foot had to defend like crazy. Eventually they gave away a corner which was very well delivered, and Thompson put through the equaliser amidst great cheering from the large Newcastle contingent in the crowd.

Once again strong and furious play ensued with each side having chances. Chatt did grand work, his feeding of the Ironopolis forward line was splendid indeed whilst in counter the East End forwards were giving the home defence a torrid time. Langley was having to make himself useful and carried out his duties creditably. A free-kick for 'hands' was awarded to Ironopolis whilst they were under the cosh allowing themselves breathing time as they got the ball away. However, they were quickly driven back again, and Collins was afforded an opportunity and whilst he struck his shot well Watts was ready for him and made a comfortable save. Ironopolis then conceded a corner, which was unfortunately for East End fruitless. Miller was next to show, attempting a long shot which went narrowly wide of the post.

Keeping up an almost constant pressure now East End were having the better of play and were making things quite warm for Watts and his defence, and on more than one occasion they were lucky in having narrow escapes. Watts made an excellent save from Sorley, and a free-kick for 'hands' looked very promising for East End, but only a corner was to come of it, which was ultimately to no avail. From then until the half time whistle East End kept Ironopolis pinned into their top third but could not break down the resolute Ironopolis defence.

After the interval East End immediately took up from where they had left off and launched a vigorous attack. They found that once again the defence was stout with Langley and Elliott serving grandly and eventually Hill got the ball away and made a splendid run up. In the East End defence Watson proved equally stout and dispelled any danger. McReddie and Seymour next put in some steady work but were unable to make much progress. Play was now becoming quite even, whilst remaining quite exciting, and always entertaining. Chatt again distinguishing himself for both his defensive display and his clever distribution of the ball.

A foul by Hill in an advanced position looked promising for East End but nothing became of the advantage with the ball ultimately being sent bye. Sticking to their task East End piled on the pressure and Watts received deserved applause for his tremendous display whilst at the other end Whitton proved to be a safe pair of hands when called upon to do so, especially when saving admirably from Hill.

Breaking out from one attack the Ironopolis forwards lined up well and some fine passing was witnessed between them which led to an opportunity for McReddie, but his shot went very narrowly wide. There was then a halt called to the game as Oliver came to grief and upon his recovery the match resumed. The re-start went well for East End as they powered forward and there ensued an almighty tussle in the Ironopolis goal mouth which resulted in Thompson managing to poke the ball through, registering their second goal, and put them in front for the first time in the match.

Ironopolis responded well and rushed down but they were repelled, and East End attacked to win a corner from which unfortunately nothing became. Play was then again put into the East End quarters and McReddie was again unlucky as his effort went agonisingly close. Working like Trojans the Ironopolis forwards were lining up beautifully and maintained severe pressure from which reward was eventually borne as Hughes was able to get away a tremendous shot which beat Whitton all the way. Tremendous cheering accompanied the equaliser! Not unsurprisingly the excitement, and tension, was very high. Neither side were prepared to accept a drawn result, both now going all out for the winner. Miller and Watson were given plenty of work to do as were their opposing backs, both sets carrying out their duties with aplomb. McReddie put in a well-placed corner for Ironopolis but nothing resulted, the same occurred following another corner. Sorley then got injured and another halt to the game was called. Whilst the previous halt had benefitted East End this one was of benefit to the homesters as in badly fading light they rushed forward and a third goal was registered for them as the ball was forced through following a melee in the East End goal. Another abortive corner to Ironopolis was the only other noteworthy action before time was called within a minute or two of the goal.

Middlesbrough Ironopolis.....3 goals.
Newcastle East End.................2 goals.

Newcastle Daily Chronicle (18/11/1892) p7d.
Athletic News (21/11/1892) p6a.
Newcastle Daily Chronicle (21/11/1892) p6e.
Northern Daily Telegraph (21/11/1892) p3e.
Northern Echo (21/11/1892) p4e.
Sheffield Daily Telegraph (21/11/1892) p7e.
Sheffield and Rotherham Independent (21/11/1892) p7d.
Shields Daily Gazette (21/11/1892) p3e.

THE NORTHERN LEAGUE
RESULTS TO SATURDAY, NOVEMBER 19 [INCLUSIVE]

Pos	Team	Pld	W	D	L	F	A	Avg.	Pts
1	Middlesbrough Ironopolis	7	6	1	0	15	4	3.7500	13
2	Newcastle East End	4	2	0	2	11	9	1.2222	4
3	Sheffield United	3	1	1	1	5	2	2.5000	3
4	Middlesbrough	3	1	0	2	4	5	0.8000	2
5	Stockton	3	0	1	2	5	8	0.6250	1
6	Darlington	4	0	1	3	3	15	0.2000	1

Game 15: Saturday, November 26, 1892   **Darlington vs Newcastle East End**

Competition: Northern League   Venue: Feethams   Gate: 1,500

Darlington   0 - 7   Newcastle East End

Scorer(s): *none*

Scorer(s): Sorley (3 mins); Wallace (5 mins, 47 mins, 80 mins); Thompson (18 mins); Reay (20mins); OG (sh)

Goal, Edward Auld; *backs*, McDonald and Frank Norris; *half-backs*, McLaine, Tommy Waites and D. Campbell; *forwards*, McPherson, Billy Fleming, J. McCrimmon, Walter Keay, McFarlane

Goal, Dave Whitton; *backs*, Peter Watson and James Miller; *half-backs*, Bobby Creilly, Willie Graham and James Collins; *forwards*, Harry Reay, Tom Crate, Willie Thompson, Jock Sorley, Joe Wallace

Referee: Mr. Tomlinson (Sheffield)

Kick-Off: 2:20 PM

After having suffered a very heavy defeat, by five goals to nil, at the hands of East End in their league fixture a fortnight ago at St James's Park the Quakers were expecting to perform better, or at least make home advantage count for something.

As Darlington were languishing at the foot of the table, without a win to their name, indeed having only secured a single point, whilst East End were in placed second in the table most observers saw this as an *"easy away-win banker"* without doubt, few, if any, though would have guessed just how right they would be! The relative position of the teams in the league ensured that this game was not that heavily attended and the Feethams ground was sparsely populated, a mere 1,500 or so within the enclosure.

East End took the leather up right from the start and made a determined attack. Auld was called upon and succeeded in repulsing three times, but the next attempt proved successful as Sorley landed nicely through. Three minutes gone and it was doubtful whether Darlington had been across the halfway line for any of them. Worse was to follow for them as within two minutes of the first goal the East End again scored! Their forwards worked upfield on the right from where a screw-kick was sent in, and Wallace headed through.

Now there was a reaction from Darlington, a quite stunned Darlington at that, as they managed to make a run down the centre, but the ensuing shot was too early, coming from too great a distance, and Whitton in the East End goal had absolutely no difficulty in catching it and had more enough time to throw it out before the Darlington forwards could get near. After some play, predominantly favouring East End, a fine run up the centre was made by their forwards. They cleverly eluded the home backs, thus enabling Thompson, who had been put through and was at very at close quarters, to drive in a shot for East End's third goal.

In what was becoming a veritable rout there followed another attack up the centre, another ball played to an East End player at close quarters, this time Reay, and another goal was registered for the visitors. Four goals in twenty minutes, Darlington were looking shell-shocked indeed. To their credit however Darlington did try. They managed an attack of their own and the ball was played to McCrimmond in a promising position, but he sent his effort well over the bar. This was but brief respite for the homesters as the leather continued to be in their quarters, albeit with the occasional break. East End pressed severely, two or three times winning some corners, all which proved fruitless. Up until the half time whistle play continued to be dominated by East End though nothing else was scored.

On changing over East End simply renewed their aggressive tactics, and much like in the beginning of the first half they were virtually camped in the Darlington third and within two minutes of the start Wallace drove in a sharp shot, which credit to Auld he managed to meet but fractionally too late, as it had already gone through. East End were in jubilation, five scored and none conceded and the majority of the second half still lay ahead of them. Strangely though this signalled a period of quite equal play, until East End got up on the left, and the leather was put through once again for what seemed like goal number six, but it was ruled out for an off-side. The next twenty minutes saw Darlington performing much better, though at no time did they look dangerous or present any real threat. Play still favoured East End and perhaps this improved performance from the homesters was more down to the visitors relaxing, knowing they were in full control. At length the leather was worked up on the right by East End, centred, then passed to the left, where Wallace met the ball perfectly and steered it beyond Auld and this time the sixth goal was scored. No more than two minutes had passed before the Darlington goal was again visited and an almighty scrimmage took place within the goal mouth, resulting in the ball going over the line and it looked like it was a Darlington player who got the final touch. An own goal therefore bringing seventh heaven to the East End and absolute dejection for the Quakers.

Darlington ....None.
Newcastle East End.................7 goals.

STOCKTON VS. MIDDLESBROUGH

There was a great deal of interest in this first League meeting of the season between these local rivals, befittingly the Victoria Ground, Stockton, despite the weather being most unpropitious, saw a crowd that numbered at least 4,000. Both teams were at full-strength and Middlesbrough debuted their new back, McCrone. The homesters won the toss and on a very soft ground Middlesbrough kicked off but it was the home forwards who looked the more dangerous, both Thompson and Townley sent in clinking shots, which found Fall alert. Then the visitors had an attack but it was only a momentary relief to their defence as the home forwards once again filed down in grand style and with the ball going over to Atkin he sent in a well-judged shot which beat Fall and the homesters took a well-deserved lead. Middlesbrough came straight back at them and in one swift attack they made a rush downfield and after some loose play in front of goal, McCabe equalised with quite an easy shot. The home forwards worked close-up, and Townley sent in a brilliant a shot, which brought about an equally brilliant save from Fall. For some time, the Stockton forwards kept up a virtual bombardment of the visitors' citadel and their second goal came as Baillie put a fine cross to the goal mouth where Thompson headed through a beauty. Having retaken the lead Stockton kept up their pressure and shot after shot was rained upon Fall, but he answered each magnificently until Thompson, working the ball right into the goal mouth, made a short pass to Crawford, which wrong-footed Fall and he put through Stockton's third goal amidst great cheering. Half-time being called directly after. On resuming Stockton took up where they had left off with their forwards attacking spiritedly. At length though the visitors got away and Shaw, in returning kicked out of defence rather weakly along the ground and Stott took easy possession, gave to Black and he thundered a shot against the crossbar. The ball however dropped back into play and in a scrimmage around the goal mouth McKnight headed through. Despite this minor setback Stockton continued to have by far the best of the game, McClung having hard lines on at least two occasions. Middlesbrough then took the leather up via their right wing and for a few moments the home citadel was in danger but not breached. Thompson, taking possession, made a fine dribble through the Middlesbrough ranks and sent a low shot along the ground which Fall mis-kicked as he went to clear sending it into his own goal. A great disappointed as his performance up until then had been of exemplary standard. That was the last point of the game, and the last noteworthy action, and the final few minutes were played out.

Stockton ....**4 goals.**
Middlesbrough ....**2 goals.**

Stockton: *Goal*, Ramsay; *backs*, Shaw and McDermid; *half-backs*, Graham, Baillie and Willocks; *forwards*, Atkin, Crawford, Thompson, McClung and Townley.

Middlesbrough: *Goal*, Fall; *backs*, Crone and McManus; *half-backs*, McCrone, Stott and Taggart; *forwards*, Blyth, W. McCabe, McKnight, Lewis, and Black.

Referee: Mr Bentley (Bolton).

Birmingham Daily Post (28/11/1892) p5f.
Newcastle Daily Chronicle (28/11/1892) p6f.
Northern Daily Telegraph (28/11/1892) p3e.
Northern Echo (28/11/1892) p4e.
Sheffield and Rotherham Independent (28/11/1892) p7g.
Sporting Life (28/11/1892) p4a.
Yorkshire Herald (28/11/1892) p6e.

THE NORTHERN LEAGUE
RESULTS TO SATURDAY, NOVEMBER 26 [INCLUSIVE]

Pos	Team	Pld	W	D	L	Goals F	Goals A	Avg.	Pts
1	Middlesbrough Ironopolis	7	6	1	0	15	4	3.7500	13
2	Newcastle East End	5	3	0	2	18	9	2.0000	6
3	Sheffield United	3	1	1	1	5	2	2.5000	3
4	Stockton	4	1	1	2	9	10	0.9000	3
5	Middlesbrough	4	1	0	3	6	9	0.6667	2
6	Darlington	5	0	1	4	3	22	0.1364	1

As to the "A's"...

	NEWCASTLE EAST END 'A' RESULTS NOVEMBER 1892			
Date	Home	Score	Away	
November 5, 1892.	Bill Quay Albion	4 - 3	Newcastle East End A	*Friendly*
November 12, 1892.	Bishop Auckland	6 - 1	Newcastle East End A	*Friendly*
November 26, 1892	Newcastle East End A	2 - 2	Shankhouse	*Northern Alliance*

In other news...

The following is a letter which appeared in the Newcastle Daily Chronicle on November 11, 1892. It speaks volumes about the braveness, *previously alluded to*, of the East End executive and the challenges they faced.

Football Apathy

Sir, - The East End officials have risen to an important occasion, and boldly offered to take over the West End ground, and glad was I when I heard of it. I have been an ardent West Ender, but with its decease I gave my loyal support to East End, and they deserve it, and I feel disappointed at many old supporters and friends of the late West End, who almost weep because it went the way of all weak bodies. The East End have had the misfortune to have three indifferent Scotch clubs here; the gates have been small, and the management are getting anxious; but I can (speaking for many) assure them that there will be a huge gate to-day, when I hope to see "good old East" reverse the defeat they got a Sheffield. Come, then, all that are interested in the sport. Get your tanners ready, and come and see a champion game. I would like, with your permission, Mr. Editor, to mention that there is a want of something to keep up the enthusiasm during the week. There is not a rendezvous in town where the supporters of the leading club beat up at, to hear the latest gossip and chat. I have many a time "sallied forth at eventime," to try and hear the latest of East End, but they of the East, are always easterly. Possibly this may account for the apathy spoken of in your popular columns during the last few days.

- Yours, &c. A West End East Ender.

December 1892

Games Played in December 1892

V	Date	F	A	R	Opposition	Competition
H	03/12/1892	5	1	W	Stockton	Northern League
H	10/12/1892	1	2	L	Middlesbrough Ironopolis	Northern League
A	17/12/1892	5	2	W	Stockton	Northern League
H	24/12/1892	2	1	W	Middlesbrough	Friendly
A	26/12/1892	0	1	L	The Wednesday	Friendly
H	31/12/1892	8	1	W	Corinthians	Friendly

Appearances & Goals ~ December 1892

Name	Total		League		Friendly	
	Apps	Goals	Apps	Goals	Apps	Goals
Collins, James	6		3		3	
Crate, Thomas "Tom"	3	2	3	2	0	
Creilly, Robert "Bobby"	6	1	3	1	3	
Graham, William "Willie"	6	1	3	1	3	
Jeffrey, Harry	5		2		3	
McIntosh, James	2	2	0		2	2
McKane, Joseph "Joe"	5	1	2		3	1
Miller, James	6		3		3	
Reay, Harry	6	5	3	2	3	3
Sorley, John "Jock"	6	4	3	3	3	1
Thompson, Willie	4	4	1	1	3	3
Wallace, Joseph "Joe"	4	1	3	1	1	
Watson, Peter	1		1		0	
Whitton, David "Dave"	6		3		3	

Season to Date (03/09/1892 - 31/12/1892 inclusive)

Name	Total		League		Friendly	
	Apps	Goals	Apps	Goals	Apps	Goals
Barker, John	1		1		0	
Collins, James	12	7	8	1	12	6
Coupar, William	1		0		1	
Crate, Thomas "Tom"	18	5	8	2	10	3
Creilly, Robert "Bobby"	19	2	7	1	12	1
Dixon, Henry	2	1	0		2	1
Graham, William "Willie"	21	2	8	2	13	
Jeffrey, Harry	18		5		13	
Kirkland, J.	1				1	
McIntosh, James	2	2	0		2	2
McKane, Joseph "Joe"	19	1	6		13	1
Miller, James	19		8		11	
Reay, Harry	16	8	7	3	9	5
Sorley, John "Jock"	17	14	7	7	10	7
Thompson, Willie	15	11	6	6	9	5
Wallace, Joseph "Joe"	16	7	6	6	10	1
Watson, Peter	5		3		2	
Whitton, David "Dave"	21		8		13	

Game 16: Saturday, December 3, 1892 — Newcastle East End vs. Stockton

Competition: Northern League   Venue: St James's Park   Gate: 3,000

Newcastle East End 5 - 1 Stockton

Scorer(s): Graham (10 mins); Creilly (12 mins); Wallace (sh); Sorley (sh); Thompson (sh)

Scorer(s): Thompson (17 mins)

Goal, Dave Whitton; *backs*, Harry Jeffrey and James Miller; *half-backs*, Bobby Creilly, Willie Graham and James Collins; *forwards*, Harry Reay, Tom Crate, Willie Thompson, Jock Sorley, Joe Wallace

Goal, Charlie Ramsay; *backs*, Bob Shaw and Robert McDermid; *half-backs*, James Graham, James Baillie and Willie Willocks; *forwards*, D.C. Atkin, Bill Crawford, Gavin Thompson, Robert McClung, Jack Jones

Referee: J.H. Strawson (Lincoln)   **Kick-Off:** 2:20 PM

Last season's Northern League meetings between these two sides had seen the Heatonians win both encounters. The first at the Victoria Ground, Stockton, where they were victorious by three goals to one (17/10/1891) and the return fixture at Heaton was won again by them, but by a slightly narrower margin of East End three goals, Stockton two goals (27/02/1892). Given that history, the fact that huge improvements that had been achieved at East End, and the comparative starts that the clubs had made to the season this was looked upon as a relatively safe bet for a home win. In fairness to Stockton though, should they win their two games 'in hand' they would equal East End's points tally so there was some importance attached to this fixture.

For the encounter today Stockton were handicapped as they were without the services of their excellent forward, Billy Townley, due to him succumbing to a heavy cold. Within their eleven they did have a very familiar face, Robert McDermid, the Scot whom it will be remembered first "crossed the border" to come to Newcastle and played for West End. Team news for East End was that they saw the return of Harry Jeffrey at the back, displacing Peter Watson who had stood in admirably for Jeffrey in the previous two games.

During the week leading up to the game the frost had been so severe that many feared for game being played at all. However, over the course of Friday evening a thaw had set in and overnight there had been a light snowfall. The ground was somewhat protected of further frost by the covering of snow and so the ground was not in as bad a condition as had been expected, heavy, but playable. It was obvious that it would eventually cut up rather bad, so it was surprising that upon winning the toss Stockton elected to play 'downhill'. There was only a moderate gathering in the St James's Park ground when Thompson kicked off for East End, but this number grew during the passage of the first half, being fully 3,000 spectators gathered before the second half.

Immediately from Thompson's kick-off the ball was quickly taken to the visitors' goal, but the old West Ender, McDermid, smartly intervened and sent the leather back into midfield from whence it was driven to the home goal. The East End defence proved capable and any danger was neatly averted. The home forwards then gathered themselves and following some good work by Reay they advanced the ball to the visitor's citadel and laid heavy siege to it. The Stockton defence however proved as equally capable as the East End one had and remained impenetrable with the ball eventually being sent bye. The goal-kick saw the ball into the midfield where it remained, toing and froing between each side for some minutes.

A break then came as Sorley ran the ball up the wing, his fellow forwards surging up in support, and once again the Stockton goal was under severe pressure, but Shaw managed to finally clear the danger. The relief to the Stocktonians was short-lived however as some clever organisation from the home forwards saw them rushing back and following a scrimmage Graham managed to shoot through and the scoring was opened.

Not unsurprisingly being very buoyed by the goal the East End forwards, well supported from their midfield, laid constant attack upon the Stockton goal. The defence of the visitors was strong but eventually they were broken again, a mere two minutes after the first, with Creilly scoring to double the homesters advantage. Soon after East End very nearly scored again, and had it not been for the exploits of McDermid they surely would have done so.

The visitors right wing put in a good run but were dispossessed strongly by Collins and he launched the ball up and play was transferred once again to the Stockton quarters. Wallace tried a shot from distance and whilst the attempt was good it passed outside and was diverted over the byline for an East End corner. This led to no advantage for East End and the ball was quickly sent up the other end for the Stocktonians to have what was now becoming a rare attempt, this however was just as ineffectual as the East End corner had been. However, it did give heart to the visitors in a manner and briefly they took the ascendancy. This was soon ended as East End attacked again, and Collins had a shot which was unfortunately ineffectual.

The Stockton left wing then made good progress and a corner was won off Jeffrey. Whilst the ball was well placed and put the home goal in a little danger the East End forwards managed to take possession and move play into the midfield. The relief to the East goal proved temporary indeed as Thompson (Stockton), returned and scored with a shot from distance.

This setback awoke the East End forwards again and Graham saw an effort well saved by Ramsay. Thompson then had an excellent effort go narrowly wide. Stockton then again drove forward, and McClung was presented with a fine opportunity which he sent wide. The home forwards once again pressed and Graham upon receiving the ball from out wide drove in a most splendid which Ramsay did well to save. Reay had an effort which went awry. At the other end Jones missed a very grand chance and in what was becoming a very exciting end-to-end finale to the half Thompson (East End) took the ball right up but shot weakly. Back to the home citadel and there was an almighty scrimmage in the goalmouth which Miller did well to get away. Each goal was being visited in turn but nothing more was scored when the interval was sounded.

On crossing over East End went straight on the attack and a shot from Crate went narrowly over the bar. Stockton then made a rush up to the home goal, but Atkin shot wide. Collins then led a charge and the attack was halted unfairly by Shaw. The free-kick was in a promising position but when it was sent in McDermid cleared the danger. Once again, the homesters drove forward and another free-kick was won as Graham (Stockton) made the foul. Collins delivered the ball in nicely and Sorley rose to head through a marvellous goal for East End.

Now they had restored their two-goal cushion the East End forwards were hungry for more and pressed incessantly. Wallace had a decent effort but sent it bye. This however signalled a period of poor play which continued until Sorley shook things up a bit with an effort from distance, which unfortunately went wide. Still having the better of matters East End forced a corner and when it was delivered in there was a scrimmage in front of the goal with Crawford eventually clearing the danger. Jones then had a run up the other end and his shot was cleverly saved by Whitton. Immediately after the home forwards forced a corner from which nothing resulted. However, Reay got possession and sent in a stinging shot which Ramsay fisted out, but Wallace was all alert and shot swiftly through.

East End were now very relaxed in their play and matters became quite even. Stockton were allowed the space and time to launch a couple of ineffectual efforts. At the other end Reay crossed in a beauty which gave Ramsay all sorts of trouble, but he eventually dealt with it. The Stockton relief was not long lived as Reay again sent cleverly towards the goal and bending his head to meet it Thompson sent it through off his shoulder.

Newcastle East End ....5 goals.

Stockton ....1 goal.

MIDDLESBROUGH IRONOPOLIS VS. MIDDLESBROUGH

The return "Derby day" on Teesside! Once again, the very keen rivalry between these two clubs attracted a big gate for this, the second of their league encounters of the season, on the Paradise Ground of Ironopolis. Though the weather was cold and damp, and the ground was in a poor and slippery condition owing to the severe frosts on Thursday and Friday, there were still around 5,000 eager spectators awaiting the teams. Surprising, despite the aforementioned conditions, they were treated to a game that was more exciting than was generally anticipated and a one of the highest qualities too. Each side strove extremely hard but neither forward line was able to breach their opposing defence and when the interval arrived it was without any score.

The second half followed the same pattern as the first and the deadlock was only broken around the 80-minute mark when Hughes scored for the homesters and it being the only goal of the game secured victory for the 'Nops which though seemingly unlucky to the visitors was just about deserved.

Middlesbrough Ironopolis.......1 goal.

Middlesbrough..........................None.

Middlesbrough Ironopolis: *Goal,* Watts; *backs,* Elliott and Langley; *half-backs,* McNair, Wynn and Oliver; *forwards,* Hill, Hughes, McArthur, Seymour and McReddie.

Middlesbrough: *Goal,* Fall; *backs,* Crone and McManus; *half-backs,* Bell, Stott and Taggart; *forwards,* Blyth, Abraham, McKnight, Lewis, and Black.

Referee: Mr W.H. Jope (Wolverhampton).

The Referee (04/12/1892) p6b.
Newcastle Daily Chronicle (05/12/1892) p6c.
Northern Daily Telegraph (05/12/1892) p3e.
Shields Daily Gazette (05/12/1892) p3c.
York Herald (05/12/1892) p8g.
Newcastle Daily Chronicle (06/12/1892) p7e.

	THE NORTHERN LEAGUE RESULTS TO SATURDAY, DECEMBER 3 [INCLUSIVE]					Goals			
Pos	Team	Pld	W	D	L	F	A	Avg.	Pts
1	Middlesbrough Ironopolis	8	7	1	0	16	4	4.0000	15
2	Newcastle East End	6	4	0	2	23	10	2.3000	8
3	Sheffield United	3	1	1	1	5	2	2.5000	3
4	Stockton	5	1	1	3	10	15	0.6667	3
5	Middlesbrough	5	1	0	4	6	10	0.6000	2
6	Darlington	5	0	1	4	3	22	0.1364	1

Game 17: Saturday, December 10, 1892   **Newcastle East End vs. Middlesbrough Ironopolis**

Competition: Northern League   Venue: St James's Park   Gate: 3,000

Newcastle East End   1 - 2   Middlesbrough Ironopolis

Scorer(s): Reay (sh)

Goal, Dave Whitton; *backs,* Peter Watson and James Miller; *half-backs,* Bobby Creilly, Willie Graham and Joe McKane; *forwards,* Harry Reay, Tom Crate, Jock Sorley, James Collins, Joe Wallace

Referee: Samuel "Sam" Kemp (Redcar)

Scorer(s): McReddie (fh); McArthur (sh)

Goal, Charles Watts; *backs,* James Elliott and Ambrose Langley; *half-backs,* Donald McNair, Robert Chatt and John Oliver; *forwards,* Jack Hill, Archibald Hughes, William McArthur, Thomas Seymour, Wallace McReddie

Kick-Off: 2:20 PM

This was the return league fixture between these two teams. Current champions Ironopolis were sitting at the top of the league once again, being undefeated, and indeed having only 'dropped' the one solitary point as a result of the goalless draw against Sheffield United in their opening league fixture. Newcastle, in second place, were already some six points behind with only three games left to play following today's match.

Today was therefore the potential "title decider", *or more realistically* the *"rubber-stamping"* of the title going back to Ironopolis. An Ironopolis win meant their lead was unassailable, a Newcastle win would give them the slightest of chances in overhauling the 'Nops, but it would involve Newcastle winning all their remaining fixtures and Ironopolis losing at least one of theirs, a very unrealistic set of scenarios indeed.

The St James's Park pitch was described as being akin to a sheet of ice with a covering of snow! Strong protests were laid at the door of the referee, but he however deemed to ignore these and declared the pitch playable hence the game was to go ahead. (*see footnote to game*).

East End won the toss and elected to play 'downhill' in the first half, it was therefore the visitors who set the ball in motion. The first real attack of the game soon followed however it was to come from the homesters who had taken early possession. This chance was unfortunately ended as Sorley was adjudged to have handled the ball whilst in right front of the goal.

Continuing to maintain the upper hand Newcastle kept up the pressure on the Ironopolis goal and another good opportunity went begging as Creilly sent the ball wide and over the line. The goal-kick eased the pressure and it was indeed from Ironopolis that the next attack came from as they made a good combined rush up the field, and after some good play Seymour sent his effort behind for a goal-kick to the homesters.

Miller then intervened in a timely manner to stop another Ironopolis rush, as did Watson soon after. Ironopolis, having their best spell of the game, continued to press until Hughes failed with a good shot. This then gave the homesters an opportunity to attack. The forward line moved nicely down and putting the ball across to Sorley he headed narrowly behind. The home team managed to keep in evidence for a while.

The visitors' forwards worked their way up the field, but again Miller was there to dispossess but conceded a throw-in in doing so. This was followed by a free-kick, in a promising position, but Ironopolis could make no advantage from it.

Sorley ran the ball smartly down, and the Ironopolis goal was greatly endangered until the ball was sent behind Wallace. Creilly then put in a capital shot which was saved by Watts, but the ball fell to Collins. He played it to Reay who was very unlucky to see his effort go narrowly wide.

McReddie and McArthur, in good combination, ran the ball up but Watson intercepted and sent the ball away from danger and into the midfield. Thence the ball was taken to the visitors' goal again and Wallace crossed to Reay and with an excellent effort he brought a marvellous save from Watts. A bold attempt, from the halfway line, by Watson saw Watts in great difficulty but managing to again make a marvellous save. Collins and Wallace were proving themselves to be dangerous, but Elliott intervened in fine fashion and the ball being taken to the other goal saw Watson and Graham having to put in some good and effective work.

Despite the conditions underfoot play was very fast, with each goal being assailed in turn. Newcastle eventually obtained a corner, but nothing resulted, and the play which followed was of an inconsequential character for a while. This was until Reay had a good chance but owing to the slippery state of both the ground beneath his feet and the ball, he made a poor shot. The home goal then was put in great danger. but Reay got possession and ran the ball down the ground and crossed to Sorley. He however failed with his headed attempt at goal. This signalled a rush upfield from the 'Nops forward line and an abortive corner was the result. Moments later Whitton was called upon, but he was equal to his allotted task.

As the interval was fast approaching it seemed like the half would justifiably end all-square but in an attack that was against the run of play Ironopolis rushed up and McReddie scored for them. There was barely time for Newcastle to react to this setback before the whistle sounded.

After a rather lengthy interval, McArthur restarted for Ironopolis, who at once made an excursion into the home territory. This, however, was frustrated by Miller who turned defence into attack as he set away Wallace and Collins who changed the scene to the top end. Collins was able to get away a very good long shot which Watts had some difficulty in getting away, the ball ultimately going behind. Play hovered round the visitor's goal where it seemed the posts had a charmed existence; several efforts were rained upon them, but the ball went anywhere but between them.

The 'Nops broke away with McReddie racing down the left at a good pace. A free kick for 'hands' afforded them a splendid opportunity. The kick was very well placed, and promptly headed through by McArthur, thus registering a second goal for Ironopolis

The visitors now pressed hard, and they seemed bound to add to their score. However, whilst Miller and Watson were forced to use the most strenuous of exertions, they were successful in clearing their line. Collins and Wallace took up on the left, and a grand centre was sent to Reay who very smartly put through amidst the most tremendous of cheering. Buoyed by this success, the home team stuck to the game and gave the Ironopolis defenders a torrid time, and any amount of work to do. They stood firm however and eventually managed to affect a counter-attack which was unsuccessful as it found Watson on top form and doing wonders on the defensive. The ball travelled up and down the field at great rate, despite the frozen and slippery state of the ground, neither side having much advantage. A rather stinging effort from Hill almost took effect, and an attack at the other end was equally dangerous.

McArthur and McReddie made a grand dribble down, and Wallace shot splendidly at the other goal, the ball just passing over the bar, a very near thing indeed. Darkness was now descending making play even more uncertain. Collins distinguished himself with a very smart run up his wing, but he held on too long and Elliott halted his progress. Play was in the midfield when time was called, and Newcastle could consider themselves very unlucky to have lost this match.

Newcastle East End ....1 goal.

Middlesbrough Ironopolis.....2 goals.

At the time it was widely reported that both teams had protested strongly that the game should not go ahead, due to the condition of the ground and the intermittent, but quite furious, snowstorms. As it transpired it was only the Newcastle committee who lodged a 'formal' appeal to the Northern League Committee. This perhaps not being surprising as having won Ironopolis would not have wanted that victory taken away from them, as a successful appeal would result in the downgrading of the game from that of a "league fixture" to one of a "club match" (friendly) and a replay would have been needed. [History of course proved it wasn't.]

There were also complaints, *this time officially from both sides*, as to the way the referee exercised his duties. Some of his decisions reportedly bordering on the absurd and causing much hilarity amongst the crowd. As to the crowd itself, the 'gate' receipts for this game reached as much as £50, quite a substantial amount given the difficult times football was facing (in general).

Newcastle Daily Chronicle (10/12/1892) p7a.
Evening Standard (12/12/1892) p7f.
Manchester Courier (12/12/1892) p3c.
Newcastle Daily Chronicle (12/12/1892) p7a.
Northern Daily Telegraph (12/12/1892) p3e.
Northern Echo (12/12/1892) p4e.
Shields Daily Gazette (12/12/1892) p3e.
York Herald (12/12/1892) p8e.

THE NORTHERN LEAGUE RESULTS TO SATURDAY, DECEMBER 10 [INCLUSIVE]									
Pos	Team	Pld	W	D	L	F	A	Avg.	Pts
1	Middlesbrough Ironopolis	9	8	1	0	18	5	3.6000	17
2	Newcastle East End	7	4	0	3	24	12	2.0000	8
3	Sheffield United	3	1	1	1	5	2	2.5000	3
4	Stockton	5	1	1	3	10	15	0.6667	3
5	Middlesbrough	5	1	0	4	6	10	0.6000	2
6	Darlington	5	0	1	4	3	22	0.1364	1

Game 18: Saturday, December 17, 1892   **Stockton vs. Newcastle East End**

Competition: Northern League   Venue: Victoria Ground   Gate: 5,000

Stockton   2 - 5   Newcastle East End

Scorer(s): Thompson (fh); tbc (sh)

Scorer(s): Sorley (fh, sh); Crate (sh, sh); Reay (sh)

Goal, Charlie Ramsay; *backs*, Bob Shaw and Robert McDermid; *half-backs*, Willie Willocks, James Graham and James Hutton; *forwards*, D.C. Atkin, Bill Crawford, Gavin Thompson, Robert McClung, Billy Townley

Goal, Dave Whitton; *backs*, Harry Jeffrey and James Miller; *half-backs*, Bobby Creilly, Willie Graham and Joe McKane; *forwards*, Harry Reay, James Collins, Jock Sorley, Tom Crate, Joe Wallace

Referee: J.H. Strawson (Lincoln)

This was the return league fixture between Stockton and East End, the first game held a fortnight ago at St James's Park had resulted in a win for the East End of five goals scored to one goal conceded. The game today, taking place at the Victoria Ground, therefore aroused great interest with the Stocktonians hoping home advantage would help them avenge that defeat and the Novocastrians hoping to "*do the double*" over their hosts. The attendance of circa 5,000 spectators was no doubt increased by the rather beautiful weather for the time of year. It was bright and sunny with just a little wind, perfect conditions for the '*association game*' albeit with the ground being slightly on the heavy side.

The homesters won the toss and the visitors kicked off, but Stockton immediately returned and applied some early pressure, only to find Jeffrey alert to the danger and he cleared the line in good style. There followed a brief excursion by the Newcastle forwards into Stockton territory, but they were smartly repulsed by an organised defence. Some interesting, and even, play then took place in midfield which both sides probing for an opening. Newcastle won a corner, but the ball was headed bye. From the goal-kick Crawford took the ball nicely up the Stockton right wing and put in a good ball for Atkin. He in turn centred it beautifully for Thompson who headed very cleverly beyond the reach of Whitton and first-blood went to the homesters.

Elated by this success the home forwards continued to aggress and made a good rush down which resulted in quite a melee in front of the Newcastle goal which they eventually managed to clear dispelling the very real danger. Then Sorley ran the ball well down and played it to Reay, but with a fine intervention he was well tackled by Hutton before he had any opportunity to shoot. The homesters were now showing grand form and the play of their forwards was especially delighting the spectators. Following another fine run down, this time led by Atkin they forced a corner, but nothing resulted.

Reay and Collins then led an attack upon receiving, and the whole of the forward line passed McDermid and with only Shaw now to stop them assumed a very dangerous position indeed. However, amidst great cheers, stop them he did, and he sent the ball clear. A truly tremendous intervention from him.

Graham and Hutton were playing a grand game for Stockton and Thompson was very much in evidence. Making a particularly fine run he made a brilliant pass through to Townley who won a corner off Miller. From it the ball was well delivered in but got away by the Newcastle defence. Getting up to near the home goal both Collins and Wallace sent in splendid shots, only to find Ramsay all there.

By a piece of very nice combined play the visitor's forwards attacked once again and Ramsay had a lively time of it indeed. Stockton, who had now been playing for some time without Willocks, their right half-back, who had twisted his knee and was forced to leave the field of play, were coping admirably with his loss and equally coping with the renewed vigour of the visiting forwards. However, it did look like that it would only be a matter of time before the equaliser was achieved and when it did arrive it arrived in the most controversial of circumstances.

Newcastle's forwards had managed to amass in front of the Stockton goal and an almighty scrimmage took place around the goalmouth. Sorley, in the midst of the melee, just managed to rush the ball over the line, *or did he*?

Ramsay scooped the ball out and threw it away and despite the heaviest of protests from the Stocktonians the referee decreed the ball had crossed the line and the point was allowed.

For some time following the Newcastle forwards had by far the best of matters but found a very resolute home defence who stuck to their task gamely, preventing any further score. At the other end, however, McClung had the Newcastle goal at his mercy, but Whitton repulsed his shot with a marvellous save and when half-time was signalled the leather was in Newcastle territory.

Following the interval, it was good to see Willocks taking his place thus restoring numerical parity. Newcastle attacked from the outset and Collins was presented with an opportunity, but Ramsay was able to fist away his shot. Immediately after Crate took possession and shot through the softest of goals to put the visitors in the lead for the first time in the game. This being barely two minutes after the restart.

This seemed to dishearten the Stockton lads, who appeared to lose all combination, while on the other hand the Newcastle players were extremely buoyed, and they played up in a splendid fashion. So much so that the home defence really had their work cut out for them now. Their woes were further compounded when Willocks, who had been kicked on the thigh, had to again leave the field of play. Sorley soon took possession and deftly got the better of Shaw, indeed simply running around him, and he scored with a beauty of a shot, Ramsay having no chance.

The Novocastrians now played like demons and shot with deadly aim. Both Crate, then Reay each added another goal, and the Newcastle forwards continued to keep up a thorough bombardment of the Stockton citadel.

At length the homesters, with great determination, became dangerous. Atkin, with a splendid piece of individualism, engineered a fine centre but try as they might they could not defeat the defence of the Reds. Townley secured possession and sent in a grand shot, but Whitton saved. Newcastle now looked a bit ragged and gave away a series of free-kicks in some dangerous positions and from one of these the ball went through, but as it had not been touched the point was disallowed. Townley again was the creator of a Stockton attack and instigated a tremendous melee in the Newcastle goalmouth during which the ball was sent through and this time it counted!

Perhaps realising that their three-goal cushion may not be as safe as they had thought, *or that they had allowed to look precarious*, the visitors returned to the attack. Vigorously they charged, and on one occasion brought about a smart save from the home custodian, but they could not add to their tally, however neither could Stockton so East End emerged as victors.

Stockton..................................**2 goals.**

Newcastle East End................**5 goals.**

Athletic News (19/12/1892) p6a.
Newcastle Daily Chronicle (19/12/1892) p6d.
Northern Daily Mail (19/12/1892) p4c.
Northern Echo (19/12/1892) p4d.

THE NORTHERN LEAGUE
Results To Saturday, December 17 [Inclusive]

Pos	Team	Pld	W	D	L	Goals F	Goals A	Avg.	Pts
1	Middlesbrough Ironopolis	9	8	1	0	18	5	3.6000	17
2	**Newcastle East End**	8	5	0	3	29	14	2.0714	10
3	Sheffield United	3	1	1	1	5	2	2.5000	3
4	Stockton	6	1	1	4	12	20	0.6000	3
5	Middlesbrough	5	1	0	4	6	10	0.6000	2
6	Darlington	5	0	1	4	3	22	0.1364	1

Game 19: Saturday, December 24, 1892   **Newcastle United vs. Middlesbrough**

Competition: Friendly   Venue: St James's Park   Gate: 3,000

Newcastle United   2 - 1   Middlesbrough

Scorer(s): McIntosh (fh); Reay (sh)

Goal, Dave Whitton; *backs*, Harry Jeffrey and James Miller; *half-backs*, Bobby Creilly, Willie Graham and Joe McKane; *forwards*, Harry Reay, James Collins, Willie Thompson, Jock Sorley, Jimmy McIntosh

Referee: A. Grundy (Whitburn)

Scorer(s): tbc (sh)

Goal, J.W. Fall; *backs*, Bob Crone and J. McManus; *half-backs*, Bell, J. Stott and J. Taggart; *forwards*, Cronshaw, R. Blythe, W. McCabe, Ben Lewis, D. Black

Kick-Off: 2:15 PM

This friendly fixture was brought off amid great interest in deference to the fact that the two teams had been drawn together in the English Cup competition to be played some weeks hence. Newcastle, [*note now "United" and not East End, the name change voted for on December 9th has been ratified by the Football Association*], were without the services of Crate who was starting a one-month suspension for having played in Scotland during the close season and they were without Wallace too. The absence of the latter giving the opportunity of a trial being handed to James McIntosh, a lad from *"the land-o-cakes"*, that's Dundee to the rest of us.

With the visitors kicking off the homesters played the start of the game against the hill but with the assistance of the wind. The visitors pressed hard in the early stages and were unlucky in not scoring, Whitton being called upon to save in brilliant fashion. Reay and Collins gained possession and changed the scene to the top goal with Crone making a saving intervention and kicking clear. Again, the visitors got down and Lewis had a grand opportunity, but his final kick was disappointing as it went wide of the post. At the opposite end Thompson had almost as good a chance and his final effort was probably better than that of Lewis, but the result was the same. The ground was as hard as iron, and any attempt at roughness was at once penalised by the referee, Mr Grundy. Sorley and Thompson combined well to produce some good work and the latter sent in a lightning shot which Fall was lucky in being able to kick out smartly. From a good cross by Reay the new arrival McIntosh headed inches over the bar. The homesters were now having decidedly the best of matters. A splendid individual run down the left by Black resulted in a fine centre into the United goal area being wasted as none of his teammates had kept pace with him and the ball was ran out. Back at the Middlesbrough goal Thompson headed in a beauty which was fumbled by their custodian, Fall, but McManus was able to intercede and kicked behind for a corner to Newcastle from which nothing arose.

Middlesbrough hen attempted to mount an attack of their own, but this was brought to a swift end by Jeffrey in good style. McIntosh sent in a hot shot which looked certain to score but Fall was equal to the effort and returned the ball strongly. Then Reay finally forced the ball through but to the disappointment of most present the whistle had earlier sounded for a foul and consequently the goal was disallowed.

Not to be denied however the home forwards once again took up the running and kept at their work. The reward came when McIntosh shot a grand goal from close quarters amid tremendous cheering. With half-time closing in Middlesbrough tried to mount an attack straight from the kick-off with Black very cleverly getting past Jeffrey and sending in a long shot which Whitton had little difficulty in kicking away.

Thompson got the second half underway for Newcastle and now that they were playing 'downhill' they took no time in trying to press that advantage. Almost immediately Sorley was presented with a good chance but failed in his attempt then McIntosh went very close with an effort. Whitton in the United goal was then called upon to do some work and he acquitted himself admirably. Middlesbrough continued to press, and the United defence stood up well, being taxed to its ultimate limit but ineffectually. The visitors then got a corner but could not capitalise upon it and the resulting goal-kick relieved the pressure albeit temporarily, for it was not long before Jeffrey had to save again. Then after what seemed like an age the Newcastle forwards, led by Sorley, ran down but were dispossessed by the timely intervention of Crone when it appeared that they had a good chance. A fruitless rush was made by the Middlesbrough forwards and then McKane, after some good tackling, sent over the line. Play was now end-to-end and after some minutes Black got in near and sent in a swift shot which Whitton fisted out only to have the ball returned, Graham eventually coming to the rescue and the ball was taken to the Middlesbrough end. Any danger was soon relieved and a free-kick allowed Middlesbrough to break back out and a veritable bombardment of the Newcastle goal followed which ended up fruitless as the United defence stood impregnable. Play then ruled in the midfield for a time. Whitton was called upon again to make a save in marvellous fashion and it was only a free-kick for 'hands' against Cronshaw that lifted the pressure on the Newcastle goal. The relief was however short-lived for gaining a free-kick of their own Middlesbrough brought about the equaliser.

The game then became quite rough, the hard ground militating against good play from either side. Newcastle then got a free-kick for 'hands' near the Middlesbrough goal. Numerous good shots were put in by the home forwards, all to no avail. Still the home forwards pressed, and Fall saved a couple of shot in wonderful style, but Reay eventually beat the Middlesbrough custodian, scoring amidst great excitement. Time was shortly called, and the game thus ended:

Newcastle United....................**2 goals.**
Middlesbrough........................**1 goal.**

NORTHERN LEAGUE

Sheffield United vs. Darlington: An attendance of around 2,000 spectators braved the bitterly cold weather and gathered to see these two teams play off their league fixture at Bramall Lane. The ground was extremely hard and slippery and winning the toss United elected to play with the sun behind them. Straight from the start the homesters pressed and a shot put in by Wallace was nicely stopped by Auld. After about ten minutes play Drummond opened the scoring. McPherson and McCrimmon broke away down the right wing for Darlington but they were driven back by Lilley and Wallace registered United's second goal. Fleming almost halved the arrears after receiving the ball from McPherson, his attempt very narrowly missing. Not long after he had another attempt with the same result and there was no more scoring up to the break.

Upon resumption the United again pressed strongly and barely three minutes had passed before Hammond registered their third goal. After a brief visit to the Sheffield quarters they were back on the attack, Auld being forced into a couple of beautiful saves. Pretty even play followed, with Darlington just about holding their own, but ultimately the quality of United shone through and Wallace scored their fourth goal.

There was a very good response from Darlington as they virtually penned in the United, but their finishing was poor with all their efforts going wide. As the game was coming to a close Hutchinson, with a fast shot, brought out a good save from Howlett but no sooner had this happened than Hammond put on Sheffield's fifth goal and the game was brought to said close.

Sheffield United........................5 goals.
Darlington ....None.

Sheffield United: *Goal*, Howlett; *backs*, Whitham and Lilley; *half-backs*, Howell, Hendry and Needham; *forwards*, Drummond, Wallace, Hammond, Davies, and Watson.

Darlington: *Goal*, Auld; *backs*, Norris and Coleman; *half-backs*, McManus, Waites and McLaine; *forwards*, McPherson, McCrimmon, Fleming, Hutchinson, and Keay.

Referee: Mr Morgan Roberts (Derby).

Newcastle Daily Chronicle (24/12/1892) p7e.
Newcastle Daily Chronicle (26/12/1892) p6e.
Northern Echo (26/12/1892) p4f.
Scottish Referee (26/12/1892) p4a.
Sportsman (26/12/1892) p4e.

	THE NORTHERN LEAGUE RESULTS TO SATURDAY, DECEMBER 24 [INCLUSIVE]								
							Goals		
Pos	Team	Pld	W	D	L	F	A	Avg.	Pts
1	Middlesbrough Ironopolis	9	8	1	0	18	5	3.6000	17
2	Newcastle United	8	5	0	3	29	14	2.0714	10
3	Sheffield United	4	2	1	1	10	2	5.000	5
4	Stockton	6	1	1	4	12	20	0.6000	3
5	Middlesbrough	5	1	0	4	6	10	0.6000	2
6	Darlington	6	0	1	5	3	27	0.1111	1

Game 20: Monday, December 26, 1892   **The Wednesday vs. Newcastle United**

Competition: Friendly   Venue: Olive Grove

The Wednesday   1 - 0   Newcastle United

Scorer(s): Brady (12 mins)

Goal, Bill Allan; *backs*, Tom Brandon and Johnny Darroch; *half-backs*, Harry Brandon, J. Brown and Bruce Chalmers; *forwards*, Harry Davis, Neill, Alexander Rowan, Alec Brady, Fred Spiksley

Referee: W. H. Stacey (Sheffield)

Scorer(s): none

Goal, Dave Whitton; *backs*, Harry Jeffrey and James Miller; *half-backs*, Bobby Creilly, Willie Graham and Joe McKane; *forwards*, Harry Reay, James Collins, Willie Thompson, Jock Sorley, Joe Wallace

Kick-Off: 2:25 PM

The weather was extremely cold and there was a heavy fog hanging over the ground. This dense fog persisted for the whole of the game making it almost impossible for anyone to follow the game in its entirety well certainly with any accuracy.

The Wednesday put forward a very strong eleven indeed, which included a new man, Bruce Chalmers on the right of the half-back line. Unfortunately for them however was that Billy Betts, their centre-half, who was down to play was taken ill at very short notice indeed, in fact so short notice that their Trainer, Neill, was the only one available to take his place.

With regards to Newcastle they were missing Crate who starts his one-month suspension from today, this after he was sanctioned for appearing in Scotland during the close season, Newcastle will undoubtedly miss his services. Other than that, they were probably at what would be deemed full strength.

The start of the match was delayed by ten minutes from that advertised. Presumably this was caused by the hasty need to substitute Betts, *though there is no discernible or official explanation*, so it was at 2:25pm that Wednesday kicked off but it was obvious from this beginning that even the players had the greatest of difficulty in following the ball through the fog. It was a rare occurrence indeed therefore that the spectators caught a glimpse of the ball. At the outset play was even and the Reds of Newcastle were the first to make anything like a real attack. They got unpleasantly close to the goal for the homesters liking but were ultimately beaten by the rear-guard and sank back into their own half. The game then turned pretty lively, given the prevailing conditions, and it was after twelve minutes of play that Brady broke through for the Wednesday and open the scoring.

Resuming Newcastle pressed but were quickly beaten back and afterwards there was no advantage on either side. For what could be seen the ball stayed mainly in the midfield and on those occasions when it did get near either goal the attackers were ineffectual, and half time was thence upon us.

Following the interval there was no improvement in the weather conditions but in trying to make the best of things Newcastle went to the front. However, before the charge of their forward quintet could cause any damage they were turned around and with defence going on the attack the Wednesday rushed up to the other end. Spiksley led this charge and ably assisted by his colleagues made matters within the East End citadel quite warm indeed. Their defence though stood up magnificently and whilst a shot or two did get past them Whitton was able to stop them.

Following this burst of excitement, the game settled down again to one of even play, held mainly in the midfield, but with each goal being visited without being endangered. This until just before time was called when the Tynesiders, desperately looking to get something out of the game, applied a piece of sustained pressure but it was too little, too late and with the Wednesday defence holding firm the game was called to a halt.

The Wednesday........................1 goal.

Newcastle United......................None.

Newcastle Daily Chronicle (27/12/1892) p6f.
Sheffield Telegraph (27/12/1892) p8c.
Sheffield and Rotherham Independent (27/12/1892) p7d.

Game 21: Saturday, December 31, 1892　　　　　**Newcastle United vs. Corinthians**

Competition: Friendly　　　　Venue: St James's Park　　　　Gate: 1,500

Newcastle United　8 - 1　Corinthians

Scorer(s): McKane (fh); Reay (fh, sh); McIntosh (fh); Sorley (sh); Thompson (sh, sh, sh)

Scorer(s): Salt (fh)

Goal, Dave Whitton; *backs*, Harry Jeffrey and James Miller; *half-backs*, Bobby Creilly, Willie Graham and Joe McKane; *forwards*, Harry Reay, James Collins, Willie Thompson, Jock Sorley, Jimmy McIntosh

Goal, E.V. Gosling; *backs*, H.C. Lawrence and N.T. Shaw; *half-backs*, Daniels, C. Wreford-Brown and A.K. Brook; *forwards*, A.H. Hossack, M.H. Stanborough, N. Perkins, J.A. Walker, R.J. Salt

Referee: Robert Campbell (Sunderland)

Kick-Off: 2:15 PM

It was generally accepted that when the holiday fixtures were announced the executive of the Newcastle club could not have secured a better combination than the Wednesday of Sheffield, the Corinthians, Everton and Glasgow Rangers. After a very narrow defeat at the hands of Wednesday, who it must be remembered are a Division 1 outfit, the programme continued today with a visit from the most famous of amateurs, Corinthians. Though it had been a season or two since they had visited these parts there was probably no more popular a team that could have been presided for the delectation of the patrons of the St James's Park enclosure today. Following a series of very heavy frosts there had been a bit of a thaw, but the ground was still hard and slippery, not very conducive conditions for the game of football it must be admitted. It was also noted that the weather was bitterly cold, which no doubt contributed heavily to the less than hoped for attendance.

The Corinthians won the toss and elected to play 'up the hill' for the first half so playing 'down the hill' Thompson got the game underway for Newcastle United.

Collins received possession and ran the ball well into the visitor's quarters, whereupon he was dispossessed by Shaw who cleared back upfield. The homesters quickly returned and Sorley was presented with an opportunity he however lifted the ball over the bar. The goal kick transferred play to midfield from whence Graham fed the ball well to the forwards who ran up smartly. An effort was saved by Gosling but unfortunately for him the ball fell nicely for McKane who returned it with a swift shot, thus scoring the opening goal.

From the kick-off following the goal the Corinthians showed great determination and their forward quintet strode together cleverly to put the home goal in some danger. Jeffrey managed to make a clearance but upon receiving Salt returned, and with what was a fine long shot put through the equaliser.

Immediately following the ball was entrenched in the visitor's top-third and some fast play was witnessed, this until the pressure was relieved when Collins sent the ball behind. Launching an attack from the goal-kick Jeffrey intercepted the Corinthian charge with a well-timed tackle, dispossessing the amateurs' forwards just when they were getting into a nice run. He placed the ball well up the field, but an attempt to score by Reay proved futile as the ball went very wide of the mark.

The visitors once more asserted themselves and Salt passed beautifully across to Walker who headed into the goal and a very smart intervention from Miller was all which prevented another point for them. From this McIntosh obtained possession and ran by himself along the wing. He however ended his own smart piece of play with a very poor shot indeed. Then play in general was poor and unimportant for some minutes, but after this relapse the home left wing made a steady progressive run, affording Sorley an opportunity but his effort was to no effect. 'Hands' against Wreford-Brown enabled Jeffrey to endanger the amateurs' goal, but the ball went outside without troubling Gosling in any manner. The Corinthian forwards, headed by Stanborough, were getting into a nice swinging run, when Jeffrey dispossessed them in excellent style. Turning defence into attack he launched the ball up the field, where, from a fine overhead serve, Gosling and his backs had a merry time of it but after some scrimmaging Reay managed to head through the second point for United.

Directly after, at the other end, Walker gave Perkins a chance, and just as he was about to avail himself of the opportunity McKane rushed in and cleared in marvellous fashion. Newcastle then asserted themselves and were having the best of play and obtained what looked like a good goal, but it was disallowed for some infringement of the rules on the part of one of the home forwards. However, United kept up the pressure giving the defence a torrid time and whilst hovering around the Corinthian goal, the heavily taxed defence inevitably collapsed, and McIntosh pushed through to put on a third point for the homesters. Credit must also be given to Sorley who put the ball across the goal for McIntosh in the smartest of manners.

McKane broke up a rush by the amateurs' forwards and Reay, taking fast up the wing, brought a corner off Shaw. The advantage was to no avail as Thompson sent the ball sailing over the bar. The Corinthians, gaining a second wind as it were, asserting themselves strongly, Salt sent in a splendid swift and low effort, but Whitton managed to make the save, being very fortunate in doing so. The home team then worked the leather up the field, and Sorley sent in a most severe shot, the ball thundering against the crossbar. It rebounded into play and Gosling was given several other shots to deal with, Reay very narrowly missing with the final one thus releasing the pressure. Moments later half time was announced.

The Corinthians opened the second half well, but they lost the ball to Jeffrey who played it well down the ground. It was received by

Thompson, who headed it over Shaw, and Sorley, rushing in, sent a lightning shot which Gosling could do little about, indeed having no chance whatsoever in preventing it going through, and a fourth point was registered to Newcastle. This fourth goal being scored within a couple of minutes from the restart. McIntosh was well served by Sorley and passed across to Graham, his shot being saved by gosling, but at the expense of a corner. The ball was well put in and some pressure was exerted upon the Corinthian citadel, and Thompson ultimately, after a scrimmage, headed the ball through for a fifth point to the homesters. The Corinthians managed to briefly assert themselves, but their attack was weak and easily broken down. McIntosh then rushed down the wing, passing at the centre to Thompson, who thence took the ball in a fine dribble right down, passing through almost the whole of the defence and scored with the greatest of ease. A most magnificent solo demonstration indeed. The visitor's team was proving to be a very poor one. They could do nothing against the fine combination play and individual skills of the home eleven. United continued to press and Collins put in a swift shot which Gosling saved and when the ball fell to Reay, he sent it bye. Sorley having the unluckiest of times just moments later as his effort missed by the narrowest of margins. Play was becoming a little faster and Reay made another good attempt which Gosling fisted out. There was proving to be no relief for the Corinthians and soon the goal fell to Thompson as he turned a neat pass from Sorley to effective account thus bringing about his hat-trick, this after the opposing backs had made a good stand against some severe pressure. The Corinthians made a little headway, but Salt sent past after Whitton had thrown out a shot by Perkins, as he did another shot from the same player. Reay completed the scoring after a titanic struggle in the Corinthian goalmouth, the defenders fighting bravely, but ultimately vainly. Perhaps not unsurprisingly, given the scoreline and the ease at which United were able to play the game, they relaxed a little too much thus allowing Corinthians in again, however an attempt by Salt was poor indeed. Whitton then conceded a corner from a shot by Perkins but any danger from this was easily cleared and that was the last noteworthy piece of action in a game that had been thoroughly dominated by the homesters

Newcastle United .... **8 goals.**

Corinthians .... **1 goal.**

Under normal circumstances a win by eight goals to one would be hugely celebrated, however, anyone who visited St James's Park this afternoon would have been sorely disappointed if their intention was to witness an interesting and exciting game. Despite making assertions to the strength and quality of the men Corinthians would send, those who arrived were described as *"the weakest team this famous club has ever sent on tour"*, certainly the weakest ever to be seen in Newcastle. Indeed, such was the superiority of Newcastle over their opponents that with very little extra effort they could easily have ran their score into double figures. The sum guaranteed to Corinthians was £50. It is understood that the secretary of Newcastle will, in writing to Mr N.L. Jackson (Corinthians), point out such facts and suggest a lower amount than the agreed be paid.

NORTHERN LEAGUE

Middlesbrough vs. Sheffield United: The pitch was playable but very hard indeed, certainly hard enough to interfere with the standard of football that could be achieved. The visitors played a moderate game in the first half-hour and the home team had plenty of chances but managed to score only the once before half-time was upon us. The goal being of strange nature indeed.

Cronshaw put in a grand shot which first struck Whitham, the Sheffield back, then hit a post and rebounded over the line beyond the reach of Howlett, who by then was perfectly perplexed as to the flight of the ball. Lewis then had an attempt which was cleared by Whitham and at the other end Fall was called upon to stop an excellent shot from Wallace. Soon back to the ascendancy the homesters, via Lewis, made a grand attempt at scoring but failed and Cronshaw eventually put the ball through for goal number two, but it was struck off due to an offside. Three corners then fell to Middlesbrough, each was fruitless, as was a corner to the United, with Needham kicking the ball wide. Fine play was exhibited by both sides under the prevailing conditions, but no more score was obtained.

On crossing over Sheffield played up well for a while, Drummond making a grand run without effect. Fall was then again called upon to make another fine save. Eventually they fell away again letting Middlesbrough in to secure their second point. Cronshaw getting the goal with a well driven screw shot. Only a few after minutes after this Sheffield managed to get a goal of their own, coming from a low swift shot by Wallace. There was to follow another 'offside' goal to Middlesbrough, from Black, and then even play was then the nature of the game until the close with nothing further being scored.

Middlesbrough ....2 goals.
Sheffield United ....1 goal.

Middlesbrough: *Goal,* Fall; *backs,* Crone and McManus; *half-backs,* Bach, Stott and Taggart; *forwards,* Cronshaw, Blythe, McCabe, Lewis and Black.

Sheffield United: *Goal,* Howlett; *backs,* Whitham and Lilley; *half-backs,* Waller, Hendry and Needham; *forwards,* Drummond, Wallace, Hammond, Davies and Watson.

Newcastle Daily Chronicle (31/12/1892) p7e.
Northern Echo (02/01/1893) p4e.
Newcastle Daily Chronicle (02/01/1893) p6f.
Newcastle Daily Chronicle (03/01/1893) p6f.

THE NORTHERN LEAGUE
RESULTS TO MONDAY, DECEMBER 31 [INCLUSIVE]

Pos	Team	Pld	W	D	L	F	A	Avg.	Pts
1	Middlesbrough Ironopolis	9	8	1	0	18	5	3.6000	17
2	Newcastle United	8	5	0	3	29	14	2.0714	10
3	Sheffield United	5	2	1	2	11	4	2.7500	5
4	Middlesbrough	6	2	0	4	8	11	0.7273	4
5	Stockton	6	1	1	4	12	20	0.6000	3
6	Darlington	6	0	1	5	3	27	0.1111	1

As to the "A's"…

NEWCASTLE EAST END/UNITED 'A' RESULTS DECEMBER 1892

Date	Home	Score	Away	
December 3, 1892.	Blyth	4 - 0	Newcastle East End A	Northern Alliance
December 10, 1892.	Ashington	3 - 4	Newcastle East End A	Northern Alliance
December 17, 1892.	Newcastle East End A	1 - 2	Willington Athletic	Northern Alliance
December 24, 1892.	Sunderland A	3 - 0	Newcastle United A	Northern Alliance
December 26, 1892.	Southwick	7 - 2	Newcastle United A	Northern Alliance
December 31, 1892	Whitburn	2 - 0	Newcastle United A	Northern Alliance

THE NORTHERN ALLIANCE 1892-93 HALF-YEAR STANDINGS

Pos.	Team	Pld.	W	D	L	F	A	Pts
1	Sunderland 'A'	15	11	3	1	50	17	25
2	Willington Athletic	12	9	1	2	34	15	19
3	*Blyth	13	10	1	2	52	22	*19
4	Rendel	10	7	1	2	36	12	15
5	Shankhouse	13	6	2	5	39	27	14
6	Southwick	10	6	1	3	31	14	13
7	Newcastle United 'A'	13	4	2	7	27	39	10
8	Seaham Harbour	10	2	2	6	17	41	6
9	Gateshead NER	10	2	0	8	13	28	4
10	Mickley	11	2	0	9	15	43	4
11	Ashington	11	1	1	9	23	40	3
12	Whitburn	8	1	0	7	5	34	2

*Blyth deducted 2 points for fielding an ineligible player.

It was confirmed that Crate, the Newcastle United Club's inside right forward, has been suspended for a month by the English Association for having played during the close season.

January 1893

Games Played in January 1893

V	Date	F	A	R	Opposition	Competition
H	02/01/1893	4	2	W	Everton	Friendly
H	03/01/1893	4	0	W	Glasgow Rangers	Friendly
H	07/01/1893	3	1	W	Bolton Wanderers	Friendly
H	14/01/1893	1	1	D	Sheffield United	Northern League
H	21/01/1893	2	3	L	Middlesbrough	FA Cup [Round 1]
A	28/01/1893	2	3	L	Stockton	Friendly

Appearances & Goals ~ January 1893

	Total		League		FA Cup		Friendly	
Name	Apps	Goals	Apps	Goals	Apps	Goals	Apps	Goals
Collins, James	5		1		1		3	
Crate, Thomas "Tom"	2		1				1	
Creilly, Robert "Bobby"	6	1	1		1		4	1
Graham, William "Willie"	6	1	1		1		4	
Jeffrey, Harry	5	1	1		1		3	
McKane, Joseph "Joe"	6	1	1		1		4	
Miller, James	6		1		1		4	
Reay, Harry	6	5	1		1	1	4	4
Sorley, John "Jock"	6	4	1		1		4	4
Thompson, Willie	5	5	0		1	1	4	4
Wallace, Joseph "Joe"	6	1	1		1		4	
Watson, Peter	1	0					1	
Whitton, David "Dave"	6	1	1		1		4	

Season to Date (03/09/1892 - 28/01/1893 inclusive)

	Total		League		FA Cup		Friendly	
Name	Apps	Goals	Apps	Goals	Apps	Goals	Apps	Goals
Barker, John	1		1				0	
Collins, James	25	7	9	1	1		15	6
Coupar, William	1		0				1	
Crate, Thomas "Tom"	20	5	9	2			11	3
Creilly, Robert "Bobby"	25	3	8	1	1		16	2
Dixon, Henry	2	1	0				2	1
Graham, William "Willie"	27	2	9	2	1		17	
Jeffrey, Harry	23		6		1		16	
Kirkland, J.	1						1	
McIntosh, James	2	2	0				2	2
McKane, Joseph "Joe"	25	1	7		1		17	1
Miller, James	25		9		1		15	
Reay, Harry	22	13	8	3	1	1	13	9
Sorley, John "Jock"	23	18	8	7	1		14	11
Thompson, Willie	20	16	6	6	1	1	13	9
Wallace, Joseph "Joe"	22	7	7	6	1		14	1
Watson, Peter	6		3				3	
Whitton, David "Dave"	27		9		1		17	

Game 22: Monday, January 2, 1893   Newcastle United vs. Everton

Competition: Friendly   Venue: St James's Park   Gate: 3,000

Newcastle East End   4 - 2   Everton

Scorer(s): Thompson (fh, fh); Sorley (fh); Reay (sh)

Goal, Dave Whitton; *backs*, Peter Watson and James Miller; *half-backs*, Bobby Creilly, Willie Graham and Joe McKane; *forwards*, Harry Reay, James Collins, Willie Thompson, Jock Sorley, Joe Wallace

Referee: Robert Campbell (Sunderland)

Scorer(s): OG [Watson] (sh); Holt (sh)

Goal, David Jardine; *backs*, Bob Howarth and Charles Parry; *half-backs*, Bob Kelso, John Holt and Fred Collinson; *forwards*, Alex Latta, Richard Boyle, Allan Maxwell, Edgar Chadwick, Fred Geary

Kick-Off: 2:15 PM

The second fixture of Newcastle's holiday programme saw Everton visiting St James's Park. They travelled up the previous night through the bitter coldness, and the snow. When they awoke the following morning, it was to the same, though the extent of the snow fall had subsided somewhat.

Despite the best endeavours of an army of volunteers, who had worked tirelessly to clear the pitch all morning, it was a losing battle as upon kick-off there was a covering of two-to-three inches of snow on the pitch.

Newcastle made two changes to the anticipated team, Wallace was put in place of McIntosh and Watson was in place of Jeffrey. Regarding the Everton, they were fielding a very strong eleven indeed, and included in their side was Bob Kelso, formerly of Newcastle West End, and he received a hearty welcome as being deserved of a good friend.

Newcastle won the toss and elected to play 'down the hill' for the first half and Maxwell started the game for the visitors. Almost immediately they were given a free-kick for a foul and their left-wing ran up with Geary putting in a grand centre. In an attempt to clear the ball Miller made a miskick, and the ball ran through to Maxwell who put in a grand shot, but Watson made a marvellous intervention to put at an end any danger. Kelso, Howarth and Holt effected another attack which was repulsed, and Wallace ran well down, and after some finessing, he had a chance. Whilst his shot was smart it was also wide. Newcastle kept up the pressure and were awarded a free-kick around the halfway mark. Miller took the kick and sent it beautifully through to Thompson, who in equally magnificent style, headed the ball through amidst great enthusiasm and cheering. The home team then got a corner, but Wallace sent behind. The visitors left-wing once again proved dangerous as they broke away and advanced towards the Newcastle goal in sharp fashion but McKane, ever alert, came to the rescue and he transferred play immediately into the Everton quarters. Thompson put in a good deal of clever work but failed to find a decent opening and played the ball on. It eventually arrived at Reay, but he sent it behind. It was in little doubt that Newcastle were enjoying the upper hand but for all their supremacy they could not further break down a very stout Everton defence. Geary and Chadwick managed to make a break-away and Graham was called upon to make a marvellous interception. Turning defence into attack he fed the ball to Thompson who ran swiftly down but was dispossessed. Newcastle immediately regained possession and Reay once again released Thompson and this time he succeeded in getting the ball through for his, and Newcastle's, second goal. After an ineffectual sortie by Geary the supremacy once again belonged to Newcastle. During this period of play they obtained a corner but could make nothing from it, though Reay did come very close with his fine shot. Jardine sent his goal-kick out long but it was returned straight away by McKane and Jardine was called upon to make another save and in doing so could only parry the ball which broke to Sorley and he put easily through for Newcastle's third goal. Soon after Newcastle gained another corner which Jardine saved, but at the expense of another, this latter one being sent over the bar by Collins. Yet another corner was to be won as Parry relieved a return from Reay and the ball fell to Howarth who conceded with his attempted clearance. This corner proved unproductive. Everton then had a period of dominancy as Geary ran up and put across a centre which Whitton fisted away. The ball was sent back in by Maxwell, but his shot was turned away by McKane in grand style. Wallace and Sorley then broke for Newcastle and made a tricky run down the wing then centred to Collins. From his shot Jardine had the most difficult of saves but expedited it to perfection. Holt then put in some good work for the visitors, but Reay got past him and put in a lightning shot that just shaved the post. Another good run up by Everton's left-wing saw Chadwick wasting the opportunity with a shot of very poor standard. Directly after Holt was called upon at the other end to make an important intervention. Latta then ran up the wing but Miller stopped his progress. As the half was coming to an end Everton were putting a great deal of pressure on the Newcastle goal. Chadwick had another opportunity but fire straight into the hands of Whitton and he cleared the ball well up the field and the interval arrived.

On resuming after the break Everton quickly assumed the aggressive and a long shot was sent in by Latta. In attempting to kick the ball clear Watson could only watch in horror as the ball skewed off his foot, beat his own goalkeeper and landed in his own net. A most disastrous start to the second half indeed for Newcastle.

Buoyed by this the Everton right-wing, who had been very quiet in the first half, launched an attack which Latta could not capitalise upon as he sent over the line. Keeping up the pressure the visitors were once again dangerous, but Miller relieved with a long kick clear following which Graham did some good work. Whitton was then called upon to make a save from an attempt by Chadwick, this he executed with his feet. Everton continued to have the upper hand until Sorley and Creilly combined to take the ball to the Everton goal. Sorley sent in a swift shot and Howarth kicked out. Collins took possession but his swift shot was wayward. The home forwards combined well but were dispossessed by Parry who sent the ball to Geary who ran down and had hard lines indeed with his final attempt.

There then followed a short lull in play which ended when Newcastle worked their way up and a merry scrimmage ensued in the Everton goal which they eventually cleared, and they broke towards the opposite goal. Sorley managed to run the ball out of danger and put in an excellent ball across the goal which Reay got on the end of and put through. Kelso was next to have an opportunity and Whitton parried away his attempt with Miller adding a further clearance. Everton returned but they had no success as they first forced Whitton into making a magnificent save and then gave away possession by committing a foul when they were again within sight of the Newcastle goal.

Serious Everton pressure then saw them win four corners in quick succession, but each was to no avail. Undismayed by this lack of success they kept up the onslaught and Holt sent in a shot which Whitton fisted out. This hit the crossbar and he caught it as it rebounded, the referee however ruled that the leather had crossed the line and a goal was awarded. Newcastle won a free-kick near the Everton goal and Collins sent the ball through but because the leather had not touched anyone else the goal was disallowed. Everton then pressed and won a corner, but Collins was there to clear. The home defence was then assailed until the end but stood resolute and there was no further scoring. The result therefore being:

Newcastle United....................**4 goals.**
Everton....................................**2 goals.**

The gate receipts for this match against Everton amounted to something like £79, the largest sum taken since the Celtic visit in September.

NORTHERN LEAGUE

Stockton vs. Sheffield United: There was a huge surprise played out at the Victoria Ground today, no-one expected such a result as the homesters winning by five clear goals, but that's exactly what they did. The start of the game gave no hint of what was to come as the visitors seemed to be comfortably in command of affairs. Then a heavy pressing by the Stockton forwards saw McClung scoring twice in quick succession, then Thompson scored one and Crawford added a fourth before the break. Things were more even in the second half, but Stockton got through again with Jones adding a fifth for them to complete a handsome victory.

Stockton...................................**5 goals.**
Sheffield United.......................**None.**

Newcastle United 1892-93: Season Zero

Stockton: *Goal*, Ramsay; *backs*, Shaw and McDermid; *half-backs*, Willocks, Graham and Hutton; *forwards*, Atkin, Crawford, Thompson, McClung and Jones.

Sheffield United: *Goal*, Howlett; *backs*, Whittam and Lilley; *half-backs*, Walter, Hendry and Needham; *forwards*, Drummond, Wallace, Hammond, Davis and Watson.

Referee: Mr Fairgreaves (Middlesbrough).

Liverpool Echo (02/01/1893) p4a.
Newcastle Daily Chronicle (03/01/1893) pp6-7.
Sheffield Daily Telegraph (03/01/1893) p8c.
Sheffield and Rotherham Independent (03/01/1893) p8b.

THE NORTHERN LEAGUE
RESULTS TO MONDAY, JANUARY 02 [INCLUSIVE]

Pos	Team	Pld	W	D	L	F	A	Avg.	Pts
1	Middlesbrough Ironopolis	9	8	1	0	18	5	3.6000	17
2	Newcastle United	8	5	0	3	29	14	2.0714	10
3	Sheffield United	6	2	1	3	11	9	1.2222	5
4	Stockton	7	2	1	4	17	20	0.8500	5
5	Middlesbrough	6	2	0	4	8	11	0.7273	4
6	Darlington	6	0	1	5	3	27	0.1111	1

Game 23: Tuesday, January 3, 1893   **Newcastle United vs. Glasgow Rangers**

Competition: Friendly   Venue: St James's Park   Gate: 3,000

Newcastle United   4 - 0   Glasgow Rangers

Scorer(s): Reay (fh); Creilly (fh); Thompson (sh); Sorley (sh)

Goal, Dave Whitton; *backs*, Harry Jeffrey and James Miller; *half-backs*, Bobby Creilly, Willie Graham and Joe McKane; *forwards*, Harry Reay, James Collins, Willie Thompson, Jock Sorley, Joe Wallace

Scorer(s): *none*

Goal, Mackenzie; *backs*, Robert Scott and Jock Drummond; *half-backs*, Robert Marshall, Andrew McCreadie and Frank Muir; *forwards*, Neil Kerr, David McPherson, Robb, John McPherson, John Barker

Referee: Robert Campbell (Sunderland)

Whilst the local eleven were able to defeat the Corinthians and Everton, the Glasgow club was placing so many international players on the field that it was thought they were sure to beat United in this the last of their holiday fixture list. Still, many of the supporters of the home team were not without confidence in their favourites, and fully 3,000 spectators paid for admission to the St. James's Park enclosure, the small boy, as usual, being strongly in evidence. Unfortunately, owing to indisposition, goalkeeper David Haddow and back Donald Gow were unable to play for the Glaswegians, their vacancies were filled by Mackenzie and Scott respectively. The McPherson brothers, John and David, both turned out for this match.

The Rangers won the toss and decided to play from the top goal, thus having the benefit of the incline in the first half, therefore Thompson, Newcastle's captain for today, got the game underway against the hill. As the game began snow was falling gently, and lightly; but in the early part of the second half a regular storm prevailed for about ten minutes, but the players stuck to their work: while the exciting play kept up the enthusiasm of the onlookers amid their bleak and wintry surroundings.

However, I digress so back to the beginning of the game. After some even exchanges Marshall assisted D McPherson and Kerr to get down on the right, and the last-named dropped the ball into the goal mouth, but the slippery surface handicapped Barker, who failed to turn the pass to account, and thus missed an easy opening. This state of affairs did not continue for long though as Graham was mainly instrumental in forcing the Rangers back, and Reay and Collins managed to get around Muir. When well up Reay centred, and as Scott miskicked, Sorley had nothing to do but guide the ball into the net. Unfortunately, though he shot straight at Mackenzie, and the ball rebounded from the goalkeeper into the field of play, Muir ultimately kicking it out of danger. United returned to the attack, and Sorley experienced hard lines in hitting the cross-bar with fast shot; while on the other wing Reay missed a nice pass from Thompson when he had an open goal. Severe pressure was put upon Scott, Drummond, and McCreadie, and at length Thompson assisted a dropping shot from McKane on its journey past the goalkeeper. Sorley and Wallace worked together with admirable understanding on the left wing; but they kept the ball too much to themselves so that Reay and Collins were often idle for several minutes together. Towards the interval the Rangers improved and for some time penned the home eleven round their own goal. The defence was equal to the occasion however, Miller being particularly clever and effective in his interventions. From a sudden break away Drummond was compelled to give Reay a corner. This was well placed, and Sorley put on the second point. With United leading by two goals to none, ends were changed.

On resuming, not only did the Rangers have to face the hill, but there was also a blinding snowstorm, making it virtually impossible to see from one side of the pitch to the other.

In the first two minutes Collins was given an opening close in, but he slipped, and Drummond cleared. The Tyneside eleven continued to have somewhat the best of the exchanges; though they found Drummond a difficult man to beat, while McCreadie played a brilliant game. After repeated disappointments Collins, Reay, and Thompson passed prettily down the field, and the centre managing to head the ball past Drummond, dodged round the back and scored a well-earned goal. A few minutes later Scot was called upon to stop a dangerous rush by Sorley and Wallace. He pulled them up; though as he banged the ball against Thompson when clearing, Sorley took the rebound and beat McKenzie. From this point the play fell off a great deal, then the game was stopped for several minutes owing to McCreadie getting accidentally kicked and winded. Occasionally the visitors raced up the field well together, and once or twice seemed on the point of scoring. They ultimately failed to break through the home defence, however, and when the final whistle blew the score stood:

Newcastle United....................4 goals.

Glasgow Rangers......................None.

Glasgow Herald (04/01/1893) p11d.
Newcastle Daily Chronicle (04/01/1893) p7b.

Game 24: Saturday, January 7, 1893 **Newcastle United vs. Bolton Wanderers**

Competition: Friendly   Venue: St James's Park   Gate: 2,500

Newcastle United   **3 - 1**   **Bolton Wanderers**

Scorer(s): Reay (fh, fh); Thompson (sh)

Goal, Dave Whitton; *backs*, Harry Jeffrey and James Miller; *half-backs*, Bobby Creilly, Willie Graham and Joe McKane; *forwards*, Harry Reay, James Collins, Willie Thompson, Jock Sorley, Joe Wallace

Referee: Robert Campbell (Sunderland)

Scorer(s): Munro (fh)

Goal, Whittaker; *backs*, Peter Bullough and John Somerville; *half-backs*, Alex Paton, Harry Gardiner and Harry Matthew; *forwards*, Wilson, Jimmy Munro, Davie Willocks, Jimmy Dickinson, Jimmy Turner

Kick-Off: 2:15 PM

Newcastle United welcomed first division opponents today, Bolton Wanderers, to St James's Park. The Wanderers, no doubt as a result of the inclemency of the weather, arrived at St James's Park close to half-an-hour late and it was agreed therefore to play the game in two halves of forty minutes each. The weather, as intimated to, was very inclement, and the ground was covered in about three to four inches of snow, making it anything but conducive to the prospect of a game where skills would out-master strength and stamina. Considering all this the gate, of fully 2,500 spectators, was quite a capital one indeed.

Wanderers won the toss and decided to play against the hill in the first half. Thompson therefore opened the game down the incline for Newcastle. Having the best of the opening exchanges it was not long before Thompson had a shot which brought about a save from Whittaker, kicking out it was soon returned by Collins, but his attempt was also saved by Whittaker. Play was then concentrated in the midfield for a while.

Turner and Dickinson then rushed up the wing but were intercepted by Miller in splendid fashion and he gave to Wallace, further clearing the danger. After a fine pass by Munro into the Newcastle goalmouth some fine play was displayed but Wallace eventually ran quickly down the field and passed across to Collins and his shot missed by barely the breadth of a hair. Miller then placed cleverly, and Thompson had a chance only to be disappointed by being ruled offside, this relieving the danger to the Wanderers goal.

Gardiner disposed the home forwards when they were in a dangerous position. Some interesting play ensued, and Whitton had to handle a shot from Munro. He had no difficulty in kicking away, and then Dickinson sent over the line. Graham saved, and then Whitton had to fist out a shot from Willocks. Bolton continued to press, and the sustained pressure eventually paid off as Munro scored with a splendid shot.

Newcastle then had a look-in and were very unlucky in not getting the ball through, Wallace failing when he had a good chance. United kept up the pressure, and gaining a free kick for hands, Creilly sent nicely in, but Thompson missed in making a good endeavour to score. United played well, and from a good centre by Reay, Wallace just failed to score. Reay also had a shot but missed. The home team rushed and gained a corner and, from a shot by Graham, Whittaker saved under difficulties. The United continued to press, but the Bolton defence remained quite resolute.

After a visit to the home goal, the United forwards, led by Thompson, worked their way down, and Wallace sent in a clever shot, which the visitors' custodian saved, play being then rapidly transferred to the other end. Hands against Reay spoiled the home team of a good chance, and the ball was quickly taken back into Whitton's hands, the home custodian clearing in wonderful fashion.

The game was fast, and Newcastle won a corner, but it was of no use to them. They, however, kept up the pressure, and some beautiful play was shown; and from a fine overhead kick by Collins, Reay equalised amidst great enthusiasm. Bolton, after the kick-off, tried their utmost, but their endeavours availed them nothing, for Wallace cleverly ran back, and dodging the backs, gave to Reay, who headed the second goal in beautiful style.

The home defenders were then given some hard work to do, but Jeffrey and Creilly worked in marvellous style. The home forwards ran down, and Wallace passed to Sorley, who headed finely, but just over the bar. Play was confined to midfield for the remainder of the half, and when the whistle went the score was: Newcastle, two goals, Bolton, one goal.

On restarting Bolton had the best of the opening play, but they could not break through Miller and Whitton, although they made several excellent attempts. The visitors returned, and Jeffrey saved in a clever manner, a free kick for hands further relieving the pressure. United then showed the way, and pressed severely, and from a cross by Collins, Sorley just missed scoring. Bolton got a corner, and the ball was nicely placed into the goal, Miller saved in grand style, and play was transferred well into the Wanderers' ground. The forwards worked in grand fashion, and Sorley and Reay took the ball to the goal and Thompson rushed the leather through, scoring a third point for the home team.

Directly after the kick-off, Thompson, Wallace and Sorley returned, the last named missing with a good shot. Jeffrey gave a corner, in dispossessing the Bolton forwards, but the concession was useless. The visitor's goal became again endangered, but the ball, after some pressure had been put on, was sent to midfield. Whittaker frustrated a shot from Thompson, and then Graham sent high over the bar. Wallace next struck the left post with a shot, and Reay had similar luck directly afterward. Both goals were endangered in turn, and Whitton had to give a corner to save an attack. He saved from the kick-in and Thompson, running up, was fouled by one of the Wanderers, but the free kick gave the home no benefit. They, however, got a corner. A foul in favour of the home team was the result, but it availed them nothing. Darkness was now setting in, to distinguish the players was, difficult. Just before the finish Whitton had to save a shot from Willocks, and time was called with the score:

Newcastle United....................3 goals.
Bolton Wanderers....................1 goal.

Game by Game ~ January 1893

It was noted that the Bolton team, after the match, dined at Mr Liddle's, Clock Restaurant, Clayton Street, at which place they stayed during their visit.

NORTHERN LEAGUE

Darlington vs. Stockton: Played before a fair company, considering the inclemency of the weather, the ground being covered in deep snow. About four minutes from the start, Darlington having got down on the left, Fleming passed over to the right and McPherson scored. Even play followed, neither side showing any superiority over the other. After about ten minutes of such play the visitors got away with Atkin and Townley racing up the right wing and when near to goal Townley took the shot and put the ball past Macdonald and the equaliser was registered. Stockton pressed and from a scrimmage in front of the Darlington goal McClung managed to head the ball home putting the visitors in front. When half-time arrived nothing further had been scored.

On resuming the homesters held a temporary advantage but soon Stockton pressed and kept the ball in the Darlington area for a period before it was eventually cleared. Darlington then had a run to the other end but were soon back defending.

This pattern of play continued until well on, and towards the end Hutchinson and McPherson took up the centre and a pass to the right for McCrimmond saw him send in a daisy-cutter which once again equalised the score. Soon after this, with time running out fast, Fleming and Reay charged up the field and the latter managed to shoot through. A very exciting end to what had been a very good game under the circumstances.

Darlington .... 3 goals.

Stockton .... 2 goals.

Darlington: *Goal*, McDonald; *backs*, Norris and McLaine; *half-backs*, McManus, Waites and Campbell; *forwards*, McPherson, McCrimmond, Hutchinson, Keay and Fleming.

Stockton: *Goal*, Barker; *backs*, Ramsey and Lindsay; *half-backs*, Shaw, Graham and Hutton; *forwards*, Aitken, Townley, Thompson, McClung and Jones.

Referee: Mr White (Newcastle).

Newcastle Daily Chronicle (07/01/1892) p7f.
Newcastle Daily Chronicle (09/01/1893) pp6f-7a.
Bolton Evening News (09/01/1893) p2d.
Manchester Courier (09/01/1893) p3g.

THE NORTHERN LEAGUE
RESULTS TO SATURDAY, JANUARY 07 [INCLUSIVE]

Pos	Team	Pld	W	D	L	Goals F	Goals A	Avg.	Pts
1	Middlesbrough Ironopolis	9	8	1	0	18	5	3.6000	17
2	Newcastle United	8	5	0	3	29	14	2.0714	10
3	Sheffield United	6	2	1	3	11	9	1.2222	5
4	Stockton	8	2	1	5	19	23	0.8261	5
5	Middlesbrough	6	2	0	4	8	11	0.7273	4
6	Darlington	7	1	1	5	6	29	0.2069	3

Game 25: Saturday, January 14, 1893 — Newcastle United vs. Sheffield United

Competition: Northern League   Venue: St James's Park   Gate: 2,500

Newcastle United   1 - 1   Sheffield United

Scorer(s): OG [Cain] (68 mins)

Goal, Dave Whitton; *backs*, Harry Jeffrey and James Miller; *half-backs*, Bobby Creilly, Willie Graham and Joe McKane; *forwards*, Harry Reay, Tom Crate, Jock Sorley, James Collins, Joe Wallace

Referee: Robert Campbell (Sunderland)

Scorer(s): OG [Miller] (70 mins)

Goal, Charles Howlett; *backs*, Harry Lilley and Bob Cain; *half-backs*, Ernest Needham, Rab Howell and Michael Whitham; *forwards*, Jack Drummond, Joe Brady, Harry Hammond, Fred Davies, Arthur Watson

Kick-Off: 2:30 PM

This was the return league fixture between these teams, the first at Brammall Lane had proved to be an utter disaster for Newcastle, being soundly defeated by five goals to none. However, they did have a drawn encounter, *of two goals each*, at the beginning of November in a friendly fixture. Perhaps that had a bearing on the attendance, with only a modest 2,500 braving the cold weather. Dependent upon which report one reads the surface conditions were described, according to some, "*rather on the hard side*" whilst to others it "*was like a sheet of ice*"!

Winning the toss Newcastle elected to play 'down the hill' and with a mild wind in their favour. At once Newcastle attacked, and getting right up the pitch, they gave Howlett a shot to save which he fisted out, but it must be said with some difficulty. He had a much easier time of it a few moments later with a rather slow shot from Sorley. Collins then sent in 'a hot one', which had the beating of Howlett but also of the post as it went very narrowly bye and missed the target. 'Hands' was given against Reay when he was in a promising position. Sheffield then broke away, and Whitton was called upon to make a save, which he did with difficulty. A corner was then won by Sheffield but from which nought arose.

Snow now began to fall quite heavily in the faces of the Sheffielders. 'Hands' was then given against Sheffield whilst they were well forward and taking the free-kick Jeffrey sent the ball well down towards the other end. The well marshalled defence of Sheffield took possession and play was once again pressed in the Newcastle top-third, but the pressure was relieved. Turning defence into attack Newcastle became the more prominent resulting in Wallace being given an opportunity but his effort went over the bar. Howlett then made two glorious saves giving a corner off the last. The ball was well delivered, and Wallace had another opportunity and this time sent it narrowly outside the posts. Sheffield were being severely penned in and another corner was won by Newcastle, but the ball went over the bar.

A free kick for foul off Cain neatly let the Newcastle men in again and Sheffield were lucky to escape the danger. Miller and Jeffrey were next called upon and under great stress acquitted themselves admirably. Sorley and Wallace were now to the front with smart dodging tactics, the Sheffield goal being endangered numerous times without succumbing. 'Hands' against Graham relieved the pressure, only, however, for it to be at once resumed, but, try as they might, Newcastle couldn't get the ball through.

Play was too rough to make the game a pleasant one and the referee halted the game and called the players together, cautioning them on the roughness of their play, and other transgressions.

On resuming, Newcastle took up the pressure, Sheffield rarely crossing the centre line it seemed. Their backs and half-backs were having to play a grand defensive game, and it was only due to them that a big score for Newcastle was not piled on. A sudden break away by Watson and Davies gave Sheffield an opening, but Hammond's final shot went wide of the mark. The respite for Sheffield was temporary as Newcastle went up the other end and a corner was conceded. From it the ball was very well placed by Wallace, but no further advantage was gained. Attacking again Reay was very unlucky in seeing his fine effort strike the crossbar. Then there was a brief sally to the other end which proved fruitless, Watson making a good shot, but Miller kicked out.

The home forwards took possession once again and made a splendid run up but Howlett cleared cleverly, and then Reay just missed with a fine shot upon returning. The goal-kick saw the ball launched high up the field where Hammond gained possession but he was easily dispossessed by Jeffrey who dribbled well up, and with some smart play being shown in front of the Sheffield goal they were thankful to see Reay's final effort going past. The snow had stopped but the players were having great difficulty in keeping on their feet, and Drummond ran the ball over the line, when the Sheffield forwards were becoming dangerous. Watson soon had another shot at the home goal and he just missed with a good shot, and directly after Miller made an excellent intervention to save another shot by the same player. The visitors then had a corner and failed to make any advantage. A rush was made to the other end, but it proved to be as fruitless. Collins was barged off the ball as he tried to progress and 'hands' against the visitors presented Newcastle with a free-kick resulting in a corner which saw McKane shooting outside the posts. A very lively scrimmage in the Sheffield goalmouth saw them defending well and ultimately Reay headed over. Sheffield were once again having great difficulty in getting out. When they eventually did their break-away saw Whitton making an easy save.

Once again play became rough, and once again the referee was forced into lecturing both teams on their rather ungentlemanly conduct.

On restarting play Newcastle continued to

press and kept the ball near the Sheffield goal but their defence was proving to be very safe. Graham had an opportunity, but Lilley saved nicely. On the odd occasions when the Sheffielders did get up the field they were always pulled up by the local backs. The referee was called upon to caution a Sheffield player for rough play and when the break arrived there had been no score.

Following the interval Sheffield had both the wind and the hill in their favour but seemed unable to take advantage as it was Newcastle who ran up and forced Lilley into making a save. Still pressing 'hands' was given against Newcastle when they were close in. The ball was sent well down then 'hands' was given against the Blades from which the ball was sent behind. Sheffield then mounted an attack which ended in them running the ball out. From a good run up Sorley crossed to Reay who again had hard lines as his shot struck the bar again. At the other end Drummond had a shot but hit it badly and it was easily got away. Jeffrey then had to concede a corner when saving what looked like a certain goal but luckily nothing came from it. Sheffield shot well in, but Miller made a marvellous intervention and a race up the other end saw Reay shooting wide. A foul against Sheffield afforded Newcastle another free-kick and from this set-piece situation they almost brought about the opening goal but were thwarted by the Sheffield defence at the last moment.

The snow now resumed, falling in the faces of the Newcastle lads, making play very difficult for them. A corner was won by Sheffield which amounted to nothing. Newcastle then got well up and Howlett made another good save. The snow then became a virtual hurricane, like a white blanket being thrown into the homesters faces. If things had been difficult for them before, they were almost impossible now. Struggling against this they bravely forced their way up, but their efforts were wasted as the ball went bye. This however led to the most bizarre of opening goals and a most welcome break for the embattled Newcastle lads.

Sheffield were awarded a goal-kick and upon taking it Howlett smashed it against one of his own defenders' heads and it rebounded past him into his own goal! If that was bizarre then the equaliser was just as strange, and it occurred within two minutes. A ball was sent across the Newcastle goal and in attempting to make a save Miller made the perfect header – *for Sheffield* – as he sent it sailing beyond his own goalkeeper and into the goal! After this the game eased up somewhat though both sides still tried for the winner but both defences were too strong. Thompson took a hard knock just before the finish and upon his recovery the final whistle went calling to an end a bruising affair which saw a goal for either side, but neither scoring for themselves.

Newcastle United .... 1 goal.

Sheffield United .... 1 goal.

It was universally agreed there was great folly in the way play was conducted. Under the prevailing conditions it was amazing no one was injured. The number of fouls and infringements committed was immeasurable and the 'serious' foul count was so high as to cause the referee, Mr Campbell, *who seems to have taken up residence at St James's Park such is the frequency of his visits*, to have words with individual players on numerous accounts and having to call the captains together.

Newcastle Daily Chronicle (16/01/1893) p6e.
Newcastle Daily Journal (16/01/1893) p7d.
North-Eastern Daily Gazette (16/01/1893) p4f.
Northern Echo (16/01/1893) p4e.
Sheffield and Rotherham Independent (16/01/1893) p7d.
Sheffield Daily Telegraph (16/01/1893) p7d.

	THE NORTHERN LEAGUE								
	Results To Saturday, January 14 [Inclusive]								
							Goals		
Pos	Team	Pld	W	D	L	F	A	Avg.	Pts
1	Middlesbrough Ironopolis	9	8	1	0	18	5	3.6000	17
2	**Newcastle United**	9	5	1	3	30	15	2.0000	11
3	Sheffield United	7	2	2	3	12	10	1.2000	6
5	Stockton	8	2	1	5	19	23	0.8261	5
4	Middlesbrough	6	2	0	4	8	11	0.7273	4
6	Darlington	7	1	1	5	6	29	0.2069	3

Game 26: Saturday, January 21, 1893　　　　　　　　Newcastle United vs. Middlesbrough

Competition: FA Cup, Round 1　　　Venue: St James's Park　　　　　　　Gate: 4,000

| | Newcastle United | 2 - 3 | Middlesbrough | |

Scorer(s): Thompson (13 mins); Reay (15 mins)

Goal, Dave Whitton; *backs*, Harry Jeffrey and James Miller; *half-backs*, Bobby Creilly, Willie Graham and Joe McKane; *forwards*, Harry Reay, James Collins, Willie Thompson, Jock Sorley, Joe Wallace

Referee: Sam Ormerod (Accrington)

Scorer(s): Blyth (43 mins); McKnight (50 mins); Lewis (sh)

Goal, J.W. Fall; *backs*, T. Bach and J. McManus; *half-backs*, Bob Crone, J. Stott and J. Taggart; *forwards*, W. McCabe, R. Blyth, J. McKnight, Ben Lewis, D. Black

Kick-Off: 2:30 PM

The North-Eastern Daily Gazette had carried the following notice on Thursday, December 22:

> *"The Middlesbrough Club have offered Newcastle United £20 in addition to the regulation 'half gate' to play their English Cup tie on the Linthorpe-road Ground instead of at Newcastle."* [p3e]

However, despite the best attempts of Middlesbrough the venue was that as was drawn, namely St James's Park.

This was already the fourth meeting of the season between these sides, with Newcastle winning all three previous games with an 'aggregate' score of six goals to two goals, so they went into this match with confidence. However, it must not be forgotten that Middlesbrough had of late been putting in some much-improved performances and were showing exceedingly good form.

The weather was dull, and the recent thaw, although making the ground a bit softer had also made it very slippery, but it was deemed to be playable.

The Teesiders were the first to enter the pitch and a big sturdy lot they seemed. Newcastle were not long in following and after a good week's training looked in good condition, but man-for-man they were slighter than their opposite number.

Middlesbrough won the toss and elected to play 'down the hill' therefore Thompson the Newcastle captain kicked off for the homesters.

Early play went in Newcastle's favour and they often looked dangerous, on occasions, but the reality was that the best of the chances that were created fell to Middlesbrough. They forced two successive corners with their attacking play. Nothing came from the first one, but the second was only got away with the greatest of difficulty by Whitton. This gave the initiative very much to Middlesbrough and it was not long after when Whitton was again called upon to make a capital, if somewhat fortuitous, save, this time with his feet, to deny Stott who had put in a such a beautiful shot. Middlesbrough then literally besieged the Newcastle goal. Shot after shot was sent in, but nothing came from any of them. Black and Lewis were proving to be particularly effective down the left side and fed the ball in well.

Middlesbrough didn't have it all their own way though, and from a long return upfield Sorley got past Bach and forced a corner for Newcastle, but again nothing came from it. Soon back on the attack Newcastle had a great chance with a shot from Collins that only just went wide. Then it was Middlesbrough's turn to attack with McKnight who got the ball in the centre and raced down the field, but Miller was able to intercept cleverly and clear the danger. Sorley then took the initiative for Newcastle when he raced down the left and passed the ball through to Reay. His shot was parried by Fall but quite feebly and Thompson got his head to the ball to open the scoring.

Only a minute later there was a most bizarre of goals; Fall caught a shot from Graham very easily, but then he just stood with the ball under his arm. Reay rushed up and crashed both him and the ball over the line and into the goal. As it was a fair charge the goal stood, and Newcastle found themselves looking quite comfortable at two goals to nil.

There was a natural, and expected, reaction to this goal from the Teesiders and they pressed strongly. Black, Lewis and McKnight all went close with well worked efforts. They were then almost given a gift of a goal as a miskick by Jeffery almost saw him scoring an own goal. Keeping up

~ 84 ~

the pressure, McCabe went down the right, passed to McKnight, his centre was met by Black who shot in a real daisy-cutter that looked all the way a goal but Whitton somehow pulled off a great save, pushing it behind for a corner. The pressure from Middlesbrough was now almost relentless and the defence of Newcastle had to be strong.

In all honesty, given the pattern of play, it looked like it was only a matter of time before there was a Middlesbrough goal and it came only two minutes before half-time. McKnight had missed with an effort but following the Newcastle goal-kick he received possession and fed the ball to Blyth in midfield. Dribbling up a couple of yards he sent in a high shot that had Whitton well beaten and passed just under the crossbar, indeed grazing it on its way through. A bad time to concede for Newcastle, but a great time to score for Middlesbrough.

After the interval things were immediately looking worrying for the homesters. Even with having the advantage of now playing downhill they couldn't get started and it was Middlesbrough, picking up from where they left off in the first half, who were first on the attack. Stott and McKnight both had rather futile shots at goal before McCabe took the ball upfield and passed to Lewis, he in turn passed to McKnight who got the equaliser with a rather magnificent shot, this after only five minutes of the restart.

Middlesbrough attacked again and forced a corner that was placed nicely in by McCabe and Whitton had a good deal of trouble in clearing the resulting scrimmage. Newcastle then had a great chance themselves when Reay give the ball to Thompson who made a good run through the centre, he went passed Bach very easily, and seemed certain to score, but Fall ran out in the nick of time and cleared the ball. Middlesbrough were then straight back on the attack, forcing a corner which was splendidly centred by McCabe, and Lewis headed the ball in for their third goal.

In taking the lead, Middlesbrough took almost complete control for quite a period of time. Their forwards were much more dominant, and Newcastle could do nothing against McKnight and Lewis. After a bit of fine short passing Middlesbrough gained another corner, taken by Lewis, but nothing came from it. In an all-out effort to force an equaliser Newcastle had a good chance that saw Crone, McKnight, and McManus all missing the ball, but between themselves Reay and Collins made a real mess of the opportunity this presented. The last five minutes of the game saw Newcastle camped in the Middlesbrough half but were unable to break down their defence.

Newcastle United ....**2 goals.**
Middlesbrough ....**3 goals.**

NB: You may find many references to Middlesbrough's first goal being scored by McKnight. The consensus however seems to point to McKnight having an opportunity but missing with his effort and upon the ball returning into play it was sent, by McKnight, to Blyth who scored.

Newcastle Daily Chronicle (23/01/1893) p6e.
Newcastle Daily Journal (23/01/1893) p7e.
Northern Echo (23/01/1893) p4d.

Game 27: Saturday, January 28, 1893   **Stockton vs. Newcastle United**

Competition: Friendly   Venue: Victoria Ground   Gate: 2,000

Stockton   3 - 2   Newcastle United

Scorer(s): Jones (fh); Townley (sh, sh)

Goal, Charlie Ramsay; *backs,* Bob Shaw and William Lindsay; *half-backs,* Willie Willocks, James Graham and Cochrane; *forwards,* D.C. Atkin, Billy Townley, Gavin Thompson, Robert McClung, Jack Jones

Referee: Richard Peel (Middlesbrough)

Scorer(s): Sorley (sh, sh)

Goal, Dave Whitton; *backs,* Harry Jeffrey and James Miller; *half-backs,* James Collins, Willie Graham and Joe McKane; *forwards,* Harry Reay, Tom Crate, Willie Thompson, Jock Sorley, Joe Wallace

Kick-Off: 2:45 PM

The combination of the Newcastle team had to be somewhat rearranged for today's match. Creilly was unable to play and Collins was put in his place, normally an inside-right but he had played at half-back too. This also saw the welcome return of

Crate who donned the jersey for the first time in five weeks, he occupied Collins's berth.

Stockton won the toss and Newcastle kicked off into the face of a strong wind. The homesters swiftly ran the ball down and an opening shot from their left wing went bye. It was not long before they had another attempt, but this was repelled and Newcastle got the ball up into the Stockton end but after some smart play Atkin and Townley carried the ball back into the Newcastle half and Miller made a very timely intervention to halt their progress. Thompson, the home centre-forward had a glorious opportunity but, just as he was about to shoot, he fell on the ball and the opportunity was gone. Immediately after this Townley sent in a smart shot from distance and Whitton had to be on top form in making a save and thus preventing an opening goal, but it was obvious to all that such a goal was on its way.

Getting possession Jones sent in a sharp shot which went over the head of Whitton and into the back of the goal and that much anticipated opener had indeed arrived.

Again, Stockton returned vigorously to the attack and Jones was within an ace of registering his, and the homesters, second point but Whitton managed to make the save. Atkin then sent in a low shot which Whitton saved and threw out, almost falling over as he did so. This constant bombardment was kept up by the home team and there were repeated attempts at increasing the scoreline but each failed either due to the stoutness of the defence or by indifferent shooting. In a rare breakout Newcastle had a fruitless visit to the home citadel and this was immediately followed up by another Stockton attack. Atkin sent in a good shot which Whitton only just got away.

Jeffrey and Miller were called upon several times to relieve attacks by Stockton and were mostly successful in doing so. Townley sent in a long which Whitton fisted out. Another of those rare Newcastle breaks saw a tame effort on the Stockton goal which Ramsay repulsed with the greatest of ease and there was no one up to support the shot. The ball was back where it had been for the majority of the half, in the Newcastle quarters, when the interval was announced.

Immediately on the restart, with the strong wind now in their favour, Newcastle went seeking for the equaliser and twice forced Ramsay into making saves. Atkin got the leather away but back it came, and Jeffrey was desperately unlucky to see his effort go inches past the post. Play continued in a fast manner, Atkin and Townley taking the ball nicely up but when presented with an opportunity Thompson sent it past.

A grand rush down by the Newcastle forward quintet resulted in Sorley managing to put the leather through and register the equaliser whilst Ramsay was given no chance to negotiate the shot.

Stockton at once retaliated and Townley cleverly headed through thus restoring their lead. Pressing again Townley hit a splendid shot through and extended Stockton's lead, making it look comfortable for them indeed. With a two-goal cushion and having been in control for most of the match this was now surely in their pocket. Knowing this perhaps they eased off a little too much and Newcastle managed to get another goal back through Sorley as the result of a swift run down the field.

Whilst this goal added a little spice to the final few minutes of the game it was all too little and too late. Within minutes time was called.

Stockton...................................3 goals.

Newcastle United....................2 goals.

NORTHERN LEAGUE

Middlesbrough Ironopolis vs. Darlington: Ironopolis brought the curtain down on their league season knowing full well that whatever happened in the games still to be played they were champions once again, reigning champions and champions elect, well done to them. They did not let any of this '*go to their heads*' as they pressed to finish the season in front of their own fans with a flourish, and a victory of four goals to one can surely be counted as such a flourish. Whilst the game started fast and even it took Ironopolis only five minutes to open their account through Seymour. Darlington fought back hard and gained a creditable equaliser from Hutchinson after a bit of a scrimmage. Henderson then had to stop a hard shot from McArthur and was indeed called upon on various occasions, on each showing grand style. Twice the 'Nops through transgressions, namely 'hands', gave away the advantage but Fleming shot over the bar on the latter. Seymour brought another tremendous save from Henderson then Darlington wasted three corners.

In the second half Ironopolis began to assert themselves with Hill putting just over the bar. A free-kick in a dangerous place for Darlington saw the same result as McLaine taking the kick sent it over the bar. At length McReddie and Seymour raced away, and the latter restored the homesters lead with a beauty of a shot that gave Henderson no chance. The 'Washers' maintained their pressure and Darlington put up a stout defence but then a free-kick was conceded by them and Langley banged it through, the ball touching several players on its journey. Just moments later McNair dribbled his was through and gave to Seymour who brought about his hat-trick and sealed a great victory for the champions.

Middlesbrough Ironopolis.....4 goals.

Darlington..............................1 goal.

Middlesbrough Ironopolis: *Goal,* Watts; *backs,* Oliver and Langley; *half-backs,* McNair, Chatt and Nicholson; *forwards,* Hill, Hughes, McArthur, McReddie and Seymour.

Darlington: *Goal,* Henderson; *backs,* McDonald and Norris; *half-backs,* McManus, Waites and McLaine; *forwards,* McPherson, McCrimmond, Keay, Hutchinson and Fleming.

Newcastle Daily Chronicle (30/01/1893) p6e.
Northern Echo (30/01/1893) p4d.
Newcastle Daily Journal (30/01/1893) p7d.
Newcastle Daily Journal (31/01/1893) p7c.

	THE NORTHERN LEAGUE RESULTS TO SATURDAY, JANUARY 28 [INCLUSIVE]								
						Goals			
Pos	Team	Pld	W	D	L	F	A	Avg.	Pts
1	Middlesbrough Ironopolis	10	9	1	0	22	6	3.6667	19
2	Newcastle United	9	5	1	3	30	15	2.0000	11
3	Sheffield United	7	2	2	3	12	10	1.2000	6
4	Stockton	8	2	1	5	19	23	0.8261	5
5	Middlesbrough	6	2	0	4	8	11	0.7273	4
6	Darlington	8	1	1	6	7	33	0.2121	3

Monday, January 30, 1893

No game for Newcastle United today but there was a game in the Northern League between Sheffield United and Stockton at Bramall Lane. In dull but fair weather there were about 3,00 spectators gathered to witness another surprising result for the Sheffielders. Most had thought that they would be too strong for the Stocktonians, especially at home, but things did not go as planned. They conceded two goals in the first half and whilst they had the better of play in the second half and pulled a goal back Stockton had it within them to score again.

Sheffield United......................1 goal.

Stockton.................................3 goals.

Sheffield United: *Goal,* Howlett; *backs,* Whittam and Lilley; *half-backs,* Howell, Hendry and Cain; *forwards,* Drummond, Needham, Wigmore, Gambles, and McCabe.

Stockton: *Goal,* Ramsay; *backs,* Shaw and McDermid; *half-backs,* Willocks, Graham and Lindsay; *forwards,* Strachan, Townley, Thompson, McClung and Jones.

Referee: Mr Fitzroy Norris (Bolton).

Newcastle Daily Chronicle (16/01/1893) p6e.
Sheffield and Rotherham Independent (31/01/1893) p8b.

	THE NORTHERN LEAGUE RESULTS TO SATURDAY, JANUARY 30 [INCLUSIVE]								
						Goals			
Pos	Team	Pld	W	D	L	F	A	Avg.	Pts
1	Middlesbrough Ironopolis	10	9	1	0	22	6	3.6667	19
2	Newcastle United	9	5	1	3	30	15	2.0000	11
3	Stockton	9	3	1	5	20	24	0.8333	7
4	Sheffield United	8	2	2	4	13	13	1.0000	6
5	Middlesbrough	6	2	0	4	8	11	0.7273	4
6	Darlington	8	1	1	6	7	33	0.2121	3

As to the "A's"...

THE NORTHERN ALLIANCE ~ NEWCASTLE UNITED 'A' RESULTS JANUARY 1893				
Date	Home	Score	Away	
January 2, 1893.	Rendel	7 - 0	Newcastle United A	Northern Alliance
January 14, 1893.	Shankhouse	5 - 1	Newcastle United A	Friendly
January 28, 1893.	Newcastle United A	5 - 0	Gateshead NER	Northern Alliance

In other news...

Early signs of "hooliganism"?

Yesterday, a large number of boys were allowed to stand in front of the press box at St James's Park while the game between Newcastle United and Everton was in progress; and by getting on the forms, shouting and swearing, rendered it rather difficult for the journalists present, three of whom travelled from Liverpool to report the game, to attend properly to their work. Might I suggest that a policeman be stationed at the gate against the box before today's game begins, with instruction to allow no one inside the fencing; while the forms placed there yesterday should be removed, as they look very inviting to the spectators near them.

Newcastle Daily Journal, 03/01/1893, [p7b].

Wolves in "Paradise"!

It was reported that there was "a disorderly scene" at the Paradise Ground in Middlesbrough where the Ironopolis were 'entertaining' Wolverhampton Wanderers. During the first half Wolves complained that a 'Nops goal was 'offside'. They complained to such an extent that they refused to play the game anymore and simply stopped. After a while, and an explanation that their goalkeeper had clearly touched the ball not once but twice, and therefore the offside decision was correct, they resumed play. Most of the assembled 2,000 spectators were naturally very angry at this stoppage. Worse was to come in the second half when Wolves twice more stopped playing, this time complaining *"that none of their claims for fouls were listened to, whilst the 'Nops got all they asked for, and this being followed in one case by blows, quite a scene ensued, and measures had to be taken by the committee to see that Wolves were not interfered with by the more irate spectators."* The final score by the way was 3-1 to Ironopolis.

Newcastle Daily Journal, 04/01/1893, [p7e].

Goodbye Old Friend...

A PRESENTATION

On Thursday evening Mr. Jas. E. Peel was presented with a purse of gold and an illuminated album, with a ring for Mrs. Peel, in recognition of his services to the East End Club. I say east End advisedly, for it is under that name that Mr. Peel will always think of our local club. A genial companion, an energetic man when service was required of him, and a great enthusiast in the cause of the club named. Mr. Peel had earned for himself the goodwill of a large number of followers of athletic sports. In going to London, he will be missed alike by "The Old Boys," cricketers and footballers, and with his wife and family will take away the good wishes of all.

TOWN MOOR *Athletic News, 09/01/1893, [p6a].*

Another goodbye, to another old friend...

THE SECRETARY OF NEWCASTLE UNITED, - Those of our readers who are interested in the Association football on Tyneside will be sorry to hear that Mr W. H. Golding retires from his position of secretary to the Newcastle United Club to-day. This young gentleman, who is an enthusiast in the game, has laboured long and successfully on behalf of the club, and his valuable services will be seriously missed by the committee.

Newcastle Daily Journal, 30/01/1893, [p7c].

Or is it?

The Middlesbrough Conspiracy Saga Begins...

RUCTIONS

The defeat of Newcastle United by Middlesbrough a week ago has done a lot of harm to the game in the Tyneside city. For myself, I must say I think the result was not in accordance with form. From private information I have been favoured with I feel quite certain that something has taken place which I cannot state specifically. That there is something distinctly wrong about the affair one does not need to inquire after the resignation of Mr. Golding, the secretary, and that (probably) of Mr. Turnbull, chairman. This is quite enough to show that the executive have inquired into the whole affair, and that there is something wrong about the business. Emphasis is given to this impression when one knows that the committee are dispensing with the services of certain players.

TOWN MOOR *Athletic News, 30/01/1893, [p7e].*

February 1893

Games Played in February 1893

V	Date	F	A	R	Opposition	Competition
H	04/02/1893	3	1	W	Stockton	Friendly
A	11/02/1893	0	4	L	Middlesbrough	Northern League
H	18/02/1893	3	2	W	Notts County	Friendly
H	25/02/1893	1	6	L	Sunderland	Friendly

Appearances & Goals ~ February 1893

Name	Total Apps	Total Goals	League Apps	League Goals	Friendly Apps	Friendly Goals
Collins, James	4		1		3	
Crate, Thomas "Tom"	4	1	1		3	1
Creilly, Robert "Bobby"	4		1		3	
Graham, William "Willie"	4		1		3	
Jeffrey, Harry	3		1		2	
McKane, Joseph "Joe"	1		0		1	
Miller, James	4		1		3	
Reay, Harry	4	1	1		3	1
Rodgers, Thomas "Tom"	1		0		1	
Sorley, John "Jock"	3	2	0		3	2
Thompson, Willie	4	1	1		3	1
Wallace, Joseph "Joe"	3	1	1		2	1
Whitton, David "Dave"	4		1		3	

Season to Date (03/09/1892 - 25/02/1893 inclusive)

Name	Total Apps	Total Goals	League Apps	League Goals	FA Cup Apps	FA Cup Goals	Friendly Apps	Friendly Goals
Barker, John	1		1				0	
Collins, James	29	7	10	1	1		18	6
Coupar, William	1		0				1	
Crate, Thomas "Tom"	24	6	10	2			14	4
Creilly, Robert "Bobby"	29	3	9	1	1		19	2
Dixon, Henry	2	1	0				2	1
Graham, William "Willie"	31	2	10	2	1		20	
Jeffrey, Harry	26		7		1		18	
Kirkland, J.	1						1	
McIntosh, James	2	2	0				2	2
McKane, Joseph "Joe"	26	1	7		1		18	1
Miller, James	29		10		1		18	
Reay, Harry	26	14	9	3	1	1	16	10
Rodgers, Thomas "Tom"	1		0				1	
Sorley, John "Jock"	26	20	8	7	1		17	13
Thompson, Willie	24	17	7	6	1	1	16	10
Wallace, Joseph "Joe"	25	8	8	6	1		16	2
Watson, Peter	6	3	3				3	
Whitton, David "Dave"	31		10		1		20	

Game 28: Saturday, February 4, 1893 — Newcastle United vs. Stockton

Competition: Friendly   Venue: St James's Park

Newcastle United   3 - 1   Stockton

Scorer(s): Reay (fh); tbc (fh); Crate (sh)

Goal, Dave Whitton; *backs*, Harry Jeffrey and James Miller; *half-backs*, Bobby Creilly, Willie Graham and Joe McKane; *forwards*, Harry Reay, Tom Crate, Willie Thompson, James Collins, Jock Sorley

Referee: Richard Peel (Middlesbrough)

Scorer(s): Jones (sh)

Goal, Charlie Ramsay; *backs*, Bob Shaw and William Lindsay; *half-backs*, Willie Willocks, James Graham and James Hutton; *forwards*, D.C. Atkin, Moody, Gavin Thompson, Robert McClung, Jack Jones

Kick-Off: 2:45 PM

A 'return' friendly was brought off between these two teams today, making it the fourth time this season that they were in opposition. Newcastle had won the two Northern League fixtures by five goals to one goal and five goals to two respectively but had lost their first friendly last weekend by three goals to two goals. So, whilst there were no league points to gained from this encounter there was certainly a bit of pride to play for.

Stockton won the toss and elected to play 'up the hill', but this put a strong wind at their backs. Thompson kicked off for Newcastle, but Stockton easily took possession and pressed upfield where they forced a corner off Jeffrey. Nothing came from the corner as Graham upon taking possession sent the ball down to Reay who put in an admirable effort which Ramsay had to be smart to save. Collins then sent in a shot at height which looked dangerous but once again Ramsay was equal to it and fisted away.

Newcastle kept up the pressure and on several occasions were very near the mark and on one occasion Sorley was within an ace of scoring with a fine overhead kick. Relief came to Stockton in the form of a free-kick which allowed them to push into the Newcastle quarters and Moody sent in a shot from distance which Whitton comfortably saved. Sorley and Collins took the ball down well with a fine dribble and there ensued an almighty scrimmage in the Stockton goal which saw several efforts blocked and Ramsay ultimately cleared. The Stockton right wing broke away and a corner was forced off McKane, but nought came of it as it was sent behind.

The Newcastle lads were having by far the best of the play and they fairly bombarded the Stockton citadel to no effect. Their reward looked a certainty, and duly arrived when after saving two shots from Sorley and Collins a fine header from Reay finally beat Ramsay. A second was not long in coming as barely five minutes had elapsed before a mass attack by the home quintet saw the backs, the goalkeeper and most importantly the ball being barged over the line. It seems no one knows for certain who got the final touch to claim the goal.

There was still no respite for the Stockton defence and Shaw and Lindsay defended like Trojans and when they were beaten Ramsay was almost inspired making some tremendous saves. Such was their performance that they prevented any further scoring, but they were mighty pleased to hear the half time whistle.

The resumption after the interval saw no change from the play at the end of the first half. Newcastle were once again the main aggressors and the Stockton defence and goalkeeper had to be on their sharpest of mettle. Ramsay made a tremendous save from Reay and then a rush up the other end saw McKane making a great saving intervention to prevent a good shot from McClung troubling Whitton. Any relief this provided for Stockton was short-lived as in no time there was great pressure put upon their defence once more and a corner was conceded. Though well placed and causing all sorts of trouble the ball was finally got away.

Jeffrey sent in a great shot from distance which Ramsay did well to fist away but the homesters immediately brought it back and with a great rush flustering the defence Reay had the opportunity to shoot which he took gladly and sent the ball through in grand style.

From the restart Stockton worked their way down but were dispossessed by McKane in good fashion. The visitors however came back and forced a corner which availed them nothing. Before they knew it, Ramsay was called back into the thick of the action. He made one great save as the ball broke out of a scrimmage in front of his goal. From this the ball was launched down the Stockton left wing and with most of the Newcastle lads still up for the last attack Jones was able to score quite easily.

Irked by this setback Newcastle again took play into the Stockton quarters and Thompson put the ball through but the point was disallowed for 'hands' against him prior to the shot. Using the free-kick Stockton cleared their lines well and Jeffrey spoiled a run from their forwards. Stockton pressed again and a free-kick for 'hands' saw them in a very dangerous position, but Collins secured the ball and ran it out of danger. Newcastle made another great push and it was only by sheer good fortune that the Stockton citadel did not succumb once more, and they escaped with only a corner for punishment from which Newcastle could do nothing. The homesters then had a good opportunity when they were given a free-kick but the ball was sent over the bar. Newcastle then had hard lines with Ramsay saving splendidly. The homesters continuing to have the best of matters but coming up against a resolute defence sums up the remainder of the play and with nothing further scored Newcastle ran out easy winners and Stockton were to consider themselves lucky not to be on the wrong side of a large score indeed.

Newcastle United....................3 goals.

Stockton ....1 goal.

Newcastle Daily Chronicle (03/02/1893) p7d.
Newcastle Daily Chronicle (06/02/1893) p6d.
Northern Echo (06/02/1893) p4e.
Newcastle Daily Chronicle (07/02/1893) p7e.

Game 29: Saturday, February 11, 1893 — Middlesbrough vs. Newcastle United

Competition: Northern League   Venue: Linthorpe Road   Gate: 2,000

Middlesbrough   4 - 0   Newcastle United

Scorer(s): McKnight (sh); McCabe (sh, sh); Blyth (sh)

Goal, J.W. Fall; *backs*, T. Bach and Bob Crone; *half-backs*, J. McManus, J. Stott and J. Taggart; *forwards*, W. McCabe, R. Blyth, J. McKnight, Ben Lewis, D. Black

Referee: J.H. Strawson (Lincoln)

Scorer(s): none

Goal, Dave Whitton; *backs*, Harry Jeffrey and James Miller; *half-backs*, Bobby Creilly, Willie Graham and Harry Reay; *forwards*, Tom Crate, Willie Thompson, James Collins, Joe Wallace

Kick-Off: 3:45 PM

What an absolute disastrous end to the Northern League season for Newcastle! This result meant that it was possible for Middlesbrough to leapfrog Newcastle into second place in the league should they win their three remaining games, they could even do it with two wins and a draw should they "up their goal average. Yes, it was most definitely not a good end to Newcastle's league season.

In some mitigation however they did only have ten men on the pitch for the whole of the game, McKane having missed the train and Newcastle travelling with no reserve. There were various stories circulating that McKane made it to the Central Station in time to travel but got locked in the toilets! How true these are I guess we'll never know, but they do put a smile on the face of a bitter disappointment.

Making a start some forty-five minutes after the advertised time, due to Newcastle's late arrival, it was the visitors who won the toss and the homesters were forced to face a rather stiffish breeze and a dazzling sun. From the kick-off Middlesbrough made a strong run upfield ending when a shot by Black was sent well in but failed. Newcastle then pressed and winning a free-kick put the home goal in danger but a bye was the result. Play was then centred around the midfield where Bach and Crone distinguished themselves, putting in some clever work, but it was Newcastle who broke out of this and advanced down their right. A great shot by Crate was spoiled by an offside decision. 'Hands' in favour of Newcastle saw them get the ball well into the Middlesbrough goalmouth but McManus managed to clear. With the return Wallace was unlucky to see his effort go narrowly over the crossbar. Black and Lewis raced away and reaching the Newcastle quarters with a fine run they were met by Jeffrey who disposed them and got the ball away. Newcastle attacked heavily, forcing Fall to make a couple of decent saves, which he did so admirably. Next it was the Newcastle goal which came under pressure, but Miller was there to rescue the situation and relieve the danger. Shortly after Whitton had to make a save from Stott whilst at the other end Fall faced two or three well placed shots which he saved in marvellous style. A corner was then won by Newcastle, but unfortunately nothing was to become of it.

Lewis was next to have an opportunity and he sent in a beauty which saw Whitton having to be all there, which he was and dealt with it cleverly and Bach missed an opportunity when he sent the ball bye. The homesters kept up the pressure but found Jeffrey and Miller in fine form and anytime their defence was reached Whitton displayed excellent form too.

At length the Newcastle forward quintet got away and Fall was called upon again. A couple of free-kicks kept the home citadel besieged but ultimately nothing resulted. Each of the goals was then visited in turn and whilst Middlesbrough had marginally the better of things one could be forgiven for forgetting that they faced only ten men, such was the stout performance of the Novocastrians, and when half time arrived there had been no score.

Following the interval Middlesbrough at once took up the running and a ball sent in by Bach, who had swopped places with Crone, was cleared by Miller. For Newcastle Wallace did some good work and advanced down the left but whilst looking dangerous could do nothing other than send the ball bye.

A Newcastle free-kick saw Creilly send the ball well into the danger area and a scrimmage ensued but the defence managed to get the ball away. Play was becoming a little on the rough side and there were countless fouls being committed in all areas of the pitch. Following one particularly rough and nasty challenge Black was so badly winded that the referee called the game to a halt until such time as he was recovered. The referee also had occasion to talk to individual players about their conduct, regarding either the severity of their challenges or purely the sheer number of fouls an individual was committing. It was noted after the game that both sides were lucky to finish it with all eleven players such was the state of play during this particular period. McCabe had a decent chance but just as he was about to take his shot when he slipped, and the opportunity was gone. Then a Middlesbrough corner saw Crone take but put behind. A quick break by Newcastle saw them gain a corner of their own but they could not make any advantage out of it.

After being on the defensive for a while the homesters rushed away and there was a fierce struggle in the Newcastle area which saw them being given relief as the ball was sent bye. The ball was soon coming back at them and Stott saw an effort go over the crossbar. McCabe then sent in a hard shot which severely tested Whitton. There was little relief now for Newcastle, the exertions of playing a man short was beginning to tell and Middlesbrough were all out to press that numerical advantage. Stott handled whilst making an attempt on goal, but the respite given by the free-kick was short-lived with the homesters coming straight back on the attack.

Play dictated that it was an almost inevitability that Middlesbrough would score, and score they did but it took an absolutely magnificent shot by McKnight to finally beat Whitton. Middlesbrough then forced a couple of corners, each abortive, and then Black put in a fine centre for McCabe to head home the second goal for them. Almost immediately after a free-kick was awarded very close in to the Newcastle goal and in the ensuing struggle McCabe managed to score once more. Play then subsided for a while until another press from Middlesbrough saw Blyth score their fourth and final point.

They held the dominant position from then until the final whistle but could make no further score as the ten-men of Newcastle battled valiantly to the end.

Middlesbrough .... 4 goals.

Newcastle United .... None.

History would show that this would be Newcastle United's last ever game in the Northern League, well their "first team" anyway. The Newcastle United "A" side still appeared in the league for a number of seasons.

Athletic News (13/02/1893) p7f.
Newcastle Daily Chronicle (13/021893) p6f.
Northern Echo (13/02/1893) p4d.
Shields Daily Gazette (13/02/1893) p3a.

Game by Game ~ February 1893

THE NORTHERN LEAGUE
RESULTS TO SATURDAY, FEBRUARY 11 [INCLUSIVE]

Pos	Team	Pld	W	D	L	Goals F	Goals A	Avg.	Pts
1	Middlesbrough Ironopolis	10	9	1	0	22	6	3.6667	19
2	Newcastle United	10	5	1	4	30	19	1.5789	11
3	Stockton	9	3	1	5	20	24	0.8333	7
4	Middlesbrough	7	3	0	4	12	11	1.0909	6
5	Sheffield United	8	2	2	4	13	13	1.0000	6
6	Darlington	8	1	1	6	7	33	0.2121	3

Tuesday, February 14, 1893

No game for Newcastle, but the Northern League fixture between Sheffield United and Middlesbrough was of great interest to them. One of Middlesbrough's three games "in hand" and those extra six points would take them above Newcastle. Should the result be a draw then Middlesbrough could still overtake Newcastle, but it would obviously more difficult for them, placings could even come down to goal average.

Sheffield United vs. Middlesbrough: These clubs played their return Northern League match at Bramall Lane today before circa 5,000 spectators. A goodly number of these being boys from Sheffield elementary schools who were admitted free of charge on their Shrovetide holiday. Sheffield were hopeful of showing off their new centre, Hill, but a sudden illness prevented this and Gallacher was tried at centre. Wallace joined Drummond on the right. Whittam, being unwell, stood down, and Mellor played at the back.

United won the toss and elected to play from the Bramall Lane end giving them a brisk breeze behind them, with the additional advantage of a very bright sun shining in the faces of their opponents.

Middlesbrough kicked off but gaining possession it was Sheffield who first attacked with Drummond putting in a long, lightning shot from the right which caused Fall some trouble. Hammond sent over the bar then McCabe dashed away on the visitors' left, getting a free kick for 'hands' close in, and only a smart piece of goalkeeping from Howlett prevented them scoring. United then made a dash away to the other end, and Gallacher put in a sharp shot which Fall saved capitally, and then skilfully avoided a rush upon himself. Play was very fast considering the soft and heavy state of the ground. Middlesbrough played well against the wind, and there was at this time little to choose between the teams. Black made a good run for Middlesbrough and put in a grand shot which Howlett saved under the bar. Sheffield then began to press, and for some time were dangerously near their opponents' goal, where Gallacher, from a pass by Wallace, put an effort just over the bar. Wallace afterwards put in a capital shot which Fall only just saved, and Hammond, from the rebound, put the ball again over the bar. United were now having the better of the play, and attacked with spirit, but found the Middlesbrough defence solid. The visitors made a brief visit to the home quarters but were soon driven back. Watson raced away, Drummond received and gave Fall another good shot to stop. Then Middlesbrough had a spell of pressing, McCabe shooting just wide, and Blyth sent over. Mellor, with a miskick, nearly put through his own goal, Howlett just stopping it on the line. Just after Lewis put in a fast, low shot, which Howlett again saved cleverly. Sheffield then played up and pressed again, Hammond had a good chance, but missed the ball. Then from a centre by Drummond, Fall had to save, and failing to get the ball clear away Gallacher pounced on it and scored for the United, amidst cheers, this after half-an-hour's play.

Middlesbrough played up now, and Mellor had to clear in the nick of time, whilst just afterwards McKnight, with a grand shot, only just missed the mark. A good run by Drummond made Fall come out and kick away. Directly afterwards Hammond put in a capital shot but Fall kicked away. United were now pressing, and Wallace just missed the mark, Gallacher next giving Fall a good shot to stop. Sheffield tried hard to score again, while they had the wind, but Middlesbrough kept them out, and just before the interval dashed away, and with Black centring well, the United goal had a very narrow escape. A rush to the Middlesbrough end again nearly lowered the visitors' citadel, and then half-time arrived without further score.

At the change of ends Middlesbrough now had the benefit of the breeze and at once began to attack. A grand screw by Black from the corner saw Howlett coming out to fist away. With the custodian now out of his goal it looked certain to fall, but Cain cleared the return. Then the red and whites played up, and with Hammond running down, Fall had to rush out to stop him. Fall then stopped a long shot by Cain which was followed by a fast one from Drummond which only just went wide, and Fall stopped another from Howell. Middlesbrough then dashed away and provided with a good opportunity Black sent in a blazing shot that was only a few inches away from scoring. Another assault by the visitors met with more success, as after some tricky play Blyth, with a capital shot the equaliser eight minutes from the change of ends. United played up, and the game became fast and furious. From a foul for pushing against one of the Middlesbrough men there was a scrimmage under the bar, but Crone and Fall each warded off the danger in turn, just as the ball was going through. The homesters attacked again, and a good shot was sent in Mather, but as the whistle had previously sounded for an off-side Fall made no effort to stop it and the point was disallowed. Play was exciting, and mainly in favour of the Sheffielders, who tried hard for the lead. Two fouls for tripping by the Middlesbrough men endangered their goal, but their defence stood solid. McManus, Crone, and Stott working hard and successfully. At length the pressure was relieved, and some good passing by the visitors ended in Blyth with a good shot only just missing,

after which McKnight gave Howlett a long one to deal with. Play now changed from end to end and was very even. Howlett stopped a shot from McCabe and Fall a one from Hammond. Fall was just afterwards smartly rushed through with the ball in his hand but just escaped by giving a corner. Play was now very vigorous, and mostly in favour of Sheffield, who faced a very determined defence. As the end drew near, United made strenuous efforts to get the winning goal. A corner was of no avail, Crone clearing. Five minutes from the finish, however, Watson put in a magnificent strong shot from near the touch line, and the ball dropped just through the top corner of the goal and gave United the lead amidst loud applause. The Sheffielders thus won a hard-fought and interesting game.

Sheffield United......................2 goals.

Middlesbrough.........................1 goal.

Sheffield United: Goal, Howlett; *backs*, Mellor and Lilley; *half-backs*, Howell, Needham and Cain; *forwards*, Drummond, Wallace, Gallacher, Hammond, and Watson.

Middlesbrough: Goal, Fall; *backs*, McManus and Crone; *half-backs*, Taggart, Stott and Bach; *forwards*, Black, Lewis, McKnight, Blyth and McCabe

Referee: Mr J.H. Strawson (Lincoln).

So, that is it folks, the panic is over! Newcastle sitting in second place on eleven points have already finished their season and Middlesbrough with those three games in hand (*including this fixture*), a potential six points, were the only side who could displace them from that second berth.

This defeat for Middlesbrough means that, even if they won their two remaining games, they could not catch Newcastle. Second place in the league for Newcastle is therefore guaranteed.

Shields Daily Gazette (13/02/1893) p3a.
Northern Echo (15/02/1893) p4d.

	THE NORTHERN LEAGUE RESULTS TO SATURDAY, FEBRUARY 14 [INCLUSIVE]						Goals			
Pos	Team	Pld	W	D	L	F	A	Avg.	Pts
1	Middlesbrough Ironopolis	10	9	1	0	22	6	3.6667	19
2	Newcastle United	10	5	1	4	30	19	1.5789	11
3	Sheffield United	9	3	2	4	15	14	1.0714	8
4	Stockton	9	3	1	5	20	24	0.8333	7
5	Middlesbrough	8	3	0	5	13	13	1.0000	6
6	Darlington	8	1	1	6	7	33	0.2121	3

Game by Game ~ February 1893

Game 30: Saturday, February 18, 1893 — Newcastle United vs. Notts County

Competition: Friendly　　　Venue: St James's Park　　　Gate: 3,000

Newcastle United　3 - 2　Notts County

Scorer(s): Willie Thompson (8 mins); Jock Sorley (fh, fh)

Goal, Dave Whitton; *backs*, Tom Rodgers and James Miller; *half-backs*, Bobby Creilly, Willie Graham and James Collins; *forwards*, Harry Reay, Joe Wallace, Tom Crate, Willie Thompson, Jock Sorley

Scorer(s): Oswald (fh); Burke (fh)

Goal, George Toone; *backs*, Jack Hendry and Andrew Whitelaw; *half-backs*, Fay Harper, David Calderhead and T. Wilkinson; *forwards*, Tom McInnes, James Oswald, Dan Bruce, Andrew McGregor, James Burke

Referee: Robert Campbell (Sunderland)　　**Kick-Off:** 3:00 PM

Esteemed visitors indeed to St James's Park today, Notts County, founded in 1862 are universally recognised as the world's oldest Football League club, predating the Football Association itself, and are one of the 12 founder members of the Football League (1888).

Newcastle made a change to their 'usual' back pairing as Jeffrey was replaced by a triallist, Tom Rodgers, who was a well-known athlete and was on the printing staff of the Newcastle Journal.

Newcastle won the toss and elected to play 'up the hill' for the first half. Without further ado the County started the ball rolling and were on the immediate offensive. They made a strong attack on the home citadel, placing it in grave danger and a shot from Burke went very narrowly over the bar. Almost a disastrous start for Newcastle and the quality of County was on display already!

Trialist, Rodgers, distinguished himself in cleverly repulsing the Notts forwards as they were endeavouring to score when close in on the Newcastle goal. This then led to the home forwards picking up the mantle and taking the action up the hill towards the opposite goal. Wallace and Sorley exchanged some pretty passing, ending with a fine centre by Wallace and a good header from Sorley which was not far away but ultimately in vain.

The play that followed was of an extremely fast nature, both sides were passing and moving, displaying excellent dribbling skills but neither could force any dominance upon the other. Each end was visited, each end was endangered, and each end ultimately prevailed. After Whitton had to deal with one grand shot from McInnes, which would leave his palms stinging no doubt, the homesters rushed up the field and swooped on the visitor's goal. With a fine shot Thompson managed to break the deadlock and Newcastle took the lead. This gave the game an even greater fillip now as Notts stove desperately to get an equaliser and for this they did not have to wait too long. Oswald sent in a well-aimed shot that had Whitton well beaten and indeed such was its direction that he stood no chance of keeping out.

Newcastle reacted well to this and for a period they made matters quite warm for Howlett and his defenders and during this period of dominance they again took the lead as Sorley put the ball through after capital combination work by Wallace, Thompson and Crate presented him with an opportunity. Sorley then added a third goal for Newcastle as they won a free-kick which was well delivered in and gave Toone all sorts of difficulty in dealing with, which he did but in doing so only parried the ball back into play. Keeping up the virtual siege on the Notts goal the home forward quintet once again opened the Notts defence for Sorley to rush through and score.

Notts were not finished though, they may have now been two goals behind, but they were never prepared to let this game go. Back they came at the Newcastle defence and with a good display of football their forward line neared the Newcastle goal and with a final rush Burke forced the ball through for their second goal. Nothing more was scored up to the break so the homesters took a slender lead into the interval.

Upon changing ends Newcastle played up very strongly and shots were fired in on regular short intervals by Creilly, Sorley, Wallace and Thompson but none of them took effect. Whenever Notts did break they found in Rodgers, Miller and Whitton an extremely robust defence which they could not penetrate. There were no goals scored in the second half, after the feast of five in the first, but this in no way distracted from the fine display of football, from both sides.

Newcastle United.....................3 goals.

Notts County ....2 goals.

Here's one for the "pub quiz" masters amongst you, Notts County represented the first 'Magpies' to play at St James's Park. Taking the nickname from their black and white striped home kit, whilst Newcastle at the time still played in the red of East End and it would not be some years before they were to adopt the same nickname. *Arguments still rage as to whether the same reason was behind Newcastle's adoption of the nickname though.*

NORTHERN LEAGUE

Middlesbrough vs. Stockton: Middlesbrough started the ball rolling and pressed heavily for the first few minutes of play keeping the ball confined mainly in the visitors' territory. Play was of a fast and furious nature. Ramsay proved his worth as a custodian and only some fine saves from him prevented a home onslaught.

At length when the ball was got away it was the Stocktonians were stopped in their tracks by Bach and there was no way through. Play was soon back in the Stockton goal-mouth but again they broke out and got down, and Jones putting the ball well and it was eventually got through by Thompson.

Pressing hard for the equaliser the homesters now came the fore and McKnight passed to Black who eluded the challenge of Ramsay and put through, parity restored.

Before very long Middlesbrough were attacking again and a hot scrimmage took place in the visitors' goal-mouth and the ball was rushed through, registering a second goal for them. Play was once again fast and exciting and just before the half ended a great press from Middlesbrough saw Black playing in McCabe who scored a third goal for them.

Following the interval Middlesbrough were the first to show and on a couple of occasions the Stockton goal was in imminent danger but Lindsay, McDermid and Ramsay were offering a splendid defence and try as they might Middlesbrough could not get the better of them. Making a break away Stockton got up and put the ball through but were despondent to have the referee rule it out for offside. This started a passage of end-to-end play during which Stockton once again managed to get the ball and this time the goal counted. It was unfortunately for them too little, too late, as soon after time was called.

Middlesbrough ....3 goals.

Stockton ....2 goals.

Middlesbrough: *Goal,* Fall; *backs,* McManus and Crone; *half-backs,* Taggart, Stott and Bach; *forwards,* Black, Lewis, McKnight, Blyth and McCabe.

Stockton: *Goal,* Ramsay; *backs,* Lindsay and McDermid; *half-backs,* Shaw, Graham and Hutton; *forwards,* Strachan, Willocks, Thompson, McClung and Jones.

The battle for third place was going down to the wire. With a single game left each Middlesbrough and Sheffield were tied on eight points with their goal averages being very similar, the Sheffielders being only marginally ahead. Indeed, the fate of the placing now lay in the hands of Darlington against whom both Sheffield and Middlesbrough had to play. Darlington of course had lost six of their eight games played and conceded thirty-three goals in the process. All eyes would be on Feethams at the beginning of April.

Newcastle Daily Chronicle (20/02/1893) p6e.
Newcastle Daily Journal (20/02/1893) p7d.
Northern Echo (20/02/1893) p4c.

THE NORTHERN LEAGUE RESULTS TO SATURDAY, FEBRUARY 18 [INCLUSIVE]							Goals			
Pos	Team	Pld	W	D	L	F	A	Avg.	Pts
1	Middlesbrough Ironopolis	10	9	1	0	22	6	3.6667	19
2	Newcastle United	10	5	1	4	30	19	1.5789	11
3	Sheffield United	9	3	2	4	15	14	1.0714	8
4	Middlesbrough	9	4	0	5	16	15	1.0667	8
5	Stockton	10	3	1	6	22	27	0.8148	7
6	Darlington	8	1	1	6	7	33	0.2121	3

Game by Game ~ February 1893

Game 31: Saturday, February 25, 1893 — Newcastle United vs. Sunderland

Competition: Friendly   Venue: St James's Park   Gate: 7,000

Newcastle United   1 - 6   Sunderland

Scorer(s): Wallace (55 mins)

Scorer(s): Gillespie (1 min, sh); Campbell (20 mins, 42 mins [Pen], 89 mins, sh)

Goal, Dave Whitton; *backs*, Harry Jeffrey and James Miller; *half-backs*, Bobby Creilly, Willie Graham and James Collins; *forwards*, Harry Reay, Tom Crate, Willie Thompson, Jock Sorley, Joe Wallace

Goal, Ned Doig; *backs*, John Gillespie and Tom Porteous; *half-backs*, Billy Dunlop, John Auld and William Gibson; *forwards*, James Gillespie, David Hannah, Johnny Campbell, Jimmy Millar, John Scott

Referee: J. Potts (Stockton)

Kick-Off: 3:10 PM

As champions of the football league the guarantee needing to be paid to bring Sunderland here today would not have been cheap, so it was good to see around 7,000 spectators crammed into a cold and damp St James's Park, a worthy crowd for worthy adversaries. This was their second visit this season, the first in September having ended in a draw of two goals apiece, so this game was eagerly anticipated.

Newcastle won the toss and elected to play 'up the hill' so without further ado at precisely 3:10pm Campbell for Sunderland set the ball rolling. For the first few moments little headway was made by either side but soon the Sunderland forwards showed good combination then disaster for Newcastle! James Gillespie and Hannah advanced towards the home goal. In making an intervention Miller slipped at the crucial moment and Gillespie was free to easily put the leather through. There was barely a minute on the clock.

From the restart the Newcastle left wing ran up cleverly and the Sunderland defence was put under intense pressure, but Reay sent behind. Graham put in some fine work for the homesters and play generally hovered around the Wearsiders goal for a time, but eventually the leather was transferred to midfield. Thence Gillespie rushed down and played in Hannah who sent in a shot from distance which challenged Whitton, but he saved albeit with some difficulty and at the expense of a corner. An intervention by Graham saved brilliantly and the ball spun out to Auld who put his shot over the bar. Jeffrey frustrated another attack by the Sunderland left wing. There was some beautiful play exhibited by the Sunderland forwards, and Campbell had a great chance, but went offside and the free-kick relieved Newcastle from severe pressure.

Collins gained possession and took the ball well up before giving to Wallace who made a bad pass. Sorley was next to show for Newcastle made a good shot which only narrowly missed. The homesters rushed up again, making a good attack, but (John) Gillespie made a saving intervention. Wallace benefitted from this but from some distance sent his shot past. Play slowed considerably after this for a while. Creilly tackled in good style, and it was from a Newcastle attack that the second goal came – *for Sunderland*!

Breaking up the Newcastle attack (John) Gillespie sent the ball long downfield where it was seized upon by Campbell. Taking it first time, he spun it towards the goal where it hit a post and bounded in before Whitton could do anything about it. About 20 minutes had elapsed and the homesters faced a real challenge now and were also facing a heckling from their own supporters dismayed at the mistakes they were making and the muddled efforts when opportunities allowed. This was no more exemplified than when Doig in the Sunderland goal as taking a kick red shirt had the temerity to attack him and was summarily flattened into the mud amid screams of laughter.

Crate did try, but his well-crafted shot went awry. Reay made a good return on the goal kick which eluded (John) Gillespie but not Doig who threw away. Almost directly after Hannah was in a collision and had to leave the field of play due to his injuries.

Wallace sent a grand cross over to Reay but when well-placed he missed the ball and a good opportunity was wasted. Sunderland then took the ball up and won a corner, from this a free-kick was awarded to them for 'hands' against Wallace but they then wasted the opportunity. Play was briefly taken to the visitor's goal, where Graham

~ 97 ~

intervened well. The home forwards tried desperately but finally Reay sent the ball over the bar. Some pretty exciting play ensued with the homesters having slightly the best of matters, but it was obvious to all this was temporary. A free-kick for a foul by Auld was easily cleared by Porteous and before you knew it the ball was back in the Newcastle quarters. Auld was tackled and fully mauled off the ball and when it spun free to Campbell, he received the same treatment, but he was awarded a penalty for his pains. Taking the spot-kick himself, he easily put the ball past Whitton. The interval was called minutes after this goal. Three goals to the good and though they were now playing with only ten men Sunderland were well in control and cruising this game.

Upon changing ends Thompson resumed the game and Wearsiders took the upper hand once more. Swarming around Whitton. As he took control of the ball Campbell charged him, both players falling in the goalmouth and Scott rushed in to take advantage of the free ball only to see his hasty effort go wide from a matter of feet, what a let-off for Newcastle.

Newcastle then took on the role of aggressors and fairly camped themselves around the Sunderland goal. Some good play was witnessed, both by their forwards and by the Sunderland defence. Eventually, following an attack which got close in, the ball was cleared some distance into the midfield where it was returned by a long kick from Graham and falling to Wallace he took possession and bustled his way through the remainder of the defence and struck it nicely past Doig.

Any thought of this signalling a Newcastle comeback were quickly dispelled as Sunderland simply moved up a gear. Their combination play was far superior, and to which Newcastle simply did not have an answer. In one sweeping attack the white-shirted Sunderland forward line easily slipped their way through the red-shirted Newcastle defence and Gillespie slid in a grand shot right between the posts to register the Wearsiders fourth goal. Newcastle again tried and had a modicum of success as they had hard lines as they pressurised Doig which saw him having to haul out one attempt and desperately clear away a second with his feet. Remembering that Hannah was still off the field of play, and Sunderland were therefore still down to ten men, if ever Newcastle were to make their numerical advantage count surely it would have been during this period, but alas it was not to be. They did manage to gain a corner but Reay's effort from it was wasted and the ball was sent into midfield by (John) Gillespie. Miller returned but this only led to the Sunderland left wing powering down and Millar sent in a shot from an oblique angle that saw Whitton having to make a save.

The passing of the remaining four Sunderland forwards was superb and they repeatedly ran through all that was put before them and only bad luck, or superb saves by Whitton, denied them. Then Millar sent in a header which Whitton caught with difficulty and threw out, the ball however did not travel far. Intercepted by (James) Gillespie he sent in a 'corker' of an effort which Whitton saved with his feet at the expense of a corner. There was a scrimmage in front of the Newcastle goal following the corner which saw Campbell have several fruitless attempts before he finally secured a good hold on the ball and getting decent purchase on it sent it crashing through and Sunderland now had five goals, woe indeed for the Newcastle players and fans.

Vainly the home forwards ran down, and a shot from Sorley was easily fisted out by Doig and the Sunderland vanguard were soon back in Newcastle territory. Play became rather slow for a period as no doubt being a man down was wearing on Sunderland and the fruitless exertions of the homesters was also taking its toll. A little excitement was registered as Creilly found himself in a nice position but Doig, once again, was able to fist out without too much difficulty. Both Graham and Reay were both unlucky as they had attempts which missed narrowly.

Sunderland pressed again and their reward was a corner which came to nothing. Wallace then made a good attempt which brought out an equally good save from Doig and threw out. The return by Graham was sent behind. Presently a corner was gained by Newcastle, but nought arose from it, nor was there anything more from a second corner. Whilst this period of play was dominated by Newcastle the Sunderland goal never looked in any real danger and there was always the feeling that even with being a man down, they had it within themselves to turn the tables at any time. This was amply displayed as following some clever work by Millar, just before time was called, Campbell scored his fourth goal, and Sunderland's sixth, ensuring the Wearsiders ran out quite ridiculously easy winners and turned their hosts as red as their shirts.

Newcastle United ....1 goal.
Sunderland ....6 goals.

Newcastle United: *Goal*, Whitton; *backs*, Jeffrey and Miller; *half-backs*, Creilly, Graham and Collins; *forwards*, Reay, Crate, Thompson, Sorley and Wallace.

Sunderland: *Goal*, Ned Doig; *backs*, John Gillespie and Tom Porteous; *half-backs*, Billy Dunlop, John Auld and William Gibson; *forwards*, James Gillespie, David Hannah, Johnny Campbell, Jimmy Millar and John Scott.

Referee: Mr J. Potts (Stockton).

Newcastle Daily Chronicle (23/02/1893) p7e.
Newcastle Daily Chronicle (25/02/1893) p7e.
Newcastle Daily Chronicle (27/02/1893) p6d.
Sunderland Echo (27/02/1893) p4a.
Newcastle Daily Chronicle (28/02/1893) p7e.

In other news...
The Middlesbrough Conspiracy Saga continues...

The Newcastle United Club. – The adjourned directors' meeting of the club was held last night, at the Viaduct Hotel, Byker, the whole of the directors being present. The allegations made against some of the players of the United were thoroughly gone into, and as there is every probability of the matter being settled in the law courts very shortly, the committee decided that they would give every facility to have the charges thoroughly investigated. – After a long discussion the chairman withdrew his resignation. – The Secretary intimated that until the matter was cleared up he could not see a way to act as secretary of the team, but after strong pressure from the committee it was agreed that Mr. Dixon, the energetic secretary of the A team, should be asked to take Mr Golding's position, and upon that understanding Mr Golding consented to undertake the duties of secretary to the A team.

Newcastle Daily Chronicle, 01/02/1893, [p7d].

In expanding upon the breaking scandal, the Newcastle Daily Journal carried the following:

"A meeting of the committee of this club (*ed. Newcastle United*) was held at Heaton last night when there was a large attendance of members. Mr Golding was ultimately prevailed upon to withdraw his resignation and will consequently go on in the good work he is doing as secretary."

As we know from the Newcastle Daily Chronicle version of events Mr Golding and Mr Dixon, secretary of the "A" team swapped roles rather than Mr Golding remaining in post. The Journal continues:

"Before the cup tie between United and Middlesbrough three letters were received by Mr Golding from a person who dwells on the banks of the Tees, who in his communications stated that some of the Newcastle men were betting on the Middlesbrough team winning the tie, and also connected a prominent supporter of the Middlesbrough Club with these transactions. At last night's meeting a letter was read by a solicitor, acting on behalf of the Middlesbrough committee, asking for the name of the correspondent in order to take legal proceedings against him."

There was also another 'bombshell' awaiting – dissolving of the club, barely two months after new incarnation! In addressing this the Journal concludes the article with:

"The United committee wish us to state that there is no grounds whatever for the rumour of the breaking up of the club; and we may expect to see the majority of the present players signed on for next season. In fact Miller has already put his signature to the necessary document."

So, there we have it, members of the Newcastle team colluding with a prominent Middlesbrough supporter to ensure a Middlesbrough victory in the FA Cup whilst making a tidy profit at the bookmakers! Surely this cannot be the case? We eagerly await any further developments...

Newcastle United 1892-93: Season Zero

Farewell to a local hero

It was reported in the newspapers today that Peter Watson left Newcastle United, (Friday, February10), to take up on an offer to play for Rotherham Town Football Club. Having only arrived in January 1891 his time with United was short but not without an incident which very much made him a 'local hero'.

On the night of Sunday, March 6, 1892, Watson had occasion to be in the Byker Bank area of Newcastle where he witnessed "several roughs" assaulting a Police Officer, PC Walton. Without hesitation Watson went to the assistance of the officer and the "roughs" were duly arrested.

Amazing scores in the Alliance

When Sunderland played Newcastle United at St James's Park on Saturday, February 25, you thought their score of six goals to one was impressive, well their "A" side absolutely smashed that! They beat Willington Athletic, second in the Alliance, whilst eight points behind Sunderland they did have two games 'in hand' over them, so the result of ten goals to nil in favour of Sunderland was mightily impressive. However, even that paled into insignificance when one looked at the score between third placed Rendel and ninth placed Whitburn. The former running out victors by no fewer than sixteen goals to nil!

The Middlesbrough Conspiracy Saga ends...

Reported in the Newcastle Daily Chronicle, and other local news outlets, the following finally puts the lid on the Middlesbrough conspiracy saga:

> "Everyone will be pleased to know that the disagreeableness which was caused by severe charges against East End players when they were defeated by Middlesbrough in the English Cup, have now been completely and amicably disproved. When the charges were made, principally against J. Miller, that player asked the committee to make a thorough investigation, and this having been done he has been exonerated from all blame, and also has been retained by the club for next season. It is a pity that the committee could not discover the originator of the libel."

As to the "A's"...

NEWCASTLE UNITED 'A' RESULTS FEBRUARY 1893			
Date	Home	Score	Away
February 4, 1893.	Newcastle United A	1 - 3	Rendel	*Northumberland Cup Semi-Final*
Newcastle United A:	*Goal*, Jos Ryder; *backs*, Rodgers and Crichton; *half-backs*, Fitzgerald, Wilde and J. Ryder; *forwards*, Grierson, Cattell, Dixon, Donaldson and Dodds		
Rendel:	*Goal*, R. Forster; *backs*, T. Campbell and T. Bell; *half-backs*, Kirk, Wardropper and Redpath; *forwards*, Southern, Purvis, Henderson, Wood and Heslop		
Played at the old East End ground at Heaton Junction.			
February 11, 1893.	Newcastle United A	3 - 3	Trafalgar	*Friendly*
Newcastle United A:	*Goal*, Jos. Ryder; *backs*, Queen and Crichton; *half-backs*, Rodgers, Taylor and J. Ryder; *forwards*, Cattell, Grierson, Dixon, Donaldson and Dodds		
Trafalgar:	*Goal*, Lowery; *backs*, O'Donnell and Atteridge; *half-backs*, Irwin, Walton and Fraser; *forwards*, J. Patten, R. Patten, H. Herdman, W. Neill and W. Atkinson		
February 18, 1893.	Howden-le-Wear	1 - 2	Newcastle United A	*Friendly*
Newcastle United A:	*Goal*, Ryder; *backs*, Wilde and Crichton; *half-backs*, Cattell, Campbell and J. Ryder; *forwards*, Halliday, Gardner, Dixon, McCann and Dodds		

March 1893

Games Played in March 1893

V	Date	F	A	R	Opposition	Competition
H	04/03/1893	3	4	L	Stoke	Friendly
H	11/03/1893	6	1	W	Annbank	Friendly
H	18/03/1893	3	1	W	Derby County	Friendly
H	25/03/1893	4	1	W	Nottingham Forest	Friendly

Appearances & Goals ~ March 1893

Name	Total Apps	Total Goals	League Apps	League Goals	Friendly Apps	Friendly Goals
Collins, James	4	1	0		4	1
Crate, Thomas "Tom"	4		0		4	
Creilly, Robert "Bobby"	3		0		3	
Graham, William "Willie"	3	2	0		3	2
Jeffrey, Harry	4		0		4	
McCabe, Frank	2		0		2	
McKane, Joseph "Joe"	4		0		4	
Miller, James	4		0		4	
Reay, Harry	3	8	0		3	8
Ryder, Joseph "Joe"	1		0		1	
Sorley, John "Jock"	4	1	0		4	1
Thompson, Willie	3	2	0		3	2
Wallace, Joseph "Joe"	4	1	0		4	1
Whitton, David "Dave"	1		0		1	

Season to Date (03/09/1892 - 25/03/1893 inclusive)

Name	Total Apps	Total Goals	League Apps	League Goals	FA Cup Apps	FA Cup Goals	Friendly Apps	Friendly Goals
Barker, John	1		1				0	
Collins, James	33	8	10	1	1		22	7
Coupar, William	1		0				1	
Crate, Thomas "Tom"	28	6	10	2			18	4
Creilly, Robert "Bobby"	32	3	9	1	1		22	2
Dixon, Henry	2	1	0				2	1
Graham, William "Willie"	34	4	10	2	1		23	2
Jeffrey, Harry	30		7		1		22	
Kirkland, J.	1						1	
McCabe, Frank	2		0				2	
McIntosh, James	2	2	0				2	2
McKane, Joseph "Joe"	30	1	7		1		22	1
Miller, James	33		10		1		22	
Reay, Harry	29	22	9	3	1	1	19	18
Rodgers, Thomas "Tom"	1		0				1	
Ryder, Joseph "Joe"	1		0				1	
Sorley, John "Jock"	30	21	8	7	1		21	14
Thompson, Willie	27	19	7	6	1	1	19	12
Wallace, Joseph "Joe"	29	9	8	6	1		20	3
Watson, Peter	6	3					3	
Whitton, David "Dave"	32		10		1		21	

Game 32: Saturday, March 4, 1893 — Newcastle United vs. Stoke

Competition: Friendly   Venue: St James's Park   Gate: 3,000

Newcastle United 2 - 4 Stoke

Scorer(s): Graham (fh); Reay (fh); Wallace (sh)   **Scorer(s):** Schofield (fh); Evans (sh); Clare (sh); Edge (sh)

Goal, Joe Ryder; *backs,* Harry Jeffrey and James Miller; *half-backs,* Tom Crate, Willie Graham and Joe McKane; *forwards,* Harry Reay, Joe Wallace, Willie Thompson, James Collins, Jock Sorley

Goal, Bill Rowley; *backs,* Tommy Clare and Thompson; *half-backs,* Davy Christie, Jack Proctor and Davy Brodie; *forwards,* Willie Naughton, Joe Schofield, Jimmie Robertson, Alf Edge, Ted Evans

Kick-Off: 3:00 PM

Once again Newcastle were able to bring First Division opposition to St James's Park, a testament to their growing standing in the footballing world perhaps, notwithstanding last week's disaster of course, but that was against the current champions of course. Stoke were always popular visitors to Newcastle and their visits to the former Heaton ground of East End had produced some fine exhibitions of football. It must be admitted that the prospects for football in the North-East were not that good at the beginning of the week as snow and then rain made a return. Matters however greatly improved and by this afternoon's kick-off the weather was bright, and a good crowd assembled.

Stoke had brought their full league team to Newcastle but at the last moment Underwood (back) and Dickson (inside-right) were withdrawn, their places being taken by Thompson and Edge respectively. From a Newcastle perspective they rested Whitton and gave his place to Joe Ryder and Creilly saw his knee break down again, so his place went to Crate. On a positive note McKane was back in his place and Collins was partnering Reay in the vanguard.

Newcastle won the toss and elected to play 'down the hill' taking advantage of both it and the wind which was not too strong but gave an advantage. Robertson started for Stoke but the ball was quickly in the possession of the United midfield and without further ado the Newcastle forward quintet were rushing smartly down. A shot was sent in by Thompson, but it was straight into the hands of Rowley. When he threw out it was returned by Wallace, but his effort went behind. The home right-wing was having some success and were well supplied by Jeffrey. This led to a decent opportunity for Reay which he unfortunately sent over. Directly after Clare made a most important intervention to halt a combined rush from the Newcastle forwards. It was then the turn of Graham to make just as important an intervention as Robertson was getting nicely away. The homesters then won a free-kick upon which they could not improve and then, in this enthralling end-to-end contest it was the turn of the home goal to be endangered as Naughton ran well up and put in a fine centre. Ryder, alert to the danger managed to kick away.

Some nice passing movement was shown by the visitors down their right wing but a timely intervention by Jeffrey put paid to that as he dispossessed them in fine style and cleared well away. A return was met by Graham and with some heavy pressing Newcastle forced a corner. From the well-placed ball scrimmage ensued in the goal mouth and Rowley showed great bravery in getting in the middle of it and coming away he was clinging onto the ball. After this Newcastle again pressed heavily and won three corners in succession and gained nothing from any of them. For this they were made to pay immediately as completely against the run of play Stoke broke away and Schofield opened the scoring with a grand shot.

Severely irked by this reverse Newcastle went all-out for the equaliser and forced a great save from Rowley. The ball was not long away from his charge as back it came and from another fierce scrimmage in front of goal Graham squeezed the leather through for Newcastle amid great excitement from the crowd. McKane then had to step in as the ball was brought into the Newcastle quarters by Edge and disposing him sent the ball into midfield. Jeffrey then put in a fine attempt as he sent a return crashing into the crossbar and the ball bounded over. Still pressing Newcastle left themselves a bit exposed and

Naughton took advantage, running the ball well into the Newcastle quarters but could not better the situation. This respite to the Newcastle onslaught was temporary indeed as back they came and the Stoke citadel was once again the centre of play. Another brief relief as Naughton and Edge again put in some good work with the later having a fine effort saved by Ryder. Once more Newcastle rushed down and some pretty play resulted in front of the Stoke goal with the ball being put through from an equally pretty shot from Reay and Newcastle were now deservedly in front! Right up until the whistle for the interval Newcastle continued to have the better of play but could not break a stout Stoke defence again.

Upon the change of ends Thompson restarted for the home team and, in attempting to pick up where they had left off, they immediately made for their opponents' goal. Rowley was forced into a great save from a beautiful shot from Wallace and in doing so conceded a corner. The ball from the corner was temporarily relieved but soon another scrimmage developed in the Stoke goal and the ball was cleared out however it was met by Wallace who returned it in grand fashion, sending the ball through to register Newcastle's third goal. Whilst maintaining the upper hand Newcastle were now finding the Stoke defence impenetrable and they once again left themselves exposed and a quick break-away led to the ball being fed to Evans whose shot beat the best endeavours of Ryder and Stoke were right back in this game. No taking the upper hand Stoke sent in several shots which whilst taxing for the home defence they proved capable and equal to them all. For a while play was even as Newcastle forced their way out of danger but could not affect any realistic attacks. They did make one good attempt, but Reay was demonstrably offside with his effort. Back at the other end Miller had to intervene and sent a long kick away. Newcastle then won a free-kick for 'hands' against Proctor but all they gained was territory. Seemingly not to have learned their lesson Stoke were able to make another quick break a Robertson had the ball in the back of the Newcastle net, but the point was disallowed for offside. Straight from the free-kick however Clare received the ball and struck it well in with considerable force, indeed such force that although Ryder managed to touch the ball, he could not keep it out and Stoke were level.

Pulsating end-to-end play followed, neither side being happy to settle for a draw. Stoke had an abortive attempt and soon after forced a corner but again nothing was gained from it. Still they pressed and their reward came as Edge, with a swift shot, beat Ryder and Stoke were in the lead within only moments to go. Indeed, there was only time for one more fruitless attack by Newcastle before time was called and an enthralling, and thoroughly enjoyable game, except for the result of course, came to an end.

Newcastle United .... 3 goals.

Stoke .... 4 goals.

Stoke arrived in Newcastle on Friday evening and put up at the Crown Hotel which they used as their headquarters during their stay.

Newcastle Daily Chronicle ((04/03/1893) p7e.
Athletic News (06/03/1893) p6a.
Birmingham Daily Post (06/03/1893) p7f.
Newcastle Daily Chronicle ((06/03/1893) p6e.

Game 33: Saturday, March 11, 1893 **Newcastle United vs. Annbank**

Competition: Friendly   Venue: St James's Park

Newcastle United   6 - 1   Annbank

Scorer(s): Reay (fh, fh, fh, sh, sh); Thompson (fh)

Goal, Dave Whitton; *backs*, Harry Jeffrey and James Miller; *half-backs*, Bobby Creilly, Tom Crate and Joe McKane; *forwards*, Harry Reay, James Collins, Willie Thompson, Jock Sorley, Joe Wallace

Referee: F. Knott

Scorer(s): Watson (fh)

Goal, Fitzsimmons; *backs*, Dunlop and Millar; *half-backs*, J. Graham, Gourlay and Davidson; *forwards*, Watson, Donnelly, Henderson, Kerr, Welsh

Kick-Off: 3:00 PM

Annbank, who should have been Newcastle's opponents back in October, finally made an appearance at St James's Park today. Current holders of the Ayrshire Cup, the Ayr Charity Cup and Ayrshire League Cup their record this season was impressive having played 27 matches they had won 23 of them and scored no less than 172 goals in the process! On January 14 they had beaten Newmilns, the team from whom both Sorley and Wallace came, by no fewer than 16 goals to 2 goals. Whilst such a score was never in anyone's mind for today perhaps Newcastle needed to be wary, though not overly so as the last time these two sides met was when East End beat Annbank at Heaton by four goals to two goals a couple of seasons ago. As more added interest to this fixture the Annbank team included none other than that famous old Preston North End half-back Johnny Graham, brother to Newcastle's Willie Graham, but they were not destined to face each other today as Willie is side-lined with an injured foot.

Newcastle won the toss and elected to play 'down the hill' so it was Henderson of Annbank who got the ball rolling. They were immediately dispossessed by McKane and he set the home forwards off and running, the ball being carried an extra few yards courtesy of a light wind and out over the line. Annbank paid a visit to Newcastle's quarters but were easily repulsed and found themselves suddenly defending desperately. Fitzsimmons being called upon and he threw out an attempt by Thompson. The Newcastle forwards were playing a clever game but found the Annbank defence quite impenetrable. Miller in making a grand save from Collins gave away a corner. From it the ball was delivered in well and a mighty scrimmage ensued in front of the Annbank goal. After some clever attacking, and stout defending, Reay was able to head through in grand style, this after only five minutes of play the homesters took the lead.

From the restart Annbank could make no headway and the homesters quickly took possession and the ball was hovering dangerously around the bottom goal. Newcastle were working well together, their combination play proving too clever for the visitors and when presented with an opportunity Reay beautifully lifted the ball over the head of Fitzsimmons and just under the bar giving the custodian no chance of making a save.

There was a brief interlude in the Newcastle pressure as Annbank made a quick trip up the field, but it was fruitless and before they knew it, they had conceded a corner to Newcastle. When the ball was delivered in Reay carried the ball clean through the goal from Fitzsimmons's very grasp but a free-kick in favour of the custodian was awarded rather than a goal to Reay. Newcastle continued to press strongly and for a while the defence and custodian where equal to the task. Fitzsimmons made a great save from a Thompson effort and threw a long way out but upon the return 'hands' was given against Graham which saw Newcastle very close in once more, but they found no success.

Watson and Donnelly had a brief sojourn upfield with the former eventually sending over the bar and a return was similarly useless. Back at the other end a good dribble by Collins afforded him an opportunity but his swift shot was well dealt with by Fitzsimmons as he fisted it far out. This led to the ball being quickly transferred into Newcastle territory and with a fine pass by Henderson possession was given to Watson who scored for Annbank, amid stunned silence in St James's Park. To be fair to Annbank though, whilst it may have been totally against the run of play, it was a finely executed goal.

The home forwards made another pretty run but were dispossessed by Graham, but Wallace regained the ball and made a good shot but unfortunately sent it over the bar. Collins then returned with a grand shot which Fitzsimmons saved and threw out, back came the return from Thompson who only just missed. The pressure on Annbank was immense and unrelenting and Newcastle were again surrounding their goal. The ball was delivered in, several players going for it, with Fitzsimmons getting there first but as he made the save, and with several players on the ground, Thompson latched onto the free ball and sent it between the posts. Directly after Fitzsimmons fisted out another effort by Thompson but Reay took possession and put on Newcastle's fourth goal. Without further ado the interval was announced.

On the changing of ends there was no changing the desire of the homesters and they immediately reapplied the pressure. Reay and Collins both had excellent attempts, but the wind had grown considerably and undoubtedly affected these. Miller and Gourlay had to make repeated interventions, which they did admirably. A couple of quick break-outs by Watson and Donnelly where deftly dealt with by Jeffrey and Miller. A free-kick for a foul seemingly let the visitors in but they could take further advantage. Collins taking a good shot on the run was unlucky to miss and Wallace sent in a cracker which Fitzsimmons had to fist away and Reay ending the move by sending behind.

The game went into a lull for a while until a nice run by the Annbank forwards saw Whitton making an important save from Henderson as did Jeffrey with a timely intervention. Collins raced away but was pulled up for offside but then in a marvellous run Wallace and Sorley dashed up and the former fed the latter for a great shot to register a fifth goal for Newcastle.

Annbank tried vainly to rally, Henderson having hard lines as he saw his effort hit the crossbar and then getting a free-kick for 'hands' near to the Newcastle goal but the homesters got the ball away. Collins made another fine run up the wing, but he sent over the bar. The wind was now very strong and interfering with play and Newcastle worked hard to keep the ball low, and the passes short. Using these tactics, they managed to work their way right up and the ball was given to Reay who registered his fifth and Newcastle's sixth goal.

Indeed, Reay later had the ball in the back of the net for what would have been his 'double hat-trick', but he was adjudged offside. Wallace just missed with an opportunity after this and the game slowed and fizzled out and the final whistle arrived with no further scoring.

Newcastle United....................**6 goals.**

Annbank..................................**1 goal.**

Newcastle Daily Chronicle (10/03/1893) p7d.
Athletic News (13/03/1893) p7a.
Newcastle Daily Chronicle (13/03/1893) p6d.
The Scotsman (13/03/1893) p7e.

Game 34: Saturday, March 18, 1893   **Newcastle United vs. Derby County**

Competition: Friendly   Venue: St James's Park   Gate: 3,000

Newcastle United   3 - 1   Derby County

Scorer(s): OG [Methven] (fh); Collins (sh); Thompson (sh)

Goal, Frank McCabe; *backs*, Harry Jeffrey and James Miller; *half-backs*, Bobby Creilly, Willie Graham and Joe McKane; *forwards*, James Collins, Tom Crate, Willie Thompson, Jock Sorley, Joe Wallace

Referee: Mr Coleman (Gateshead)

Scorer(s): tbc (fh)

Goal, John Robinson; *backs*, Jimmy Methven and Joseph Leiper; *half-backs*, Ernest Higginbottom, Archie Goodall and Ralston; *forwards*, Samuel Mills, William Storer, John Goodall, John Stuart McMillan, Thomas Little

Kick-Off: 3:30 PM

First Division opponents once again for Newcastle, this time in the form of that well-known midland outfit, Derby County. Maybe well-known, but they were totally unknown in one sense as this was their first visit to Newcastle so there was a good deal of interest shown in this friendly fixture. It was interesting to note that Derby would be playing the Goodall brothers, both playing for the countries of birth, Ireland for Archie and England for John, this peculiar circumstance arising from their family travels as their father was a corporal in the Scottish Fusiliers.

Derby won the toss and elected to play 'up the hill' for the first half and therefore Thompson set the game under motion for Newcastle. They made their intentions clear as a rapid movement saw a very early opportunity fall to Creilly, but he sent over the bar. Directly following this Sorley took possession and sent in an effort which went bye. From the goal-kick 'hands' was given against Miller. This saw the ball being brought to the area around the home goal where a scrimmage developed but the ball ultimately being sent behind. Derby pressed again and Little, after some good play, sent his attempt high over the bar. Newcastle then had a quick look-in and a splendid effort from Thompson was saved equally splendidly by Robinson and he repeated that with a save from Wallace.

At the other end J. Goodall sent a shot over the bar and further pressure from Derby was only relived when a free-kick for a foul was awarded against them. The homesters then worked their way back upfield and pressure was now on the

Derby citadel, but it was once more a foul which relieved the pressure. Derby could do nothing more with the free-kick as Collins took possession of it and ran it out of danger. Wallace then gave Robinson a sharp shot to save and with a good clearance he got play up to the other end. An intervention by Miller saw the Newcastle left-wing carry the ball high up and the ball was crossed into the centre for Wallace. He sent in a fine shot which Robinson rushed out to prevent it going in but he missed it completely and Methven dashed to make a hasty clearance and was horrified to see it hit his custodian and rebound between the posts.

Play became fast and furious for a while each side having opportunities but none that were clear cut or incisive. Neither side, it could be said, could gain any degree of superiority over the other long enough to affect any further score. With half time approaching it did look to one and all that Methven's unfortunate 'own goal' would be the only one of the half. That was until Derby went down and forced a corner which was well delivered into the Newcastle goalmouth and in the ensuing melee it was rushed through for the equaliser. Not long after the interval was called.

Upon resumption of play Goodall set the ball rolling for Derby but in their haste to get forward they lost control and the ball was ran out. End-to-end play of a very fast nature followed which eventually afford Sorley an opportunity which he sent in beautifully, but Robinson just managed to pull off a save. From his clearance the ball was quickly returned as Wallace played it to Collins who scored with a lightning strike that this time Robinson had no chance of getting to.

The fast, even play continued but with Newcastle gradually to gain an upperhand though finding the Derby defence to be of admirable quality. Several shots were sent in by seemingly the whole of the Newcastle forward quintet but at each the defence repelled or Robinson saved. Wallace had a decent attempt following a rush but sent over the line and in what was an increasingly rare occurrence the Derby forwards broke out, but McCabe pulled off a tremendous save. Wallace appeared to have scored with a fine return shot but was adjudged offside and Thompson sent a shot behind. A free-kick looked to have put the homesters in a promising position but it availed them nothing. For a brief while the ball was kept away from the Derby citadel and they did manage to have an attempt on the Newcastle goal, but McCabe had stayed alert and relieved any danger. Newcastle worked the ball back up to the other and another free-kick was awarded in their favour. This was cleared but at the expense of a corner. The ball was well delivered but Jeffrey sent it behind. Just before time was called Newcastle were assembled around the Derby goal and there was a combined rush by the forward line the led by Thompson who carried the ball through thus ensuring there would be no come back this time for Derby.

Newcastle United....................3 goals.
Derby County..........................1 goal.

Athletic News (20/03/1893) p6c.
Derby Daily Telegraph (20/03/1893) p3g.
Newcastle Daily Chronicle (20/03/1893) p6e.
Newcastle Daily Journal (20/03/1893) p7d.
Northern Echo (20/03/1893) p4b.

Game 35: Saturday, March 25, 1893 **Newcastle United vs. Nottingham Forest**

Competition: Friendly   Venue: St James's Park

Newcastle United   4 - 1   Nottingham Forest

Scorer(s): Graham (3 mins); Reay (fh, fh); Sorley (sh [Pen])   **Scorer(s):** Pike (sh)

Goal, Frank McCabe; *backs*, Harry Jeffrey and James Miller; *half-backs*, Bobby Creilly, Willie Graham and Joe McKane; *forwards*, Harry Reay, Tom Crate, Jock Sorley, Joe Wallace, James Collins

Goal, Dennis Watkin Dan Allsopp; *backs*, Archibald Ritchie and Adam Scott; *half-backs*, Thomas Hamilton, Harvey and Peter McCracken; *forwards*, Arthur Shaw, Alexander Higgins, Neil McCallum, Horace Pike, Tom McInnes

Referee: W. Tiffin*   **Kick-Off:** 3:00 PM

When these two teams met last season, it was in the FA Cup and "United" were still "East End" and

Forest were in the Football Alliance and went on to become champions. Anyway, the result was a narrow 2-1 defeat for East End and Forest went on to reach the semi-final where they were finally beaten - *after two replays* - by the eventual winners West Bromwich Albion.

Forest won the toss and elected to play 'up the hill' in the first half. So, it was in fine weather, and before a large gathering, that Sorley got the 'battle of the reds' underway. The Newcastle 'reds' immediately put pressure on the 'reds' of Forest and their defence did well to them at bay. After three minutes of this onslaught Sorley gave a clever back-pass to Graham who put through with a clinking shot and the homesters had a very early lead.

From the restart Reay took possession and sent over to Wallace who's attempt went bye. Reay again got possession, but McCracken intervened and put the ball out. Shaw and Higgins then had a run up, but Jeffrey easily cleared. Reay put in a return from which Wallace forced corner, which was cleared. From a free-kick the ball was sent through by Jeffrey, but no score resulted. Forcing their way to the other end Forest had an attempt by McInnes well saved by McCabe and in the next minute McInnes had another attempt but sent it over. Back at the other end Crate put in a good ball which Sorley headed just over. In an exciting period of end-to-end play, we were next at the Newcastle goal, but the final effort by Shaw went wide. The ball was then put through at the other end by Reay, but this point was chalked off for offside.

Newcastle again pressed and a sharp struggle followed in the Forest goal, Allsopp performing heroics as he saved again and again. A rush downfield led by Collins was followed by a display of excellent passing between the forwards and Sorley centred finely for Reay who, denied his previous goal, made no mistake with his shot and penetrated what had become an almost impregnable defence.

McInnes made a dash up resulting in a free-kick for 'hands' but Newcastle easily cleared the danger. Newcastle then rushed down. Wallace centred, and Sorley put the ball narrowly over. Following the corner, a free-kick was awarded to Newcastle for a foul on Creilly. Jeffrey took the free-kick and sent it nicely in for Reay to head through and give Newcastle a very comfortable three goal cushion.

Keeping up the pressure Newcastle tried again, and Wallace was unlucky with a very close shot. On the counter-attack Shaw beat McKane and shot but Miller headed away but only as far as McInnes, but he shot wide. Crate had a shot at the other end, Allsopp clearing. Crate then fouled McCallum but when the kick was sent in Creilly intervened. Back at the Forest goal a corner was conceded by Scott and when the ball came in there was an almighty melee in the Forest goalmouth with Allsopp finally clearing. Forest got up again but McKane intervened then another melee in the Forest goal saw some desperate defending and Allsopp thrice having to save. With Newcastle in full control the half time whistle went.

Upon changing ends McCallum kicked off for Forest but they were immediately pushed back as Newcastle forced the play. Crate centred, and Creilly sent in a shot which Allsopp fisted out for a corner. Well delivered it led to a Newcastle free-kick which Allsopp was able to save from Sorley. Forest then got down, and McCallum sent the ball over. They had another effort, on target from Shaw, which McCabe saved well. Wallace sprinted up the field and hit the side of the net with good shot. The local forwards pressed again, and Scott made a great intervention to stop Reay. Forest broke away and their progress was stopped unfairly by Jeffrey and a free-kick was awarded. Whilst it was cleverly delivered in it was equally cleverly cleared.

The home forwards then charged up, but Reay sent past. A corner was then won by Newcastle, and by McCracken another, with Crate shooting past. McCallum and Pike then brought the ball down, but Jeffrey cleared, and Wallace sprinted up and was fouled. From the free-kick Allsopp saved finely twice. The homesters then went in for a spot of long shooting, but the visitors' backs were solid, McInnes and Pike then taking the ball down the field. McKane cleared and when the ball fell for Scott, he crossed it back in. A free-kick resulted and from it McInnes gave to Pike who shot through reducing the arrears for Forest.

Newcastle then forced the play, and corner was won, but cleared. Wallace sent in a fine shot with Allsopp throwing away cleverly. Forest became lively for a while, but Jeffrey cleared nicely and took the ball right up the field, Graham sending in. Some exciting work followed in the Forest goal, Allsopp having to save several shots. A penalty kick was awarded to Newcastle following a foul by McCracken. The spot-kick was taken by Sorley who easily restored the three-goal cushion for Newcastle.

Immediately upon restarting Newcastle regained possession and the Forest goal was bombarded once more. Collins sent in a hot shot and was desperately unlucky to see it smash into the upright. Play from then until the end was in favour of the homesters, the ball kept near the Forest goal, but little quality was displayed by either side and what had turned out to be a very one-sided affair ended without further scoring.

Newcastle United................4 goals.

Nottingham Forest.................1 goal.

It was noted that some little unpleasantness was drafted in the game towards the end and after the departure of Higgins several of the Forest players had to be escorted from the field of play by the police. The exact cause leading to this unsavoury event was not apparent, although the general summation was that it undoubtedly stemmed from the rough play the Foresters had exhibited in the closing stages of the match.

*The referee for this game was reported as being Mr Campbell of Sunderland in the Saturday edition of the Newcastle Daily Chronicle, however in the Monday edition the referee was reported as being Mr W. Tiffin.

Newcastle Daily Chronicle (25/03/1893) p6f.
Athletic News (27/03/1893) p6b.
Newcastle Daily Chronicle (27/03/1893) p6f.
Nottingham Evening Post (27/03/1893) p4d.
Nottingham Daily Express (27/03/1893) p7c.

As to the "A's"...

NEWCASTLE UNITED 'A' RESULTS MARCH 1893					
Date		Home	Score	Away	
March 4, 1893.		Hebburn Argyle	6 - 2	Newcastle United A	Friendly
Hebburn Argyle	*Goal*, Thos. Cain; *backs*, G. Toward and F. Owens; *half-backs*, P. Inglis, J. Donald and N. Stephenson; *forwards*, W. Richardson, W. White, C. McShane, W. Stewart and A. Flynn				
Newcastle United A:	*Goal*, Whitton; *backs*, Armstrong and Crichton; *half-backs*, Cattell, Quinn and I. Ryder; *forwards*, Dodds, Gardner, Dixon, McCann and Nugent				
March 11, 1893.		Mickley	4 - 0	Newcastle United A	Northern Alliance
Mickley:	*Goal*, Winchester; *backs*, McCoull and Stokoe; *half-backs*, Paisley, Best and Mills; *forwards*, Bailey, Blackburn, Bailey, Middleton and Howdon				
Newcastle United A:	*Goal*, J. Ryder; *backs*, Rodgers and Crichton; *half-backs*, Fitzgerald, Wilde and I. Ryder; *forwards*, Nugent, Gardner, Dixon, Cattell and Dodds				
March 18, 1893.		Newcastle United A	1 - 2	Rendel	Northern Alliance
Newcastle United A:	*Goal*, Joseph Ryder; *backs*, Rodgers and Crichton; *half-backs*, Fitzgerald, Wilde and J. Ryder; *forwards*, Dodds, Gardner, Dixon, Anderson and Quinn				
Rendel:	*Goal*, R. Forster; *backs*, T. Campbell and T. Bell; *half-backs*, W. Price, J. Wardropper and R. Redpath; *forwards*, G. Southern, T. Purvis, R.A. Henderson, B. Wood and J. Heslop				
March 25, 1893		Sunderland A	2 - 2	Newcastle United A	Friendly
Sunderland A	*Goal*, Thompson; *backs*, Jenkinson and Walker; *half-backs*, Ford, Robertson and Taylor; *forwards*, Hunter, Hogarth, Dowe, Lockie and Ledger				
Newcastle United A	*Goal*, J. Ryder; *backs*, Rodgers and Crichton; *half-backs*, Fitzgerald, Wilde and I. Ryder; *forwards*, Stokoe, Gardner, Batey, Dixon and Quinn				

In other news...

Signing back on...

Good news for the supporters of football in this district, especially those of Newcastle United. Willie Graham, centre half-back in the Newcastle United eleven, has decided to stay with the club for another season and put 'pen to paper' to formalise his decision. One newspaper quoted as saying:

"In Graham the committee possess one of the best centre half-backs that is to be found at present, and they may well feel pleased at being able to keep such a sterling player with them."

Newcastle Daily Journal, 03/03/1893, [p7e].

Not a good day for our goalkeepers...

On Saturday, March 4th, Newcastle's two main goalkeepers 'swapped' places, Ryder, the reserve, stepped up to play for the first team and Whitton dropped down to play for the "A" team, it was not good news for either. As is reported Ryder conceded four goals in a seven-goal thriller against Stoke but Whitton fared even worse! In a match between Hebburn Argyle and Newcastle United "A", at Hebburn, the score was 6-2 in favour of the homesters.

April 1893

Games Played in April 1893

V	Date	F	A	R	Opposition	Competition
H	01/04/1893	5	0	W	London Casuals	Friendly
A	04/04/1893	3	3	D	Stockton	Friendly
H	08/04/1893	0	0	D	Liverpool	Friendly
H	12/04/1893	0	4	L	Sunderland	Friendly
H	15/04/1893	7	2	W	West Bromwich Albion	Friendly
A	17/04/1893	2	5	L	Everton	Friendly
H	22/04/1893	5	0	W	Accrington	Friendly
H	26/04/1893	1	0	W	Middlesbrough Ironopolis	Friendly
H	29/04/1893	5	0	W	Preston North End	Friendly

Appearances & Goals ~ April 1893

Name	Total Apps	Total Goals	Friendly Apps	Friendly Goals
Collins, James	9	9	9	9
Crate, Thomas "Tom"	9	5	9	5
Creilly, Robert "Bobby"	9		9	
Graham, William "Willie"	8	1	8	1
Jeffrey, Harry	9		9	
McCabe, Frank	1		1	
McKane, Joseph "Joe"	9		9	
Miller, James	9		9	
Pattinson, J	3	2	3	2
Quinn, Charles "Charlie"	1		1	
Reay, Harry	6	1	6	1
Sorley, John "Jock"	5	7	5	7
Thompson, Willie	6		6	
Wallace, Joseph "Joe"	7	1	7	1
Whitton, David "Dave"	8		8	

Season to Date (03/09/1892 - 29/04/1893 inclusive)

Name	Total Apps	Total Goals	League Apps	League Goals	FA Cup Apps	FA Cup Goals	Friendly Apps	Friendly Goals
Barker, John	1		1		0		0	
Collins, James	42	17	10	1	1		31	16
Coupar, William	1		0		0		1	
Crate, Thomas "Tom"	37	11	10	2	0		27	9
Creilly, Robert "Bobby"	41	3	9	1	1		31	2
Dixon, Henry	2	1	0		0		2	1
Graham, William "Willie"	42	5	10	2	1		31	3
Jeffrey, Harry	39		7		1		31	
Kirkland, J.	1						1	
McCabe, Frank	3	0			0		3	

Newcastle United 1892-93: Season Zero

Name	Total Apps	Total Goals	League Apps	League Goals	FA Cup Apps	FA Cup Goals	Friendly Apps	Friendly Goals
McIntosh, James	2	2	0		0		2	2
McKane, Joseph "Joe"	39	1	7		1		31	1
Miller, James	42		10		1		31	
Pattinson, J	3	2	0		0		3	2
Quinn, Charles "Charlie"	1		0		0		1	
Reay, Harry	35	23	9	3	1	1	25	19
Rodgers, Thomas "Tom"	1		0		0		1	
Ryder, Joseph "Joe"	1		0		0		1	
Sorley, John "Jock"	35	28	8	7	1		26	21
Thompson, Willie	33	19	7	6	1	1	25	12
Wallace, Joseph "Joe"	36	10	8	6	1		27	4
Watson, Peter	6	3	3		0		3	
Whitton, David "Dave"	40		10		1		29	

Game 36: Saturday, April 1, 1893   **Newcastle United vs. London Casuals**

Competition: Friendly   Venue: St James's Park

Newcastle United   5 - 0   London Casuals

Scorer(s): Pattinson (sh); Collins (sh, sh, sh); Crate (sh)

Goal, Dave Whitton; *backs*, Harry Jeffrey and James Miller; *half-backs*, Bobby Creilly, Tom Crate and Joe McKane; *forwards*, Harry Reay, James Collins, Willie Thompson, J Pattinson, Joe Wallace

Scorer(s): *none*

Goal, Seton; *backs*, Lodge and Nelson; *half-backs*, Grieveson, Topham and Pares; *forwards*, Sharples, Robinson, Knox, Hillary, Simpkins

Kick-Off: 4:00 PM

Though the Casuals were a well-known and well-respected amateur outfit the attendance to see them today at St James's Park was small. However, when one considers that this was a Bank Holiday weekend and there were many other attractions available to the public, it was perhaps not too surprising to see such a 'disappointing' gate.

Thompson got the ball rolling for Newcastle and, without any further ado, they pressed the Casuals continually back and back, but could not gain any tangible return for their efforts.

Somewhat encouraged by the lack of incisiveness shown by Newcastle in front of goal, and no doubt buoyed by their own defensive display, the Casuals worked their way down on the right and from the move they earned a corner off Miller. From the corner the ball was expertly driven in but ultimately it reaped no reward for the visitors as Newcastle's defence gained control of the ball and Reay was able to bring the ball away, running well upfield but again to no great advantage.

Play was in general very slow and unexciting, but the boredom was slightly relieved when the visitors had an effort with Pares sending in a corker of a shot which Whitton did well to fist out. He was once more called into action as Jeffrey dispossessed a god run forward by the Casuals but a return from this by Knox was of the highest quality, as was Whitton in again making a magnificent save. The visitors kept up the pressure which was only relieved when 'hands' was given against Robinson.

The relief was very short-lived indeed as Sinclair returned with a good shot but sent it narrowly wide. As did Sharples some moments later. Having much the better of play now the confidence of the Casuals grew exponentially, and they continued to press. Knox had another good effort but failed to score with his shot.

Newcastle then broke away and had a period of pressing themselves, but the defence of the amateurs proved very stout indeed and they soon turned defence into attack as they worked the ball back into home territory. It was only a case of 'hands' against one of the Casuals that relieved the pressure once more.

Newcastle then had a great charge and the ball was taken well into the Casuals grounds, but Lodge made a great intervention and cleared in grand style. The homesters had hard lines in not scoring then the amateurs shook St James's Park when from a free-kick Lodge sent the ball through but as it had not touched anyone the point was disallowed. Newcastle were very lucky to be going into the break without conceding, and with the amateurs not conceding either a half that was quite staid ended without any score.

On changing ends and restarting Newcastle now had the hill in their favour and they immediately rushed down, and Thompson played a nice pass to Pattinson who put through and scored amidst great applause. A very early goal to settle the nerves of the homesters, *and their fans*!

Newcastle again attacked, and a free kick was awarded to them a couple of yards out from the goal. Cleverly Collins pushed it through off one of the Casuals and the explosive start to the second half continued. Another rush by the Newcastle forward line presented Crate with a good opportunity and he duly dispatched his shot well past Seton to register a third goal. What had been an impregnable defence in the first half was now quite crumbling in the second. Grieveson made a good run up to the Newcastle goal, but his shot was quite feeble, Jeffrey heading it away in grand fashion. Newcastle were soon back up the other end where Lodge put in a block saving grandly but at the expense of a corner. The ball was sent in and Seton saved splendidly, which he was called upon to do a second time with an effort from Thompson. Another corner was forced by Newcastle from which Reay sent behind. Seton again saved finely from another Thompson effort but the homesters continued to press until McKane, after putting in a terrific shot, sent outside. Newcastle had all the best of the game now and yet another corner was won, but from this Lodge saved splendidly. Newcastle just kept pressing and following Pattinson putting in a fine cross Collins scored the fourth goal for Newcastle.

By this time the amateurs were completely crushed, they had very little to offer in means of attack and the pressure on their defence was immense. Whilst the Casuals defence was holding out well it seemed only a matter of time before it cracked once more and sure enough Collins was able to get his hat-trick as he put through to register a fifth goal for Newcastle. With nothing else being scored the game ended with a five-nil victory to the homesters, not something one would have predicted at the end of the first half.

Newcastle United....................5 goals.
London Casuals.........................None.

Daily Telegraph (03/04/1893) p7c.
Newcastle Daily Chronicle (03/04/1893) p7b.
Sporting Life (03/04/1893) p4d.

Game 37: Monday, April 3, 1893　　　　　　　**Stockton vs. Newcastle United**

Competition: Friendly　　　　Venue: Victoria Ground　　　　Gate: 1,500

Stockton　　3 - 3　　Newcastle United

Scorer(s): Thompson (fh); McClung (fh, sh)

Goal, Charlie Ramsay; *backs*, William Lindsay and Robert McDermid; *half-backs*, Bob Shaw, James Graham and James Hutton; *forwards*, Strachan, Bill Crawford, Gavin Thompson, Robert McClung, Jack Jones

Referee: Mr. Kellcher (South Bank)

Scorer(s): Crate (fh); Graham (fh); Collins (fh)

Goal, Dave Whitton; *backs*, Harry Jeffrey and James Miller; *half-backs*, Bobby Creilly, Willie Graham and Joe McKane; *forwards*, Harry Reay, Tom Crate, Willie Thompson, Charlie Quinn, James Collins

This holiday fixture was played off at Stockton before about 1,500 spectators in splendid weather.

Newcastle kicked off and at once worked the ball well down, but a fine intervention and return by Lindsay transferred play to the Newcastle quarters. The Novocastrians kept up a brisk attack upon the Stockton goal, and Crate put well in, but Lindsay was there again and headed away. Shortly after Quinn had an effort which he sent behind.

The Stockton forwards replied and placing

the leather in the Newcastle goal Whitton performed magnificently to effect a save. Back now at the other end and McDermid intervened to save a dangerous rush from the Newcastle forwards by kicking well away.

Play was fast and very even for some time. The leather travelled very quickly between the two goals by reason of good combinations displayed by the respective forward quintets.

After several fruitless attempts by Newcastle a hot shot was sent in by Crate and beat Ramsay, and the visitors were one goal to the good. Shortly after the opening goal Graham added a second for Newcastle with a strong low shot, which Ramsey, knowing he was well beaten, made no effort stop.

The game was now a much more exciting affair, and Stockton retaliated strongly. After several scrimmages had occurred in the Newcastle goalmouth the leather was put through by (G) Thompson following another scrimmage and the deficit had been reduced.

Stockton kept up a spirited attack upon the Newcastle goal and had hard luck in not scoring on more than one occasion. Several times they sent in excellent shots, but the Newcastle defence was magnificent in getting them away in marvellous fashion on each occasion. Against the run of play Newcastle broke away fast and with a flying visit to the Stockton quarters a third goal was scored by Collins. Back on the attack came Stockton and this exciting game just got a little more exciting as McClung put through a beauty and once again the deficit was reduced to a single goal. Play continued to be very brisk, each side putting in a lot of hard work and being rewarded with some excellent efforts, but neither side could increase their score and the interval arrived.

Upon changing ends, the second half was opened by Newcastle and they made a strong effort to score, but all attempts were unavailing. Stockton then had a look in, but Jeffrey and Miller at the heart of the Newcastle defence prevailed and relieved with some strong kicking. Stockton forced a corner which Strachan delivered in well, but the ball was worked out of play. Fast end-to-end play ensued for a while but without any result for either side, the attacks having no sting in them. After one prolonged attack by Stockton a beauty of a cross was sent in by Jones and McClung headed through the equalising goal.

Newcastle made some gallant efforts to restore their lead but Lindsay and McDermid were proving to be absolute rocks and forming an impenetrable defence. A quick break by Stockton's right wing ended with Strachan sending in a splendid shot which only just cleared the bar, a lucky escape for Newcastle indeed. Both teams tried hard for a winning goal but both attacks met with excellent defences and the game ended drawn which on reflection is probably the fairest result there could have been.

Stockton ....3 goals.

Newcastle United ....3 goals.

Northern League

Darlington vs. Sheffield United: The beautifully fine weather, the other attractions available in the town and nearby areas, surely affected the attendance as it was not as expected, there being only around 2,000 witnessing the game.

Keay got the game underway for the homesters but it was the visitors who first proved dangerous through Davis but a good intervention from Bird relieved the pressure. Next Wallace put in a low shot which was got away by the feet of Barker. A break down the right by Hill made matters look ominous for Darlington but Norris this time intervened. Play was then in midfield until Waites headed the ball forward to Keay, he passed to McLaine who struck a stinging shot which gave Lilley no chance, one-nil to the homesters!

Pressing their advantage Darlington won a corner as McPherson screwed in a shot which Lilley caught but was bustled over the line, they could not however make more advantage from it.

Sheffield then pressed forward, and Hill dallied far too long when well placed in front of goal and he was dispossessed by Norris rushing in. Wallace put in a beauty which was well held by Barker under the charge of Gallacher. Then Hutchinson and Fleming who got away cleverly, and the former's shot was unlucky as it rattled and rebounded off the shins of Lilley who knew little about it. This game was turning out to be a real little corker as Hill shot well but Barker saved equally well. Darlington won a corner from which nought arose and Hill cleared well. Wallace then hit a beauty which Barker was lucky to fist out. The equalising goal when I came was a beauty! Hill took possession and ran three-quarters the length of the pitch and swerving past both backs shot through, a worthy goal indeed. The homesters tried to restore their lead but McPherson failed badly with a shot when well placed. Not a minute later and instead of having their lead restored they were behind, and it was through that man Hill again, this time with a grand snapshot. McLaine had three consecutive shots but failed with all. Gallacher was then injured in a collision with McDonald and had to retire. There was no more scoring up to the break

After the interval United were restored to eleven men as Gallacher returned and it was they who took up the pressing and Hill put in a nasty one which Barker had some difficulty getting away. Fleming rushed up the left and put in a good centre which won Darlington a free kick for 'hands' close in goal, but nothing came of it, and the visitors pressed again. For some time neither side could raise any advantage, and then Fleming put in a fine shot which Lilley pushed over the bar. From the resulting corner the ball was got away and Campbell was horrified to see his attempted clearance go straight to Davis who smashed in United's third goal. Very even play followed, both sides having chances and both defences holding up well. Gradually it was United who were getting the better of things, but they were never truly dominant. This was amply demonstrated as from conceding a corner Darlington were able to turn defence into attack and a fine oblique shot from Fleming was pushed away by Lilley but a rushing McLaine finished the score. Taking great heart from this Darlington pressed hard and won a corner which was futile as was a subsequent corner by United who saw Cain shoot wide from Gallacher's delivery. A free-kick close in resulted in another corner for the homesters but again they could not improve matters. Continuing to have the best of the play, marginally, Darlington could not find a way through and nothing further was scored.

Darlington .... 2 goals.
Sheffield United .... 3 goals.

Darlington: *Goal*, Barker; *backs*, McDonald and Norris; *half-backs*, Bird, Waites and Campbell; *forwards*, McPherson, McLaine, Keay, Hutchinson, and Fleming.

Sheffield United: *Goal*, Lilley; *backs*, Mellor and Lilley; *half-backs*, Walley, Hendry and Cain; *forwards*, Drummond, Wallace, Hill, Davis and Gallacher.

Referee: Mr Douglas (Gateshead).

Newcastle Daily Chronicle (04/04/1893) p4d.
Northern Echo (04/04/1893) p4a.

THE NORTHERN LEAGUE
RESULTS TO SATURDAY, APRIL 04 [INCLUSIVE]

Pos	Team	Pld	W	D	L	F	A	Avg.	Pts
1	Middlesbrough Ironopolis	10	9	1	0	22	6	3.6667	19
2	Newcastle United	10	5	1	4	30	19	1.5789	11
3	Sheffield United	10	4	2	4	18	16	1.1250	10
4	Middlesbrough	9	4	0	5	16	15	1.0667	8
5	Stockton	10	3	1	6	22	27	0.8148	7
6	Darlington	9	1	1	7	9	36	0.2500	3

Tuesday, April 4, 1893

Northern League. Darlington vs. Middlesbrough: The concluding match of the Northern League was played out today at Feethams. In beautiful weather around 1,500 spectators gathered to witness the event. Darlington commenced pressing and Keay put in a stinger, which Fall got away cleverly. The game became fast and exciting, perhaps slightly in favour of the homesters. McLaine came very near scoring, and then a long return from McDonald bounded just under the bar, and though, Fall managed to touch it and Fleming headed it finally through, no more than ten minutes from the start. Keay then had a couple of good efforts. Darlington kept the upper band and obtained three corners in quick succession, but without scoring. The visitors occasionally broke away but could not equalise and half-time came with Darlington a goal front.

Upon resuming each goal was attacked in turn and Fleming missed a fine chance, putting the ball straight into Fall's hands. After fifteen minutes of play Fleming put right the goalmouth and the ball was headed in McPherson, putting Darlington two in front. Within the next minute Fleming put in three hot ones in quick succession, but all were got away. Norris saved cleverly when Johnson was dangerous, and the homesters once again resumed the aggressive. At length Middlesbrough obtained a corner, which fell on McDonald's foot and rolled easily through.

Darlington .... **2 goals.**
Middlesbrough .... **1 goal.**

Northern Echo (05/04/1893) p4a.

THE NORTHERN LEAGUE
RESULTS TO TUESDAY, APRIL 04 [INCLUSIVE]

Pos	Team	Pld	W	D	L	F	A	Avg.	Pts
1	Middlesbrough Ironopolis	10	9	1	0	22	6	3.6667	19
2	Newcastle United	10	5	1	4	30	19	1.5789	11
3	Sheffield United	10	4	2	4	18	16	1.1250	10
4	Middlesbrough	10	4	0	6	16	17	0.9412	8
5	Stockton	10	3	1	6	22	27	0.8148	7
6	Darlington	10	2	1	7	11	36	0.3056	5

Game 38: Saturday, April 8, 1893 — Newcastle United vs. Liverpool

Competition: Friendly   Venue: St James's Park   Gate: 1,000

Newcastle United 0 - 0 Liverpool

Scorer(s): *none*

Goal, Dave Whitton; *backs*, Harry Jeffrey and James Miller; *half-backs*, Bobby Creilly, Willie Graham and Joe McKane; *forwards*, Harry Reay, Tom Crate, Willie Thompson, James Collins, Joe Wallace

Referee: Mr Robert Campbell (Sunderland)

Scorer(s): *none*

Goal, Matt McQueen; *backs*, Andrew Hannah and Duncan McLean; *half-backs*, John McCartney, Joe McQue and Jim McBride; *forwards*, Malcolm McVean, Tom Wyllie, John Miller, Jock Smith, Hugh McQueen

Kick-Off: 2:45 PM

Having a blank weekend in their calendar the Newcastle United executive managed to secure a fixture against the newly established Merseyside club, Liverpool. As the fledgling outfit were trying to find their feet in the shadow of their illustrious city counterparts, Everton, and having had their application to join the football league dismissed almost 'out of hand' this was seen as a decent test of the quality of the Merseyside newcomers.

Liverpool won the toss and elected to play 'down the hill' in the first half. Ralph Carr, the well-known oarsman, and one-time custodian for Newcastle East End, was received with very great enthusiasm from those gathered as he took the ceremonial kick-off this afternoon. Starting well Liverpool soon showed their mettle as they pressed strongly. A warm attack on the home goal brought about a splendid save by Whitton, and such was the strength of the attack that he was almost charged through as he held onto the ball.

Between themselves Crate and Reay worked the ball up to the other end, but McBride was very quick with his interception. In a second rush moments later, McLean was the one with the lightning interception. Smith and McLean then progressed towards the Newcastle quarters down the left wing in grand style but the final shot, coming from McLean, went easily wide of the target. A free-kick for 'hands' put the Liverpool citadel under some danger and the ball went through however as it had not toughed anyone there was consequently no score given, hard lines for Newcastle. Not disheartened Newcastle once again took up the attack and for several minutes they put severe pressure on the visitors and McQueen pulled off an almost miraculous saves on at least two occasions. This caused great excitement in the crowd. Play from then until the half time whistle was of a fast and end-to-end nature. Each goal being endangered, each defence prevailing. Whilst neither side could get an upperhand, nor could either side score, when the interval did arrive the crowd applauded both teams off the pitch in recognition of their efforts.

Upon changing ends Newcastle now had the hill in their favour and proceeded to have by far the better of play, pressing their opponents most severely for some minutes. However, try as they might, the defence of the Merseysiders was grand indeed. McBride then picked up an injury and had to retire which brought about a redoubling of effort by Newcastle in order that they may make some advantage of their numerical supremacy. Crate went close as he sent narrowly over the bar with an overhead shot then Wallace went even closer as he hit the right post with a splendid effort. Newcastle won a free-kick close to the visitor's goal, but it was to no avail. Some minutes later a corner gave them the same return. The pressure coming from Newcastle was now relentless and they had very hard lines on several occasions. Shot after shot was sent into the Liverpool goal but time and again the defence of the Merseysiders was magnificent. McLean rescued an almost certain goal from a decent effort by Reay. A cross was well delivered by Collins, but Reay headed just over bar, the goal kick relieving the pressure for some moments. Right up until the end of play Newcastle kept up the severe pressure but McLean and Hannah were wonderful in defence and McQueen, the custodian, was in absolute splendid form. For a game that had produced no goals it had never once lacked excitement.

Newcastle United ....None.

Liverpool ....None.

Athletic News (10/04/1893) p6a.
Liverpool Mercury (10/04/1893) p7j.
Manchester Courier (10/04/1893) p7d.
Newcastle Daily Chronicle (10/04/1893) p7c.
Newcastle Daily Journal (10/04/1893) p4d.
Sporting Life. Newcastle v. Liverpool. 10/04/1893) p3d.

Game 39: Wednesday, April 12, 1893 — Newcastle United vs. Sunderland

Competition: Friendly   Venue: St James's Park   Gate: 3,000

Newcastle United   0 - 4   Sunderland

Scorer(s): none

Goal, Frank McCabe; *backs*, Harry Jeffrey and James Miller; *half-backs*, Bobby Creilly, Willie Graham and Joe McKane; *forwards*, Harry Reay, Tom Crate, Jock Sorley, James Collins, J Pattinson

Referee: F. Hardisty (Middlesbrough)

Scorer(s): Millar (fh, sh); D. Hannah (fh, fh)

Goal, Ned Doig; *backs*, Tom Porteous and Robert Smellie; *half-backs*, Hughie Wilson, Billy Dunlop and William Gibson; *forwards*, Jimmy Hannah, John Harvey, Jimmy Millar, David Hannah, John Scott

Kick-Off: 6:15 PM

Following the severe defeat at the hands of Sunderland in February, a six-one thrashing at St James's Park, this match was arranged at supposedly the express behest of the Newcastle players. They wanted this match so that they could prove that the February result was not a fair reflection of their current status and/or standing.

Given it was a six-one defeat one can feel for them, but Sunderland are after all the current Football League champions, and they are indeed '*champions elect*' for this season, having handed out heavier defeats to some of their Division One opponents. Taking all that into account Newcastle really had nothing to feel too dismayed about regarding the February result. However, they wanted their chance, they got their chance, and they spectacularly blew their chance!

The Wearsiders, and a few of their supporters, travelled the short distance to Newcastle during the afternoon as the kick-off was arranged for 6:15 p.m. There were serious apprehensions about the lateness of the kick-off due to the potential fading light and the very real possibility of this game ending in darkness. However, the Newcastle executive had indicated the timing was to allow 'shop workers' and such like to attend, so irrespective of the concerns 6:15pm it remained, and it was admittedly a very good crowd for a weekday evening. Sunderland won the toss and elected to play 'down the hill' in the first half and County Councillor Routledge initiated proceedings on behalf of Newcastle.

From the very outset the homesters made several smart attacks and upon two occasions Doig had to save in the neatest style imaginable. The Wearsiders are not League champions for nothing though, and they showed up strong in defence and then broke away in true champion fashion. Their forward quintet made a grand rush down brushing aside any challenges from the homesters and getting right up to the Newcastle citadel Millar had the easiest of shots to put the visitors a goal to the good, with barely five minutes on the clock!

Another Sunderland attack was stopped when Collins and Jeffrey dispossessed Scott in grand style. Play had subsided into a very even pattern where both teams pressed without much strength and each defence repelled without too much effort. Newcastle won a free-kick in Sunderland territory and Miller put the ball in well. There was a fine display of heading on the part of the Newcastle forwards but eventually it was to no avail as the ball ended up back in the midfield area. Sorley then had an effort which was threw out by Doig. Sunderland then pressed and after numerous shots had been repulsed by the home defence (D) Hannah manged to put the ball through for Sunderland's second goal.

McCabe was called into action and made a good save from a long shot by Millar and the return was sent behind by Harvey. Newcastle then had a period where they had the best of matters but in getting up to the Sunderland citadel Jeffrey put the ball behind. In a bit of 'route one' football the goal kick went to Gibson and he put it in the middle for (D) Hannah to put through a splendid shot and Sunderland were three-nil up.

The interval was short indeed as no time was lost in restarting and upon the change of ends Newcastle now had the advantage of playing 'downhill' and exerted all pressures to make that advantage count. They put on an unrelenting display of forward-facing football. A smart shot from Graham was repulsed and the headed return by Reay went bye. In the next attack it was Reay again who tested Doig with a magnificent shot which he had great difficulty in dealing with. Sunderland then had the upperhand for a period but were ineffectual.

The home defence was kept under pressure and shot after shot was sent back by them.

However, the perseverance of the Sunderland attack finally paid off as Dunlop put a shot well into the goal where Millar connected with it well and sent it through for Sunderland's fourth goal.

Millar again proved dangerous as McCabe had to fist away an effort by him. Creilly found Sorley with a good ball upfield and he in turn gave to Crate but his shot just missed. Several times Newcastle then got close but were very weak in front of goal. For this they almost paid the price as a rush from the Sunderland forwards saw the ball once again in the Newcastle goal, but the point was disallowed for an offside. That of course would have been a five-goal margin to the Wearsiders which is what they recorded the last time which had prompted the Newcastle players 'demanding' this game. Oh, cruel is fate.

Harvey made a decent effort which was unsuccessful and the Wearsiders continued to press. On more than one occasion there were hot scrimmages in from of the Newcastle goal and McCabe made at least three excellent saves during these. He had to make another save from Millar too and as the anticipated darkness settled in the game dragged on to a very uninteresting finish with Newcastle having totally failed in their objective. The gulf between the two sides remained and was obvious to all observers, Newcastle now needed to regroup and re-focus for the challenges that lay ahead.

Newcastle United .... None.
Sunderland .... 4 goals.

This was the third meeting between these two sides this season, the first in September resulting in a two-two draw, the second, the aforementioned February meeting, and today's encounter, all the meetings being at St James's Park.

As the September meeting was against "Newcastle East End" it does not really count as a "Tyne-Wear" Derby, as technically those are between Newcastle United and Sunderland, so today is the second Tyne-Wear Derby with Sunderland having won both with an aggregate score of 10-1 to the Wearsiders!

That is of course if you count 'friendlies' as being 'countable' games. Most people don't, and personally neither do I, but it has the potential of being a 'canny' pub-quiz teaser for you, so keep

Game by Game ~ April 1893

that one, well those two actually, "in your back pocket" ready and available.

Newcastle Daily Chronicle (12/04/1893) p7d.
Newcastle Daily Chronicle (13/04/1893) p7c.
Sunderland Echo (13/04/1893) p4c.
Athletic News (17/04/1893) p6c.

Game 40: Saturday, April 15, 1893 — Newcastle United vs. West Bromwich Albion

Competition: Friendly   Venue: St James's Park

Newcastle United 7 - 2 West Bromwich Albion

Scorer(s): Sorley (fh, sh, sh, sh); Wallace (sh); Reay (sh)

Goal, Dave Whitton; *backs*, Harry Jeffrey and James Miller; *half-backs*, Bobby Creilly, Willie Graham and Joe McKane; *forwards*, Harry Reay, Tom Crate, Jock Sorley, James Collins, Joe Wallace

Referee: Mr Coleman (West Hartlepool)

Scorer(s): Boyd (fh, fh)

Goal, Josiah Joe Reader; *backs*, Charles Perry and Thomas McCulloch; *half-backs*, Willie Groves, Thomas Perry and Jack Taggart; *forwards*, William Isiah Bassett, Roderick Roddy McLeod, Henry Boyd, Thomas Pearson, Alfred Geddes

Kick-Off: 3:00 PM

Top-flight opposition again for Newcastle United as Division One side West Bromwich Albion visit St James's Park. After the abject despondency of the Sunderland game in mid-week this was not going to be the easiest of ways to bounce back for Newcastle. In striking contrast to that game Newcastle pulled out all the stops to thrash their exulted visitors, this even after being behind at break. In rather glorious weather Newcastle welcomed back Whitton in goal and Wallace at outside-left as the only two changes from Wednesday's nightmare defeat. It was the visitors who won the toss and elected to play 'down the hill' in the first half so Newcastle got the ball rolling. West Brom soon took possession and pressed strongly but nothing came from their efforts. Then a great rush by the Throstles forwards was repulsed by McKane. Newcastle then pressed but their assault on the visitors' goal was nullified by Reader sending well out from an effort by Wallace.

Newcastle pressed again and were having slightly the better of things but with little success. Groves made an important intervention to clear splendidly. The play that followed was end-to-end but quite sloppy, and there was little to no pace from either side.

Some pretty passing on the part of the West Bromwich right wing ended with the ball going over the byline. Whitton then saved splendidly from Bassett and then Perry sent an effort bye. Creilly put in some excellent play and then McKane let the visitors in with a horrendous mis-kick but Collins came to the rescue and cleared the ball from danger. Newcastle then once again had a period of holding the upperhand and Sorley brought a grand save from Reader at the expense of a corner. West Bromwich then pressed and Creilly initially got the ball away but Boyd following down returned and scored very cleverly.

A free-kick for 'hands' against Groves let the homesters back in once more but the result was far from satisfactory. The West Bromwich right wing put in some good work, but Jeffrey rushed in and dispossessed them. He played the ball through to Reay quite smartly and he in turn gave to Sorley who shot through and scored a splendid equalising goal. Such was the quality of the shot that it gave Reader no chance of making a save.

Collins dribbled up well and passed to Wallace who sent the ball high over the bar. At the other end West Brom won a corner and from a nicely placed delivery Boyd scored to put the visitors once more in front. Not too long after the half time whistle went.

On changing ends Boyd got the second half underway for the visitors who were now fighting up the hill. After some pretty play from them Collins dispossessed and sent to Wallace, he put in a grand shot, but Reader threw out. Newcastle pressed again but a foul by Sorley relieved the pressure on the visitors. Graham then sent in a nice cross for Collins who sent his effort high over the bar.

An attack by the visitors was broken up by McKane as he dispossessed the Albion forwards and made up a good deal of ground. For a while it seemed like the advantage was wasted but eventually the ball was sent to Sorley who headed through. There were vociferous appeals for an offside, but these were dismissed by the referee.

Newcastle soon regained possession and Reay had a good opportunity but sent his effort wide, as did Collins not too long after. 'Hands' against Sorley gave the briefest of respite to the Albion goal, but it was brief indeed as back came Newcastle on the press but their efforts this time were abortive. A long swift shot was sent in by Collins and Reader made a magnificent save with his feet, kicking out in a marvellous fashion. Reay then had the ball back in the Albion goal but this time the point was disallowed for offside. Not disheartened Newcastle pressed again and won a corner off Perry, but this came to nought.

Then it was the Throstles who won a corner, but the ball was run out of danger by Reay. McKane then sent the ball wide but from a free-kick taken by Jeffrey the ball fell to Sorley who scored for his hat-trick and Newcastle's third goal.

After a fine run down by Wallace the ball was given to Reay who put in a fine centre for Sorley who, spearheading a dramatic Newcastle turn-around, scored both his and Newcastle's fourth goal of the game. Following quickly on the heels of Sorley's fourth goal Newcastle secured a fifth goal courtesy of a fine shot by Wallace. Reader was called upon to make some further splendid saves as Newcastle were relentless in the pressure they exerted upon the visitors and it was not too long before goal number six arrived as Newcastle won a corner. The ball was well placed, and Newcastle pressed and from a fine pass by Graham to Sorley he scored his fifth and Newcastle's sixth goal.

Not long before time was to be called a swift shot was sent in by Reay and the Newcastle fans were in "seventh heaven" having turned around a deficit at half time into a crushing victory.

Newcastle United....................7 goals.

West Bromwich Albion..........2 goals.

Newcastle Daily Chronicle (15/04/1893) p7d.
Athletic News (17/04/1893) p7a.
Newcastle Daily Chronicle (17/04/1893) p7a.

Game 41: Monday, April 17, 1893   **Everton vs. Newcastle United**

Competition: Friendly   Venue: Goodison Park

Everton   5 - 2   Newcastle United

Scorer(s): Gordon (fh, fh, fh, sh); Hartley (fh)

Goal, David Jardine; *backs*, Charles Parry and William Lindsay; *half-backs*, John Holt, Alec Stewart and John Walker; *forwards*, Edgar Chadwick, Alf Milward, Abraham "Abe" Hartley, Patrick Gordon, John Bell

Scorer(s): Collins (sh); Crate (sh)

Goal, Dave Whitton; *backs*, Harry Jeffrey and James Miller; *half-backs*, Bobby Creilly, Willie Graham and Joe McKane; *forwards*, Harry Reay, Tom Crate, Jock Sorley, James Collins, Joe Wallace

Kick-Off: 6:00 PM

This was the "return" friendly between Newcastle and Everton, the first being at St James's Park back in January which Newcastle won by four goals to Everton's two goals. The Division One side were therefore certainly out for revenge. They had within their ranks a new signing who needed no introduction to the Newcastle fans, full-back William Lindsay, late of Stockton. Whilst this was his debut for Everton it represented his fourth game against Newcastle this season, interestingly for him he had won one, drew one and lost one so this would be his personal 'season decider'.

The attendance was described as being no better than moderate and it was Sorley for Newcastle who at promptly 6pm got the game underway on a dull evening on Merseyside.

Play was in this first period very much in favour of the homesters with Bell having a couple of efforts, each of which he put over. A break from the Newcastle right saw them take territory high up to the Everton citadel but their forwards were weak and easily prevented from scoring. Bell, Hartley and Gordon, for Everton, made repeated incursions into Newcastle territory and on one such occurrence Gordon opened the scoring for Everton.

Following the goal there was some very warm play indeed in front of the Newcastle goal as

Everton tried to press their advantage. Whitton made some capital saves, notably from Parry, Bell and Hartley. Newcastle could barely get out of their quarters during this period and their spasmodic attempts were easily countered and Everton gained another goal, this time through Hartley. Continuing to be pressured Newcastle could do almost nothing against the relentless Everton pressure. Again, and again they pressed, and Gordon sent in a wonderful shot that hit the post but only moments later had better luck as he struck for Everton's third goal.

Reeling from all this Newcastle were desperately trying to make sense of what was going on around them whilst being totally incapable of doing anything about it. Everton were running riot and had virtually all of the play. Holt sent a smashing shot in and Whitton did extremely well to fist it out. This brought about a brief rally from Newcastle and Reay and Crate combined to work their way down however no matter what Newcastle tried Walker and Holt were more than equal to any challenge they posed, and the Everton goal was never in any real danger.

Everton were awarded a free-kick and from this being well placed Gordon was able to head through for his hat-trick and Everton's fourth. Play continued to be in favour of Everton up until the whistle went for half time, but more due to their relaxing rather than the efforts of Newcastle, they did not add to their tally.

Upon the change of ends Hartley got the game underway for Everton and they immediately went on the offensive only to be checked by Jeffrey. Turning defence into attack he launched the ball upfield where it was delivered to Sorley, but his attempt was weak and easily gathered by Jardine.

Bell and Gordon then raced up to the Newcastle goal but Jeffrey and McKane defended well and eventually drove them back. Play was then concentrated around the midfield for a period until Newcastle got a free-kick in an advanced position. McKane unfortunately sent his effort from it over the bar. Everton were at this juncture playing rather apathetically and this was allowing Newcastle to hover around their goal area. Jardine had to save a smart shot from Reay but other than that the shooting of the Newcastle forwards was weak indeed and Everton knew they were not in any danger.

As if to prove a point after all the blustering from the Newcastle forwards an incisive dribble down by Hartley saw the ball being played into Gordon who scored his fourth and Everton's fifth goal as he sent a shot through, well out of the reach of Whitton.

Reay and Crate tried vainly to fight for Newcastle, but Everton always had the measure of them, Parry being in quite exceptional form and stopped any dangerous rallies in grand style. A small turning point happened in the game about ten minutes from time when Milward was hurt and had to retire from the fray.

Now facing only ten men, *a still very relaxed ten men who had a five-goal cushion it must be said*, Newcastle began to have a little more success in their attacks. However, it was still only just before time that they got any reward as there was a scrimmage in the Everton goal and Collins was able to push the ball through. This was closely followed by a second goal from Crate almost on the whistle. This 'mini rally' was however far too little, far too late, and the feeling was that even conceding two goals in quick succession, even being reduced to ten men, Everton had more than the capability to handle anything Newcastle could have mustered and the result was never in any doubt of being anything other than an emphatic Everton victory.

Everton..................................5 goals.

Newcastle United....................2 goals.

Newcastle's Harry Reay must have made quite an impression on the Everton executive as almost immediately after this game it was announced that he had officially become an Everton player! Methinks that the deal had been talked about for some time prior to this game however and the timing of the transfer was coincidental, if not somewhat mischievously partially planned.

Liverpool Echo (17/04/1893) p4b.
Liverpool Mercury. Everton v. Newcastle. 18/04/1893) p7b.
Daily Chronicle. Everton v. Newcastle United. 18/04/1893) p7d.
Newcastle Journal. Everton v. Newcastle United. 18/04/1893) p7f.
Northern Daily Telegraph. Yesterday's Matches. 18/04/1893) p7d.

Wednesday, April 19, 1893 — Newcastle United vs. Stockton

The strange story of the game that never was!

These teams were expected to face each other tonight in a 'return' friendly fixture. The kick-off was arranged for 6:10pm, which much like the Sunderland game last Wednesday, was timed principally for shop workers and such like to attend. The teams were announced in the morning's press, Newcastle United being represented by, Whitton, Jeffrey, Miller, Creilly, Graham, McKane, Collins, Crate, Thompson, Sorley and Wallace whilst the Stockton team would be: Ramsay, Shaw, McDermid, Hutton, Graham, Crawford, Atkin, Townley, Thompson, McClung and Jones.

So, everything was set, everything was arranged, and guess what? Due to some *'misunderstanding'* the Teesiders failed to appear! As put by the Newcastle Daily Chronicle *"the Teesiders did not put in an appearance"*, not sure as to when the Newcastle executive were made aware of the 'non-appearance' or whether any spectators turned up at St James's Park or not, a curious thing indeed!

Further mystery then surrounded this 'non-fixture' when the Athletic News reported that perhaps the reason for Stockton's non-appearance was not one of a 'misunderstanding' at all, but one of the Stockton management not being able to raise a team! Professionalism was being abandoned by the club and several players had already left or were in the process of being in talks with other clubs and did not wish to jeopardise any chance of a move. Lindsay as we know had left for Everton, playing for them on Monday against Newcastle. Graham and Crawford had made appearances at Grimsby looking ready to move their as had Jones, though he had also an offer from Sheffield Wednesday to consider and had been made groundsman at Stockton Cricket Club. Shaw and Ramsay had both been approached by Bootle. Was there anyone left at Stockton? It certainly sounds more plausible than a "misunderstanding".

Newcastle Daily Chronicle (19/04/1893) p7d.
Newcastle Daily Journal (19/04/1893) p7c.
Athletic News (24/04/1893) p6c.

Game 42: Saturday, April 22, 1893 — Newcastle United vs. Accrington

Competition: Friendly   Venue: St James's Park

Newcastle United 5 - 0 Accrington

Scorer(s): Crate (fh); Pattinson (fh); Collins (fh, sh, sh)

Goal, Dave Whitton; *backs*, Harry Jeffrey and James Miller; *half-backs*, Bobby Creilly, Willie Graham and Joe McKane; *forwards*, Willie Thompson, Tom Crate, J Pattinson, James Collins, Joe Wallace

Referee: Mr Coleman (Gateshead)

Scorer(s): *none*

Goal, Mason; *backs*, Hodge and Ditchfield; *half-backs*, Bowie, Matthews and Shuttleworth; *forwards*, T. Lee, Whitehead, Cookson, H. Lee, Kirkham

Kick-Off: 3:00 PM

Owing to the involvement of Accrington in the League 'Test Matches', (*the equivalent of today's Play-Offs*) they had to unfortunately send a "second eleven" to complete this engagement. Under these circumstances the game at St James's Park was robbed of the greater part of its interest, this being having, once again, another Division One side as their opposition. Still, with the weather being fine there was a reported 'fair attendance' of spectators.

Newcastle won the toss and were indeed the first team to take up the aggressive. It was with surprising ease that the first goal arrived within minutes of the kick-off. Having pressed heavily the home team were almost encamped around the Accrington goal and from a scrimmage Crate scored the opening goal. Credit needed to be given to Pattinson who did a grand job of occupying the Accrington custodian, Mason, during proceedings.

Another opportunity arose for Newcastle when 'hands' gave them a free-kick in front of the Accrington goal but from this nothing positive resulted. Within the succeeding play it was Newcastle who undoubtedly had the best of matters and when the second goal arrived it was nothing more than had been expected. Pattinson sent in a long, but swift, shot which beat Mason quite easily but after the ball had gone through there were appeals for offside leading up to the goal, this appeal not being upheld Newcastle had a two-goal lead and were already looking very comfortable.

Play then became very slow and with Newcastle perhaps relaxing just a little too much Accrington rallied somewhat and a sally into the Newcastle quarters by the by the Accrington forwards was temporarily dangerous but ultimately fruitless. Perhaps a little shaken the Newcastle forward quintet decided that they had better *"put in an appearance"*, but they came up against a solid defence. Newcastle won a corner, but nothing came from it. Collins then sent in quite a grand shot which brought an intervention from Hodge, who saved in grand style. Collins then had another attempt which he sent behind.

Mason saved splendidly following a rush by the Newcastle forwards, but ball eventually finding its way to Graham who sent his attempt over the bar. The home team continued to press heavily but were unable to score past a resolute defence though Pattinson went very close with a good shot which only just missed. Newcastle maintained their upperhand and it was just before the interval that Collins scored their third with a grand shot from distance.

Upon the changing of ends Newcastle quickly got a corner, but it was of no avail, and then a rush down by the Accrington forwards was equally fruitless. In the best period of the game for them they continued to press but found Jeffrey and Miller working hard in defence of their goal. Some severe pressure was then put upon the Accrington goal, and testament to the strength displayed by the Accrington defence it was another long shot which defeated them. Collins this time sending in a shot from distance and Newcastle's fourth point was registered. Though now four goals to the good there was no let-up in the pressure exerted by the homesters. Continuing to press Thompson saw his looping effort go over the bar and fall on the roof of the net. In a brief respite Accrington were able to break away and a great rush ensued towards the home goal, but Jeffrey intervened to end any hope for the visitors. Newcastle relentlessly pressed and with Pattinson again doing grand unselfish work and keeping the Accrington custodian occupied and unable to react to a grand long shot by Collins he brought about his hat-trick and a fifth goal for Newcastle. Right up until the final whistle Newcastle kept up the pressure but were unable to score again, and the game ended with them having a victory over Division One opposition once again, and a comprehensive victory it was too.

Newcastle United.....................5 goals.

Accrington ....None.

Just out of interest the Accrington 'first team' engaged in their Test Match with Sheffield United at a neutral venue, Nottingham, and were unfortunately beaten too, though by a much smaller margin, one goal, and it being the only goal of the game.

Newcastle Daily Chronicle (22/04/1893) p7e.
Manchester Courier (24/04/1893) p3c.
Newcastle Daily Chronicle (24/04/1893) p7b.
Newcastle Daily Journal (24/04/1893) p7c.

Game 43: Wednesday, April 26, 1893 — Newcastle United vs. Middlesbrough Ironopolis

Competition: Friendly   Venue: St James's Park

Newcastle United   1 - 0   Middlesbrough Ironopolis

Scorer(s): Collins (sh)

Goal, Dave Whitton; backs, Harry Jeffrey and James Miller; half-backs, Bobby Creilly, Willie Graham and Joe McKane; forwards, James Collins, Tom Crate, Willie Thompson, Jock Sorley, Joe Wallace

Referee: Robert Campbell (Sunderland)

Scorer(s): none

Goal, Charles Watts; backs, James Elliott and Ambrose Langley; half-backs, Robert Bob Gordon, Donald McNair and John Oliver; forwards, Frost, Archibald Hughes, William McArthur, Thomas Seymour, Wallace McReddie

Kick-Off: 6:10 PM

Crowned as Northern League champions for the third year in a row, in a season where they dropped only a single point, Middlesbrough Ironopolis visited St James's Park this evening. This match was the fifth meeting between these two sides this season, Ironopolis had won the two league fixtures and Newcastle had won the two friendly fixtures, so a season decider it was to be. As befitting the occasion both teams were strongly representative of the 'best elevens' they could muster.

As had been mentioned on the few occasions already when the kick-off had been advertised as being "post 6pm" there were very many objections to such lateness knowing full well that the end of the game would be played out in virtual darkness, or definitely have the potential to do so. As a result, the attendance was "thin".

Newcastle played against the hill in the first half but despite this handicap they held the strong eleven of the Ironopolis at bay quite easily for the first fifteen minutes or so. They not only displayed a supreme defence they also showed by far the better dribbling skills, they were stronger in their runs and their passing was most pleasing on the eye. It was all the Ironopolis could do to contain the homesters, which given they, Newcastle, had lost the previous two encounters, was not what was expected at all. During this period of supremacy Newcastle had the hardest of lines in their efforts to score. On one occasion the Newcastle forward quintet surrounded the Ironopolis goal, and after repeated attempts to put the ball through their looked to be an almost goal. A splendid shot in by Crate appeared certain to draw first blood; but at the very moment the ball was to cross the line Sorley had ran across the goal mouth, and the ball struck him and bounded back into play! What an unfortunate incident for Newcastle and what a great let-off for Ironopolis.

The Ironopolis then won a free-kick which allowed them to break away, Whitton fisted out the first effort and Oliver sent the second over the bar. However, the reprieve for their defence was temporary as they were quickly driven back again. Sorley just missed with a shot and Crate again had very harsh luck as his stinging shot looked destined for the top corner but somehow Watts managed to fist it over the cross-bar. The resulting corner was cleared, but immediately afterwards Newcastle made another endeavour to score. Several shots were fired in rapidly, but they all failed to defeat Watts, who was in rare form indeed, and he needed to be as he was most definitely the hardest worked man on the field. Try as they might though when the interval arrived the supremacy of Newcastle counted for nothing as both teams went in equal with no score.

Upon the changing ends Newcastle went straight back to their task, and now with the benefit of the hill, attacked sharply. Once again, the Ironopolis goal was besieged, and once again their defence, and Watts, stood firm and resolute. Newcastle were having no problems whatsoever in getting into decent shooting distance and positions, but each time they found the defence and Watts impregnable. Time after time he was called upon to exercise all his ingenuity and skill to throw away the balls sent in by Sorley, Collins, Thompson, Crate, and Creilly. The game then took on a far more even nature and was played out mainly in the midfield. Ironopolis it seemed where more than happy to keep the ball there, relieving their defence as it did whilst not wishing to expose that same defence should they press forward as they had seen how easy Newcastle could overwhelm them. From Newcastle's part it seemed like they had run out of ideas and were equally happy not to see their defence put under any pressure. So, it looked to all and sundry that this game was going to end in a stalemate.

All that changed with one frantic, and terrific, tussle right in front of the Ironopolis posts. The ball ping-ponged around and eventually came out to Collins whereupon he sent in a long shot which was rushed through and thus scored the first point of the game. As it turned out this was the only score of the game, so it ended with the result being a victory for Newcastle.

Newcastle United .... 1 goal.
Middlesbrough Ironopolis .... None.

Newcastle Daily Chronicle 26/04/1893) p7d.
Newcastle Daily Chronicle (27/04/1893) p7e.
Newcastle Daily Journal (27/04/1893) p7c.
Athletic News (01/05/1893) p2f.

Game by Game ~ April 1893

Game 44: Saturday, April 29, 1893 — Newcastle United vs. Preston North End

Competition: Friendly   Venue: St James's Park   Gate: 2,000

Newcastle United   5 - 0   Preston North End

Scorer(s): Sorley (fh, fh); Collins (fh, sh); Crate (sh)

Goal, Dave Whitton; *backs,* Harry Jeffrey and James Miller; *half-backs,* Bobby Creilly, Willie Graham and Joe McKane; *forwards,* James Collins, Tom Crate, Willie Thompson, Jock Sorley, Joe Wallace

Referee: Robert Campbell (Sunderland)

Scorer(s): none

Goal, James Trainer; *backs,* Nicholas John Nick Ross and James Holmes; *half-backs,* William Billy Greer, Moses Sanders and Robert Bob Holmes; *forwards,* John Jack Gordon, John Jack Barton, James Daniel Jimmy Ross, Hugh Paddy Gallacher, George Drummond

Kick-Off: 3:00 PM

The directors of Newcastle could not have been happier at securing Preston North End as the closing act in what had been a tumultuous season. Having started the season as "East End", at a new ground, St James's Park, and transitioned into the "United" midseason, the famous and popular North End seemed the perfect opportunity to say goodbye to the 1892-93 season.

In what was the finest weather they would therefore have been more than a little disappointed that there was but a meagre attendance, circa 2,000, to witness the curtain call. Newcastle won the toss and elected to play 'down the hill' in the first half and without further ado Gallacher started the ball rolling for Preston. Immediately taking possession the Newcastle forwards and ran down to the Preston citadel but they themselves were dispossessed, and (J) Ross dribbled the ball back up the field. He did well to pass through the half-back line and get himself into a decent shooting position but ended up shooting behind. Newcastle soon exerted themselves again and gave Trainer some sharp work to do, saving splendidly a long shot from Thompson but in doing so conceded a corner. The ball from the corner was temporarily cleared, but Sorley returned, and had a good chance. He however, missed and the ball going out again came to Graham who sent behind. Newcastle continued to press and following a great combined effort from the forward quintet Graham passed to Sorley who in turn sent the ball through in grand style, and the opening goal, deservedly, was Newcastle's. Without resting on their laurels, the homesters continued to press and theirs was the upperhand in every department. During this period of total dominance came a goal of the highest quality. Receiving the ball Collins sent in a shot of such speed, accuracy and pace, that even a custodian of the undoubted talent of Trainer could not hope to save. As soon as the ball had been kicked off, Newcastle relentlessly ran Preston down and after some fine play between the Newcastle forwards Sorley sent in a shot which Trainer had to throw out but the ball went to Collins who returned with a swift shot which only narrowly missed.

Preston then had a rare sortie forward. Led by (J) Ross they worked their way up and forced a corner, but this was ultimately of no advantage to the visitors. Newcastle got a couple of abortive corners of their own, Thompson only just missing from the delivery of the second. The homesters then won a free kick, and the ball was placed nicely by Jeffrey. A scrimmage ensued but Trainer saved smartly. Another sortie from the Preston forwards saw Whitton having to throw out a shot by Gordon, but 'hands' against Graham let Preston in once again, Whitton once more saved. Collins then ran down and passed all his opponents, but Trainer returned his shot, Graham then sending behind. With no more than a minute to go before the interval Sorley sent through a clinking shot thus registering his second goal of the game and Newcastle's third. Not many people would have fancied Newcastle being 3-0 up at the break against such opposition!

On restarting, play was confined to the midfield for some time before Newcastle once again took on the role of aggressors and pressed into the Preston area, but Wallace sent bye with his effort. Creilly worked the ball back again, but on playing in Crate he sent behind. Preston ran down, but McKane made a timely intervention and taking possession the ball was delivered back into the midfield. Thence Newcastle worked up on the right and gained a corner, but the ball, after being well placed, was sent past.

Play was a little faster after this, but Sorley missed when he had a splendid chance. Trainer saved grandly a shot from Thompson, and the return from Collins was sent behind. Newcastle again applied sustained pressure and from a grand return passed splendidly, but Wallace's final shot went past. Trainer then had to save, which he did excellently whilst under severe pressure. Preston forced a corner, but this was saved by Whitton then (J) Ross was unlucky to see his splendid strike hit the crossbar.

The succeeding play was for a time quite poor until a smart move from Newcastle saw Collins running the leather up the wing. Being blocked off he gave the ball to Crate. Both continued to roll forward and Crate returned the ball to his partner who with a fine, hard strike put on Newcastle's fourth goal.

This brought about a changing of positions up front for Preston as Nick Ross was sent up front to join his brother Jimmy in the attack. Preston appeared to be much the sharper in this new formation and within the closing period they had more possession and territory than they had enjoyed all game. It was however far too little, far too late.

Preston pushed forward and a shot was sent in which Whitton fisted away grandly. This allowed Newcastle to rush up and getting the ball into the Preston goalmouth there was a huge scrimmage during which Crate forced the ball through and Newcastle now had five goals to their credit. Not long after this time was called.

Newcastle United....................5 goals.

Preston North End....................None.

It was noted that Preston where only in "exhibition mode", with the result of the match inconsequential to them. Whilst Newcastle played well throughout it was seldom that Preston put forth any real effort, the Ross brothers, Grier, Drummond and Gordon being their most conspicuous.

Athletic News (01/05/1893) p2f.
Newcastle Daily Chronicle (01/05/1893) p7a.
Preston Herald (03/05/1893) p6d.

As to the "A's"...

\multicolumn{4}{c}{NEWCASTLE UNITED 'A' RESULTS APRIL 1893}
Date	Home	Score	Away
April 1, 1893.	Willington Athletic	4 – 1	Newcastle United A — *Northern Alliance*
Willington Athletic:	\multicolumn{3}{l}{*Goal*, A. Mann; *backs*, A. Bell and M. Delaney; *half-backs*, J. Fotheringham, J. Bell and A. Broadfoot; *forwards*, G. Brown, R. McLucas, J. Rice, J. Merrillees and J. Cummings}
Newcastle United A:	\multicolumn{3}{l}{*Goal*, Ryder; *backs*, Rodgers and Crichton; *half-backs*, Fitzgerald, Taylor and Quinn; *forwards*, Stokoe, Donaldson, Dixon, Simm and Dodds}
NB: This match kicked-off almost an hour late.			
April 5, 1893.	Newcastle United A	4 – 0	Willington Athletic — *Northumberland Charity Shield*
April 8, 1893.	Newcastle United A	1 – 3	Blyth — *Northern Alliance*
Newcastle United A:	\multicolumn{3}{l}{*Goal*, W. Ryder; *backs*, Rodgers and O'Donnell; *half-backs*, Quinn, Wilde and J. Ryder; *forwards*, Stokoe, Gardner, Dixon, Simm and Dodds}
Blyth:	\multicolumn{3}{l}{*Goal*, Lowery; *backs*, Gillie and Rice; *half-backs*, Southern, McCrory and Nicholson; *forwards*, Gilmour, Patten, Graham, Herdman and Murton}
Referee: Mr F. Knott. **NB:** Played at St James's Park directly at the conclusion of the first-team game against Liverpool.			
April 15, 1893.	Newcastle United A	4 – 1	Mickley — *Northern Alliance*
Newcastle United A:	\multicolumn{3}{l}{*Goal*, W. Ryder; *backs*, Rodger and Crichton; *half-backs*, Fitzgerald, Quinn and Ryder; *forwards*, Stokoe, Gardner, Dixon, Simm and Dodds}
NB: Played at St James's Park directly at the conclusion of the first-team game against West Bromwich Albion.			

Rendel Suspended

A representative committee of the Northumberland Football Association met at Yielder's Café, Bigg Market, Newcastle on Wednesday, April 12, Mr Geo. Hall presiding. The main item of interest (*to us*) is that of Rendell FC. On Saturday, April 08 they were supposed to play Shankhouse in the final of the Senior Challenge Cup but failed to arrive. They sent a telegram, *which arrived fifteen minutes **after** the game was supposed to start,* announcing their refusal to participate. They were ordered to pay the expenses incurred at Blyth that day and were suspended until the end of the present season

Tables & Statistics

Newcastle United 1892-93: Season Zero

The Northern League 1892-93 Final Standings

P	Team	Plyd	Home					Away					Total					G-Avg.	Pts
			W	D	L	F	A	W	D	L	F	A	W	D	L	F	A		
1	Middlesbrough Ironopolis	10	5	0	0	12	5	4	1	0	10	1	9	1	0	22	6	3.6667	19
2	Newcastle United	10	3	1	1	15	5	2	0	3	15	14	5	1	4	30	19	1.5789	11
3	Sheffield United	10	3	1	1	13	5	1	1	3	5	11	4	2	4	18	16	1.1250	10
4	Middlesbrough	10	4	0	1	12	5	0	0	5	5	12	4	0	6	17	17	1.0000	8
5	Stockton	10	2	1	2	14	12	1	0	4	10	15	3	1	6	24	27	0.8889	7
6	Darlington	10	2	0	3	7	16	0	1	4	4	20	2	1	7	11	36	0.3056	5

The Northern League 1892-93 ~ Final Results, All Fixtures

Date	Day	Home	Score	Away	Venue
1892-09-10	Saturday	Middlesbrough	3 - 0	Darlington	Linthorpe Road
1892-09-24	Saturday	Sheffield United	5 - 1	Newcastle East End	Bramall Lane
1892-10-01	Saturday	Stockton	3 - 3	Darlington	Victoria Ground
1892-10-01	Saturday	Newcastle East End	3 - 1	Middlesbrough	St James's Park
1892-10-08	Saturday	Sheffield United	0 - 0	Middlesbrough Ironopolis	Bramall Lane
1892-10-15	Saturday	Middlesbrough Ironopolis	2 - 0	Middlesbrough	Paradise Ground
1892-10-22	Saturday	Middlesbrough Ironopolis	3 - 2	Stockton	Paradise Ground
1892-10-29	Saturday	Middlesbrough Ironopolis	1 - 0	Sheffield United	Paradise Ground
1892-11-05	Saturday	Darlington	1 - 4	Middlesbrough Ironopolis	Feethams
1892-11-12	Saturday	Newcastle East End	5 - 0	Darlington	St James's Park
1892-11-12	Saturday	Stockton	0 - 2	Middlesbrough Ironopolis	Victoria Ground
1892-11-19	Saturday	Middlesbrough Ironopolis	3 - 2	Newcastle East End	Paradise Ground
1892-11-26	Saturday	Stockton	4 - 2	Middlesbrough	Victoria Ground
1892-11-26	Saturday	Darlington	0 - 7	Newcastle East End	Feethams
1892-12-03	Saturday	Middlesbrough Ironopolis	2 - 0	Middlesbrough	Paradise Ground
1892-12-03	Saturday	Newcastle East End	5 - 1	Stockton	St James's Park
1892-12-10	Saturday	Newcastle East End	1 - 2	Middlesbrough Ironopolis	St James's Park
1892-12-17	Saturday	Stockton	2 - 5	Newcastle East End	Victoria Ground
1892-12-24	Saturday	Sheffield United	5 - 0	Darlington	Bramall Lane
1892-12-31	Saturday	Middlesbrough	2 - 1	Sheffield United	Linthorpe Road
1893-01-02	Monday	Stockton	5 - 0	Sheffield United	Victoria Ground
1893-01-07	Saturday	Darlington	3 - 2	Stockton	Feethams
1893-01-14	Saturday	Newcastle United	1 - 1	Sheffield United	St James's Park
1893-01-28	Saturday	Middlesbrough Ironopolis	4 - 1	Darlington	Paradise Ground
1893-01-30	Monday	Sheffield United	1 - 3	Stockton	Bramall Lane
1893-02-11	Saturday	Middlesbrough	4 - 0	Newcastle United	Linthorpe Road
1893-02-14	Saturday	Sheffield United	2 - 1	Middlesbrough	Bramall Lane
1893-02-18	Saturday	Middlesbrough	3 - 2	Stockton	Linthorpe Road
1893-04-03	Monday	Darlington	2 - 3	Sheffield United	Feethams
1893-04-04	Tuesday	Darlington	2 - 1	Middlesbrough	Feethams

Northern League Games: 10			
Won	5	50%	
Drew	1	10%	
Lost	4	40%	

Northern League Goals: 49		
Scored	Conceded	GD
30*	19†	11
*Inc. 2 Own Goal(s)	†Inc. 1 Own Goal(s)	

Northern League Game Progression			
	Result		
Standing at Half Time	Won	Drew	Lost
Ahead	4	0	2
Level	1	1	2
Behind	0	0	1

Goal Distribution						
	Scored			Conceded		
	Ttl	FH	SH	Ttl	FH	SH
Home	17	9	8	8	3	5
Away	15	7	8	14	2	12
Total	32	16	16	22	5	17

Tables and Statistics

SEASON 1892-93 OVERALL APPEARANCES & GOALS STATISTICS

Name	Total Apps	Total Goals	League Apps	League Goals	FA Cup Apps	FA Cup Goals	Friendly Apps	Friendly Goals
Barker, John	1		1		0		0	
Collins, James	42	17	10	1	1		31	16
Coupar, William	1	0		0		0	1	
Crate, Thomas "Tom"	37	11	10	2	0		27	9
Creilly, Robert "Bobby"	41	3	9	1	1		31	2
Dixon, Henry	2	1	0		0		2	1
Graham, William "Willie"	42	5	10	2	1		31	3
Jeffrey, Harry	39		7		1		31	
Kirkland, J.	1						1	
McCabe, Frank	3		0		0		3	
McIntosh, James	2	2	0		0		2	2
McKane, Joseph "Joe"	39	1	7		1		31	1
Miller, James	42		10		1		31	
Pattinson, J	3	2	0		0		3	2
Quinn, Charles "Charlie"	1		0		0		1	
Reay, Harry	35	23	9	3	1	1	25	19
Rodgers, Thomas "Tom"	1	0	0		0		1	
Ryder, Joseph "Joe"	1	0	0		0		1	
Sorley, John "Jock"	35	28	8	7	1		26	21
Thompson, Willie	33	19	7	6	1	1	25	12
Wallace, Joseph "Joe"	36	10	8	6	1		27	4
Watson, Peter	6	3	3		0		3	
Whitton, David "Dave"	40		10		1		29	

SEASON 1892-93 ALL NEWCASTLE EAST END/UNITED GAMES

V	Date	F	A	R	Opposition	Competition
H	03/09/1892	0	1	L	Celtic	Friendly
H	07/09/1892	2	2	D	Sunderland	Friendly
H	10/09/1892	4	1	W	Middlesbrough Ironopolis	Friendly
A	17/09/1892	2	1	W	Middlesbrough Ironopolis	Friendly
A	24/09/1892	1	5	L	Sheffield United	Northern League
H	01/10/1892	3	1	W	Middlesbrough	Northern League
	06/10/1892	1	3	L	Stockton	Friendly
A	08/10/1892	1	0	W	Middlesbrough	Friendly
H	15/10/1892	7	0	W	South of Ayrshire	Friendly
H	22/10/1892	2	0	W	Heart of Midlothian	Friendly
H	29/10/1892	4	1	W	Mossend Swifts	Friendly
H	05/11/1892	2	2	D	Sheffield United	Friendly
H	12/11/1892	5	0	W	Darlington	Northern League
A	19/11/1892	2	3	L	Middlesbrough Ironopolis	Northern League
A	26/11/1892	7	0	W	Darlington	Northern League
H	03/12/1892	5	1	W	Stockton	Northern League
H	10/12/1892	1	2	L	Middlesbrough Ironopolis	Northern League
A	17/12/1892	5	2	W	Stockton	Northern League
H	24/12/1892	2	1	W	Middlesbrough	Friendly

Newcastle United 1892-93: Season Zero

					SEASON 1892-93 ALL NEWCASTLE EAST END/UNITED GAMES	
V	Date	F	A	R	Opposition	Competition
A	26/12/1892	0	1	L	The Wednesday	Friendly
H	31/12/1892	8	1	W	Corinthians	Friendly
H	02/01/1893	4	2	W	Everton	Friendly
H	03/01/1893	4	0	W	Glasgow Rangers	Friendly
H	07/01/1893	3	1	W	Bolton Wanderers	Friendly
H	14/01/1893	1	1	D	Sheffield United	Northern League
H	21/01/1893	2	3	L	Middlesbrough	FA Cup [Round 1]
A	28/01/1893	2	3	L	Stockton	Friendly
H	04/02/1893	3	1	W	Stockton	Friendly
A	11/02/1893	0	4	L	Middlesbrough	Northern League
H	18/02/1893	3	2	W	Notts County	Friendly
H	25/02/1893	1	6	L	Sunderland	Friendly
H	04/03/1893	3	4	L	Stoke	Friendly
H	11/03/1893	6	1	W	Annbank	Friendly
H	18/03/1893	3	1	W	Derby County	Friendly
H	25/03/1893	4	1	W	Nottingham Forest	Friendly
H	01/04/1893	5	0	W	London Casuals	Friendly
A	04/04/1893	3	3	D	Stockton	Friendly
H	08/04/1893	0	0	D	Liverpool	Friendly
H	12/04/1893	0	4	L	Sunderland	Friendly
H	15/04/1893	7	2	W	West Bromwich Albion	Friendly
A	17/04/1893	2	5	L	Everton	Friendly
H	22/04/1893	5	0	W	Accrington	Friendly
H	26/04/1893	1	0	W	Middlesbrough Ironopolis	Friendly
H	29/04/1893	5	0	W	Preston North End	Friendly

The Northern Alliance…

	THE NORTHERN ALLIANCE 1892-93 FINAL STANDINGS								
Pos.	Team	Pld.	W	D	L	F	A	G.Avg	Pts
1	Sunderland 'A'	21	16	3	2	73	24	3.04167	35
2	*Blyth	22	15	1	6	81	36	2.25000	*29
3	Willington Athletic	20	13	2	5	59	33	1.78788	28
4	Southwick	18	13	1	4	56	26	2.15385	27
5	Rendel	18	10	3	5	64	28	2.28571	23
6	Shankhouse	18	10	2	6	58	34	1.70588	22
7	Gateshead NER	21	6	2	13	49	55	0.89091	14
8	**Newcastle United 'A'**	**20	6	2	12	39	55	0.70909	14
9	Mickley	21	5	3	13	31	72	0.43056	13
10	Seaham Harbour	19	4	3	12	29	74	0.39189	11
11	Ashington	19	3	2	13	35	76	0.46053	8
12	Whitburn	18	3	2	13	18	78	0.23077	8

*Blyth deducted 2 points for fielding an ineligible player.
**The home games vs. Southwick and Whitburn were not played.

Blyth Deducted 2 Points

A meeting of the Northern Alliance committee was held at Mr W. Liddle's Clock Restaurant, Clayton Street, Newcastle, on Wednesday, October 12, 1892. Mr T. Watson presided and representatives from: Blyth, Gateshead NER, Willington Athletic, Seaham Harbour, Sunderland A, Shankhouse, and Southwick were present. The main item of interest (*to us*) was the protest lodged by Gateshead NER against Blyth for playing goalkeeper Thomas Burns in their fixture on Saturday, September 24th, when they (*Gateshead*) claimed, he was not eligible to play. The protest was upheld and unanimously resolved by the two points gained by Blyth in winning said encounter being deducted.

Player Profiles

[First Team]

Barker, John

Barker has the distinction of being with all three "Newcastle's", i.e. Newcastle West End, Newcastle East End and Newcastle United, though he never made an appearance for Newcastle United. His single appearance, which qualifies him a place in our "Season Zero" was in the Northern League for Newcastle East End and both of those criteria don't qualify for "official" status, so therefore Barker may not appear in other records you see.

BRIEF BIOGRAPHY			
Born:	ud	Died:	circa 1925
Place of Birth:	England		
Position:	Forward		
Debut:	01/10/1892 v Middlesbrough		
Last Game:	01/10/1892 v Middlesbrough		
NEWCASTLE APPEARANCE DATA			
Appearances	1		

The statistics above include Northern League fixtures for the 1892-93 season but DO NOT include any friendly fixtures.

It is rumoured that at one stage Barker was suspended by United after he refused to take part in training! However true, *or false*, that rumour happens to be we do know Barker was a "bit of a character" and was not averse to a bit of controversy.

Whilst we may not know much, one thing we do know with absolute certainty, is that Barker, whilst playing for Newcastle West End, was suspended by the Football Association, this on October 02, 1889 until November 03, 1889 for "*misconduct on the field*". At the same time the Football Association also suspended James Miller, of Newcastle East End, until November 17, 1889, for the same incident. Presumably Miller's misconduct was worse than Barker's given he received a longer suspension. They must have "made up" with each other though, as both ended up playing together for Newcastle United.

Collins, James "Jimmy"

Collins, described as being a "fleet of foot forward", has a something of quite rare 'hat-trick' at Newcastle - he played for all three Newcastle's, i.e. Newcastle West End, Newcastle East End and Newcastle United, *this unlike John Barker (above) who was "on the books"*, Collins actually played for all three.

BRIEF BIOGRAPHY			
Born:	c.1872	Died:	02/01/1900
Place of Birth:	Scotland		
Position:	Inside-Right		
Debut:	24/09/1892 v Sheffield United		
Last Game:	20/02/1897 v Loughborough Town		
NEWCASTLE APPEARANCE DATA			
Appearances	52	Goals	12

The statistics above include Northern League fixtures for the 1892-93 season but DO NOT include any friendly fixtures.

He first played for Newcastle West End, and when Newcastle East End incorporated what was left of West End, he remained with the team, therefore he became an "East End" player. Then after changing their name in December 1892 from Newcastle East End to Newcastle United, to reflect said incorporation of West End into East End and alleviate the alienation felt by many former West End supporters, he became a "United" player thus completing his 'hat-trick'.

He also has the honour of playing in Newcastle East End's first ever game at St James's Park on Saturday, September 3rd, 1892 a friendly fixture against Celtic. the honour of playing in the Northern League fixture against Middlesbrough Ironopolis, on 10/12/1892, when East End first became, *albeit unilaterally*, known as "United", and he played in the first game where East End were officially sanctioned by the Football Association to call themselves 'United', that being on 21/12/1892, a FA Cup tie against Middlesbrough. So, there's another little 'hat-trick' for him. It should be noted that whilst he played in all ten Northern League fixtures of the 1892-93 season, these are not included in 'official' figures, as well this he played in 31 'friendly' fixtures in the same season, (*again, these not counted in official figures*), however, he did play in the above FA Cup [Round 1] defeat to Middlesbrough, which **is** counted in "official" figures so you may see it quoted as him appearing only the once in the 1892-93 season.

At the end of the 1892-93 season Collins left St James's Park to join Football League Division 1 side Nottingham Forest only to return 1895. After another couple of seasons with Newcastle he moved to Kent and the Southern League, with first Sheppey United and then with Chatham.

It was sadly reported that Collins died of Tetanus, commonly referred to as "lockjaw" in his day, this after contracting the disease in a Southern League game between Chatham and New Brompton, Collins playing for the former. During this game Collins reportedly fell on a piece of flint thus cutting himself and the wound becoming infected. His date of death is reported as being 02/01/1900.

Coupar, William

Unfortunately, information is sparse on Coupar, even as to how to spell his surname. This is variously spelt as Couper, Cooper or Coupar, consensus however points to the latter. Also, hailing from Middlesbrough, it is noted that the "Ironopolis" team of the day had a player called Peter Coupar, and it is unknown whether there exists a relationship between the two.

The only thing we do know for certain about Coupar is that he was quoted as being a valued member of Newcastle East End's reserves and was called upon to play in the friendly against Middlesbrough on 08/10/1892 due to them having quite an extensive injury list.

Indeed, it is that friendly which earns him his place in this record of "Season Zero" but do not be surprised if he is not mentioned elsewhere in other publications based upon Newcastle United as in that particular fixture Newcastle were still "East End" not "United".

It is also recognised that most 'official' records do not start until the 1893-94 season when Newcastle United were in the Football Association League Division Two, so again Coupar would not be included.

Crate, Thomas "Tom"

Crate is one of Newcastle's early heroes. He has the distinction of being Newcastle East End's first ever scorer at St James's Park, this when he put through the opener against Sunderland on 07/09/1892, a friendly fixture which ended a draw of two goals each. He was to unfortunately miss out on the opportunity of playing in "Newcastle United's" first ever game, due to the fact that he was suspended by the Football Association for one month, from December 22, 1892. This suspension arising from him having played during the "close season".

BRIEF BIOGRAPHY	
Place of Birth:	Ayrshire, Scotland
Position:	Inside-Right
Debut:	24/09/1892 v Sheffield United
Last Game:	05/01/1895 v Burton Swifts
NEWCASTLE APPEARANCE DATA	
Appearances 50	Goals 18

The statistics above include Northern League fixtures for the 1892-93 season but DO NOT include any friendly fixtures.

Also, *though not chronicled here*, he went on to become Newcastle United's first ever scorer in the Football League, achieving this feat when he scored in the game against Woolwich Arsenal on 02/09/1893 at Plumstead. A game that what was itself quite historical as it was the first Football League game to played in London.

Crate was also part of probably the most bizarre incident in Newcastle's history when every single player in the first-team was sacked! This came about following the infamous "friendly" match against Middlesbrough which led to the whole of the first-team being dismissed by the Committee in charge at Newcastle. For it was after that fateful 2-2 draw at Linthorpe Road (09/09/1893) that there was a huge dispute at the club over a cut in wages which was demanded of all the players, from the £2 per week they were currently being paid. This incident being accredited as the overriding factor in his move away from St James's Park. He initially stayed in the North-East however, playing for a range of local sides but was to return home to his native Ayrshire where he worked in the coal mines.

Creilly, Robert "Bobby"

Creilly was a stalwart of the early Newcastle East End teams. Although ostensibly a half-back, Creilly was probably Newcastle's first ever 'utility man', having the ability to play "anywhere and everywhere" and doing so with great aplomb it must be said.

He played in Newcastle East End's first game at St James's Park, the friendly v. Celtic, he played in the self-entitled "United's first game at St James's Park, the Northern League fixture vs. Middlesbrough Ironopolis, on 10/12/1892, and he played in the now officially entitled "Newcastle United" first game at St James's Park, a friendly encounter vs. Corinthians on 31/12/1892. He

BRIEF BIOGRAPHY		
Born:	c.1873 Died:	09/04/1907
Place of Birth:	Scotland	
Position:	Half-Back	
Debut:	24/09/1892 v Sheffield United	
Last Game:	15/04/1895 v Burton Wanderers	
NEWCASTLE APPEARANCE DATA		
Appearances 68		Goals 2

The statistics above include Northern League fixtures for the 1892-93 season but DO NOT include any friendly fixtures.

also played in Newcastle United's first game in the Football League, the aforementioned fixture vs. Woolwich Arsenal in 1893.

Dixon, Henry

Unfortunately, information is sparse indeed on Dixon. We know he was at Newcastle West End, joining circa 1889 and was still with them at the time of their demise. Subsequently he was retained by Newcastle East End upon them taking over at St James's Park and presumably he was still at Newcastle when they became "United", though that is not guaranteed as he is quoted as playing football for the Science & Art College team and also playing cricket with both the White Rose and Bath Lane clubs. Whilst his favoured position was in the centre of the forward five, he could, as and when required, play in either the inside-left or inside-right positions.

About the only thing we do know regarding Dixon with absolute certainty is that he was a valued member of Newcastle East End's reserves and was called upon to play in the friendlies against Middlesbrough on 08/10/1892 and South of Ayrshire on 15/10/1892. Indeed, it is those friendlies which earn him his place in this record of "Season Zero" but do not be surprised if he is not mentioned elsewhere or in other publications based upon Newcastle United as in those particular fixtures Newcastle were still "East End" not "United". Also, it is be recognised that most 'official' records do not start until the 1893-94 season when Newcastle were both, now most definitely entitled "United", and were in the Football Association League, namely Division Two of that league.

Graham, William "Willie"

Arriving at the beginning of the 1892-93 season, *our "Season Zero"*, Graham was one of the first signings for Newcastle East End following their move into West End's old ground of St James's Park, and there he was to prove to be a mainstay in East End's transition from Northern League to Football Association League football.

A coalminer by trade Graham was a strong half-back, preferring to be in the middle of the three, but prepared to play anywhere. He is a member of the "Fantastic Four Club" as he played in Newcastle East End's first game at St James's Park, the friendly v. Celtic, he played in the self-entitled "United's first game at St James's Park, the Northern League fixture vs. Middlesbrough Ironopolis, on 10/12/1892, and he played in the now officially entitled "United" first game at St James's Park, a friendly encounter vs. Corinthians on 31/12/1892. He also played in Newcastle United's first game in Football Association League football, the fixture vs. Woolwich Arsenal on 02/09/1893 a Plumstead.

His natural leadership abilities made him club captain and it is generally acknowledged that he was instrumental in the shaping of the fledgling "United".

BRIEF BIOGRAPHY	
Born:	12/01/1866 Died: 12/03/1937
Place of Birth:	Dreghorn, Ayrshire, Scotland
Position:	Half-Back
Debut:	24/09/1892 v Sheffield United
Last Game:	12/09/1896 v Small Heath
NEWCASTLE APPEARANCE DATA	
Appearances 109	Goals 13

The statistics above include Northern League fixtures for the 1892-93 season but DO NOT include any friendly fixtures.

Jeffrey, Harry

Jeffrey played for all three of the "Newcastle" teams, West End, East End and United. A local lad he played non-League football for various in the area before joining Newcastle West End in 1886. At the demise of Newcastle West End club, he was retained by Newcastle East End and when Newcastle became "United" he was an integral part of the set-up already.

He played in East End's first ever game at St James's Park, vs Celtic, and he played in Newcastle

BRIEF BIOGRAPHY	
Born:	c. 03/1867 Died: 16/02/1930
Place of Birth:	Newcastle upon Tyne, England
Position:	Right-Back
Debut:	24/09/1892 v Sheffield United
Last Game:	12/01/1895 v Woolwich Arsenal
NEWCASTLE APPEARANCE DATA	
Appearances 55	Goals 3

The statistics above include Northern League fixtures for the 1892-93 season but DO NOT include any friendly fixtures.

United's first game in the Football Association League, vs Woolwich Arsenal in 1893, which incidentally was also the very first Football League game ever to be played in London. Unfortunately for Jeffrey, and Newcastle, just as he had established himself as the regular right-back he was forced to give up the game because of a leg injury sustained against Sunderland in a friendly fixture on 19/01/1895 at St James's Park. Jeffrey was trying to block an advance and in doing so received a very heavy kick on the leg, totally accidental, from Scott which saw him carried off the field. In very fair play the Sunderland representatives made it known immediately that they would have no objection to Jeffrey being replaced, this at a time when there was no such thing as substitutes, *even in friendlies under normal circumstances*. Newcastle took advantage of their offer and after a few minutes Beattie came on in place of Jeffrey. At the time it was reported that his injury was not serious but it later became known that he suffered damage to both his knee-cap and his ankle and after a lengthy period of being "very ill" he had to retire from the professional game, this after only three good seasons.

Kirkland, J.
Kirkland joined Newcastle East End in the August of 1892 from Scottish side Dunlocher Hibernian. He appeared in many *"practice"* matches but only made the one appearance in the first team, and that was in the 'Charter Day' celebratory game against Stockton. As that game was a friendly it should not be surprising if you do not see Kirkland mentioned in other listings of Newcastle East End/United players.

Other than that, very little seems to be known about Kirkland apart from that he went on to appear for Bootle and Bury. He was a member of the Gigg Lane squad that won the League Division title in the 1894/95 season, making five appearances for Bury that season.

McCabe, Frank
McCabe was East End's understudy to Matt Scott during the 1890-91 season. Due to the form displayed by Scott there were very little, if any, opportunities for McCabe in the first team, this despite being a goalkeeper of no little talent himself. It appears that he left East End at the end of that season and he seemed to "drop off the radar" for a while only to return to St James's Park in early 1893 as a "trialist". He took the place of Whitton for two friendlies in March of that year and another in the April. This last game being against Sunderland and it was a heavy defeat, of four goals to none.

That was his last appearance for Newcastle as he was not retained at the end of the season, and he went on to play in non-league football with East End Wednesday and reportedly the Newcastle Barmen, a loose combination of amateurs drawn from around Tyneside.

McIntosh, James
Information is sparse on McIntosh. According to the Newcastle Daily Chronicle he arrived as a 'trialist' from *"the land-o'cakes"*, (that's Dundee to the rest of us), in December 1892. He made his one and only appearance for Newcastle in the friendly against Middlesbrough in which he performed well and scored the first goal. It was understood that an agreement had been reached with his 'parent' club, Dundee Harp, to make the trial a permanent transfer and therein lies a quaint tale…

It is reported that when Newcastle tried to register him with the Football Association, they refused to allow it due to them not recognising any team in the association called "Newcastle United"! This little snippet is from the Newcastle Daily Chronicle, (1893-01-10, p7e):

> *"The change of name of the East End Club to Newcastle United was sanctioned at a meeting of the English Association. It therefore seems singular that when Mr W.H. Golding sent up to register Macintosh of Dundee, a reply was received from Mr Alcock's office stating that they had no knowledge of such a club as Newcastle United."* adding, perhaps slightly tongue-in-cheek, *"Do they keep a record of the doings at the English Association meetings?"*

Whilst both McIntosh and Newcastle waited for the saga of his registration to be sorted it is reported he did appear in several 'reserve' fixtures in the Northern Alliance. Then, for whatever reason, even though the name change was sorted, McIntosh still never signed for Newcastle and he returned to Scotland.

McKane, Joseph "Joe"

You can't help it but McKane will always be known as the player who missed the train!

A riveter by trade, in the shipyards on the Tyne, McKane has a strong association with Newcastle. Described as being "*quick to the tackle*" he was to swiftly endear himself to the Newcastle faithful. He appeared in Newcastle East End's first appearance in the FA Cup 'proper', this against Nottingham Forest on January 16th, 1892 at Nottingham, a game East End were to lose 2-1. He

Brief Biography	
Date of Birth	c1869
Place of Birth:	Scotland
Position:	Half-Back
Debut:	24/09/1892 v Sheffield United
Last Game:	15/12/1894 v Rotherham Town
Newcastle Appearance Data	
Appearances	51

The statistics above include Northern League fixtures for the 1892-93 season but DO NOT include any friendly fixtures.

also played in Newcastle East End's first ever game at St James's Park on Saturday, September 3rd, 1892, against Celtic. Add to this the fact that he also played in Newcastle United's first game in the Football League, against Woolwich Arsenal in 1893, which incidentally was also the very first Football League game ever to be played in London. An impressive list of "firsts" for him indeed.

He was an 'ever present' in Newcastle's first season in the Football League (1893-94), playing in all 28 of their league games and their two FA Cup ties. A great regular in the first two seasons of "United's" League existence.

However, as eluded to, McKane has quite an anecdotal, and unfortunate, association with one of our North-East neighbours, Middlesbrough and a train.

The day was Saturday, February 11, 1893 and Newcastle were going to Middlesbrough for what would be their last ever fixture in the Northern League. In those days there were no such things as substitutes and money was very tight and Newcastle, like many other teams when travelling away would usually only take with them the eleven players who would be in the team, and occasionally a 'reserve' player. For Newcastle at the time though the funds were not there for them on this occasion. The team met at Newcastle Central Station to catch the train to Middlesbrough and for some reason McKane missed the train! There are various humorous stories about him getting locked in a toilet! How true these are it is impossible to say but it does put a smile on a desperate occasion as Newcastle had to play the whole match with only ten men and were soundly beaten 4-0!

Miller, James

Miller was a right-back of some note and had captained Newcastle East End. When Newcastle became 'United' he remained part of the new team and switched to left-back during their first season in the Football League. Miller, apart from being a very credible player, was a bit of a character it must be admitted.

Brief Biography	
Place of Birth:	Scotland
Position:	Right-Back
Debut:	24/09/1892 v Sheffield United
Last Game:	18/11/1893 v Northwich Victoria
Newcastle Appearance Data	
Appearances	20

The statistics above include Northern League fixtures for the 1892-93 season but DO NOT include any friendly fixtures.

Whilst playing in a Newcastle "Derby" match between West End and East End there was a fracas between Miller, then of East End, and John Barker, then of West End, soon to be team-mates in "United", but for now very much in opposition to each other. The upshot of the incident was that Miller was suspended by the Football Association, this on October 02, 1889 until November 17, 1889 for "misconduct on the field". The punishment for Barker was a suspension until November 03, 1889.

On another occasion Miller, very much akin to Barker, was suspended by United, this after announcing that he didn't like training and refused to take part in such! This suspension basically ended his career at St James's Park as he never made another appearance.

Forward thinking defender? Whilst still very much a part of the Newcastle set-up Miller, perhaps thinking well ahead, took over possession of the Wheat Sheaf Inn on Lime Street, in the Ouseburn area of Newcastle in the April of 1893. Our "Season Zero" is also a very special season to Miller, for during it he got married. This is how it was announced in the local press:

> "Followers of football in the North will universally tender their congratulations and best wishes for happiness and prosperity to James Miller, the clever popular back of the Newcastle United Club, on the occasion of his marriage, which took place on Monday to a young lady belonging to Heaton."
>
> (Newcastle Daily Chronicle, 18//01/1893)

Pattinson, J

Unfortunately, little can be found on Pattinson, not even a reliable source as to what his forename was, all references that I've been able to find simply use his initial, that being "J" of course. What we do know for certain was that Pattinson was a member of the Newcastle East End reserve, or "A" team and was called into action for the first-team during the closing month, April, of the 1892-93 season, our "Season Zero".

Ostensibly a half-back he was tried out across the forward during the three games in which he played. Against the London Casuals he was at inside-right, against Sunderland he was at outside-right and against Accrington he was at centre-forward.

In his three games he scored two goals, one in the first and one in the last, so it was unusual not to see him again in the first team. As all three games Pattinson played in were "friendly" fixtures it is highly likely that you will not see him appearing in other records so don't be surprised if you indeed don't. His inclusion in our "Season Zero" though is essential to its completeness.

Quinn, Charles "Charlie"

Quinn was a local lad who had two stints at St James's Park. In his first stint he made the single appearance in our "Season Zero", against Stockton in the April, but when Newcastle entered the Football League the following season, (1893-94), he was a regular team member. However, he was played in a variety of positions across the forward line. His very versatility had the detrimental side effect of him not being able to 'command' any one position within the first-team.

BRIEF BIOGRAPHY		
Born:	c. 1875	
Place of Birth:	Newcastle upon Tyne, England	
Position:	Outside-Right	
Debut:	23/09/1893 v Burton Swifts	
Last Game:	14/09/1895 v Liverpool	
NEWCASTLE APPEARANCE DATA		
Appearances	26	Goals	5

The statistics above include Northern League fixtures for the 1892-93 season but DO NOT include any friendly fixtures.

Whilst he appeared frequently for the reserves, he needed first-team action and this saw him move to the 'newly named' Manchester City, formerly Ardwick, in December 1894. His time there was unfortunately not a happy one as he once again failed to gain a place in the first-team so he moved back to St James's Park in 1895. His second stint at Newcastle though wasn't as successful as his first, as he made only one appearance, and that was in a 5-1 thrashing at the hands of Liverpool. Quinn subsequently slipped down into 'non-league' football with Blyth, Gateshead NER (works team) then Ashington.

Reay, Harry

Reay was one of the pioneers of the "association code" game in the North East. A locally born lad he came to prominence playing for Shankhouse Black Watch and then Newcastle East End. He was with East End when they became 'United' in 1892 and indeed captained them on several occasions.

BRIEF BIOGRAPHY		
Born:	c. 1870	
Place of Birth:	Durham, England	
Position:	Outside-Right	
Debut:	01/10/1892 v Middlesbrough	
Last Game:	11/02/1893 v Middlesbrough	
NEWCASTLE APPEARANCE DATA		
Appearances	10	Goals	4

The statistics above include Northern League fixtures for the 1892-93 season but DO NOT include any friendly fixtures.

Though the only 'league' games Reay played in for Newcastle East End/United were Northern League games, many don't consider that competition to be worthy of inclusion in 'official' statistics.

However, Reay still gets and entry in said 'official' statistics as he appeared, *and scored*, in the FA Cup tie against Middlesbrough on 21/01/1893 which ultimately ended in defeat for Newcastle. So, you may find, *actually undoubtedly will find*, many references to Reay having only one appearance for Newcastle and scoring only the one goal, as per the 'pull-out' box but to that you must add the other appearances he made in previous seasons and the other 32 of our "Season Zero".

Reay's final appearance for Newcastle was in a friendly against Everton at Goodison Park, on 17/04/1893. The next morning most Newcastle fans were surprised to read in the morning papers that Reay had been transferred - to Everton! Must have made some impression, though goodness knows how as Newcastle were thoroughly thrashed by Everton 5-2, with their two goals coming only after Everton went down to ten men through injury.

Rodgers, Thomas "Tom"

Rodgers was another recruit from *"the land o'cakes"*, (Dundee to you and I), and was first played as a 'trialist' in a friendly match with Notts County on February 18, 1893 owing to the unavailability of Harry Jeffrey. It took him a while to get his 'full' first-team debut, November 1893, but once he did, he remained the regular left-back for the rest of the season and into the beginning of the next.

BRIEF BIOGRAPHY	
Born:	17/08/1871 Died: 13/03/1946
Place of Birth:	Perth, Scotland
Position:	Left-Back
Debut:	25/11/1893 v Liverpool
Last Game:	20/10/1894 v Leicester Fosse
NEWCASTLE APPEARANCE DATA	
Appearances	24

The statistics above include Northern League fixtures for the 1892-93 season but DO NOT include any friendly fixtures.

There are varying stories as to what happened next with Rodgers, some sources are quoted as saying that as he never really settled in England place, upon losing his place he returned to Scotland, this was around the beginning of in 1895. Other sources have him as remaining in Newcastle for over 40 years working as a print compositor for a local newspaper.

As always, take your pick, but considering that when he made his "unofficial" debut, [*the aforementioned friendly against Notts County*], he was on the printing staff of the Newcastle Journal, and that he reportedly died in Newcastle in 1946, the latter of the two choices seems the more likely.

NB: You may see various references to the spelling of his surname, there are cases of him being called "Roger", or "Rodger" and the plural of both, i.e. "Rogers" and "Rodgers", however the consensus of opinion is most definitely "Rodgers" as is presented here.

Ryder, Joseph "Joe"

Ryder, born in the Westgate area of Newcastle, was one of four brothers who were to feature quite prominently in various local non-league sides but he and his older brother Isaac, an inside-left, were to be at St James's Park at the same time, but were to never appear in the same senior side. Ryder had originally joined Newcastle West End, circa 1890, and upon their demise and incorporation was retained by Newcastle East End and was with them when they became "United". However, now having to compete

BRIEF BIOGRAPHY	
Born:	15/08/1873 Died: 11/11/1945
Place of Birth:	Newcastle upon Tyne, England
Position:	Goalkeeper
Debut:	23/09/1893 v Burton Swifts
Last Game:	08/09/1894 v Burton Swifts
NEWCASTLE APPEARANCE DATA	
Appearances	2

The statistics above include Northern League fixtures for the 1892-93 season but DO NOT include any friendly fixtures.

against the likes of Whitton, Lowery and Ward for the custodian's position chances were few and far between for him. He made his "unofficial" debut against Stoke in the friendly on 04/03/1893, which is the game which earns him his inclusion in this publication and unfortunately conceded four goals in a seven-goal thriller. His "official" debut came the season after, against Burton Swifts, 23/09/1893, and he had to wait for almost a full year before he made his next appearance, 08/09/1894, and again it was against Burton Swifts. On both occasions Ryder conceded three goals. Ryder returned to non-league football and appeared for various local Tyneside clubs before ending up at Willington Athletic F.C. However, in the August of 1895 Ryder was to return to St James's Park, for the "Alliance" side, when Newcastle United starting paying their 'reserves', much to the chagrin of many amateur sides, not least Willington of course.

Sorley, John "Jock"

Sorley was captain of Newcastle East End and upon the formation of the new "United" he remained with the team. He therefore has the honour of playing in East End's first ever game at St James's Park, vs Celtic on 03/09/1892, the first game of the "unofficially" entitled 'United' against Middlesbrough Ironopolis, on 10/12/1892, in the Northern League, the first game of the now "officially" entitled 'United', a friendly against the Corinthians on 31/12/1892 and to complete the "fantastic four" he played in United's first ever Football League game when they joined Division 2 in 1893 against Woolwich Arsenal, a game in which he scored the equalising goal to ensure United took a share of the points. You could indeed say it was a "fabulous five" as the game against Woolwich was the first Football League game played in London.

BRIEF BIOGRAPHY			
Born:	26/02/1870	Died:	10/07/1945
Place of Birth:	Muirkirk, Ayrshire,, Scotland		
Position:	Centre-Forward		
Debut:	24/09/1892 v Sheffield United		
Last Game:	02/09/1893 v Woolwich Arsenal		
NEWCASTLE APPEARANCE DATA			
Appearances	10	Goals	8

The statistics above include Northern League fixtures for the 1892-93 season but DO NOT include any friendly fixtures.

Unfortunately, however the new 'United' were beset by financial problems, *this, said by many, being more a legacy of Newcastle West End than of their own making*, but it meant Sorley moving from the Tyne to the Tees as he was sold to Middlesbrough. When one considers that during the course of the 1892-93 season Sorley played eight of the ten Northern League fixtures and scored seven goals and that he also appeared in twenty-four 'friendly' fixtures, and scored an amazing twenty goals, that is one heck of a return by anyone's standard!

Our "Season Zero" is also a very special season to Sorley, for during it he got married. This is how it was announced in the local press:

"*All football supporters and players in the North-East will join in congratulations to J. Sorley, the well-known and clever forward of Newcastle United, on his marriage which took place yesterday, to a young lady belonging to Newcastle.*" (Newcastle Daily Chronicle, 30/03/1893)

Thompson, William Pringle "Willie"

Thompson was a Blacksmith by trade and played football with local non-league sides such as Bedlington Burdon, Ashington Rising Sun and the famous Shankhouse Black Watch before moving to Newcastle East End circa 1889.

Thompson, though only 5 foot 7 inches tall was once, rather curiously, described as being "*a lanky individual*" one can only assume from that description that Thompson must have been of slim build! He was also described as possessing

BRIEF BIOGRAPHY			
Born:	c. 10/1867	Died:	c. 09/1928
Place of Birth:	North Seaton, Northumberland, England		
Position:	Inside-Left		
Debut:	24/09/1892 v Sheffield United		
Last Game:	09/01/1897 v Leicester City		
NEWCASTLE APPEARANCE DATA			
Appearances	98	Goals	46

The statistics above include Northern League fixtures for the 1892-93 season but DO NOT include any friendly fixtures.

"lightning fast pace" and was able to use either foot with extreme power and accuracy. His goalscoring record of 46 goals in only 98 matches is testament to that fact. It certainly made him an early crowd favourite at St James's Park. He could play anywhere along the forward line, but his preferred positions were inside-left or centre-forward. It was in the latter position that he became the first Newcastle United player to score a hat-trick. This being in the return League Division 2 fixture against Woolwich Arsenal on 03/09/1893. A very memorable game and one for the annals of history as not only did Thompson score a hat-trick but so did Joe Wallace. As mentioned, that game was the 'return fixture' against Woolwich Arsenal, the first match being the season opener at Arsenal's Manor Field ground at Plumstead making it Newcastle United's first ever Football Association League game and the first such game ever to played in London. Yes, Thompson is a definite 'history maker' at Newcastle. It was reported that Thompson dropped back down to non-league football with Jarrow and then Ashington late in his career.

Player Profiles

Wallace, Joseph "Joe"

Wallace was a 'pocket dynamo' at only 5 foot 4 inches tall, making him one of the shortest players to have donned the colours of Newcastle. Though being of diminutive stature he was credited with having great footballing acumen and was commonly termed "*clever wee Wallace*" in varying press circles.

Making a name for himself in local football, in Ayrshire, with the delightfully named Glenbuck Cherrypickers, Wallace was enticed 'south of the border' and joined Newcastle East End around the same time as Watson and Sorley, circa 1891. The name Glenbuck Cherrypickers, originally Glenbuck Athletic (circa 1870), was said to derive from either the fact that the local men, from Glenbuck and Muirkirk, served in the 11th Hussars in the Boer War who themselves were named the "Cherry Pickers", or that almost all of the men associated with the club, be they players or officials, worked in the local pits where one of the jobs was sorting the good coal from stones, hence them being nicknamed 'cherry-pickers'.

BRIEF BIOGRAPHY			
Born:	c. 1870	Died:	c. 10/1941
Place of Birth:	Hurlford, Ayrshire, Scotland		
Position:	Inside-Left		
Debut:	24/09/1892 v Sheffield United		
Last Game:	12/04/1895 v Burslem Port Vale		
NEWCASTLE APPEARANCE DATA			
Appearances	53	Goals	27
The statistics above include Northern League fixtures for the 1892-93 season but DO NOT include any friendly fixtures.			

In any event he very soon became a firm favourite at East End and the newly entitled "United". He was a stalwart of Newcastle's first two seasons in the Football League. With his silky skills there was also a deep determination that saw him quite prepared to 'mix it up' when the occasion warranted and was never shy of the tackle. Testament to this was the bruising Newcastle 'Derby' of October 1891 when East End played West End and Wallace was injured, his shoulder being so badly put out that after consultation with a doctor he was laid up for some weeks.

Upon leaving United at the end of the 1894-95 season Wallace remained in Newcastle and joined local non-league club, Rendel, who were based in the Benwell area of Newcastle. It is sadly reported that Wallace was to fall on hard times once he left football altogether and at one stage received financial assistance and was bought clothing by Newcastle United (Joannou, 2014, p291).

Wallace deservedly has his place in Newcastle's history books as he only just missed out on being Newcastle United's first ever hat-trick scorer. 'Just' being the operative word as it was Willie Thompson who beat him to it, and both hat-tricks were scored in the same game, the six-nil thrashing of Woolwich Arsenal on 30/09/1893. Also, he played in Newcastle End's first game at St James's Park the friendly against Celtic on 03/09/1892, he played in Newcastle United's first game in the Football League, against Woolwich Arsenal on 02/09/1893. With this fixture being at Woolwich's Manor Field ground in Plumstead, it was the first Football League game to be played in London. Finally, as previously mentioned he played in the game which saw Newcastle United record their first 'double hat-trick', and indeed was one of the hat-trick scorers himself.

Watson, Peter

Watson was signed to Newcastle East End in January 1891 around the same time as Joe Wallace and Jock Sorley and he appeared regularly for them. Increasingly though he was seen very much as a reserve to Harry Jeffrey. This eventually brought about a move to Rotherham Town. For the purposes of our records this meant that Watson only made three 'league' appearances for Newcastle, but these were in the Northern League, and he made a further four appearances in 'friendly' fixtures. As such games do not get counted in 'official' statistics Watson may not appear in some records regarding Newcastle United. So, his time with United was short but not without an incident which very much made him a 'local hero'.

On the night of Sunday, March 6, 1892, Watson had occasion to be in the Byker Bank area of Newcastle where he witnessed "several roughs" assaulting a Police Officer, PC Walton. Without hesitation Watson went to the assistance of the officer and the "roughs" were duly arrested. The following Thursday Watson was presented with "a beautiful silver-mounted briar pipe" by PC Walton on behalf of the Ouseburn Division of the Newcastle Police Force. Well done Watson, proud to hear of it.

Whitton, David "Dave"

Though he only made eleven appearances in our "Season Zero" Whitton has the hat-trick of playing for Newcastle West End, Newcastle East End, and Newcastle United. He also goes into the history books at Newcastle United as their first ever goalkeeper.

He first played for Newcastle West End, and when Newcastle East End incorporated what was left of West End, he remained with the team, therefore he became an "East End" player. Then after changing their name, in December 1892, from Newcastle East End to Newcastle United, *to reflect the incorporation of West End into East End and alleviate the alienation felt by many former West End supporters*, he became a "United" player and therefore completed his "hat-trick".

The day after the meeting which saw the change of name the brand new "Newcastle United" played their first game, (*debatable*) against Middlesbrough Ironopolis, and Whitton was the goalkeeper. If that is still not enough for you, as the name change to United was not sanctioned by the Football Association until the friendly against Corinthians on 31/12/1892, (*again debatable*) then Whitton was the goalkeeper once again. However, we do have the conundrum that as the Ironopolis fixture was in the Northern League it does not count in 'official' statistics, nor does the Corinthian game, as it was a 'friendly', however, to finally close the argument we have a "Football Association Challenge Cup" tie, colloquially known as the "English Cup" and to us now as simply the FA Cup, against Middlesbrough which is counted in 'official' statistics and Whitton was the goalkeeper that day too.

As indicated of all of Whitton's appearances in the 1892-93 season only the Middlesbrough cup tie counts in the eyes of most 'official' statisticians, so you may see his data quoted as a being that single appearance FA Cup tie.

The End Bits...

Game Changer 1: Friday, December 9, 1892 — *arise Newcastle United*

One of the most important days in the history of our beloved Newcastle United, for it was on this day that a meeting of the Newcastle East End executive was held with the main item of concern being a change of the name of the club. There had been talk of many supporters of the 'old' West End club having taken great umbrage at East End taking over St James's Park, *as had been anticipated*, so this meeting was of the greatest of interest. Befittingly there was a large gathering indeed. Here is a brief synopsis of the meeting, as reported in the Newcastle Daily Chronicle the following day:

> "Newcastle East End Football Club. – A meeting of the executive of this club was last evening held in the Bath Lane Lecture Hall, Corporation Street, Newcastle, for the purpose of taking into consideration the advisability of changing the name of organisation which lately took possession of the ground at St James's Park, Leazes, Newcastle, formerly held by the now defunct West End Club.
>
> Mr Alexander Turnbull presided, and there was a very large attendance of those interested in Association football present – The Chairman, in opening the proceedings, expressed his satisfaction at witnessing such a magnificent gathering present on such a stormy evening, and thought that it augured well for the future of Association football in Newcastle. In referring to the object of the meeting, he said at the time the negotiations were in progress between the representatives of the West End and East End Football Clubs for the transference of the ground, it was tacitly understood between them that the name of the club should be altered, and the time had now arrived when some general and representative name should be chosen. (Hear, hear and applause.)
>
> He was sure that the shareholders did not look forward to any profit, their only object being to see the game played in Newcastle as it ought to be played. (Hear, hear.) Their sole object was to bring together a team to hold their own against any team in any other part of the country. (Hear, hear and applause.) This object could only be obtained by the entire and unanimous support of all parts of Newcastle. (Hear, hear.)
>
> In considering the proposed alteration of the name of the club several had been suggested. The first was "Newcastle" – (A voice: "Right") – the next was "Newcastle Central" whilst others believed it should be "Newcastle City" others the "City of Newcastle" and others "Newcastle United". (Hear, hear and applause.)
>
> It had, however, been decided to leave the selection of the name to the meeting, and in doing so he said he was confident from the attention they had given to his remarks that everything would pass harmoniously and quietly to the end. – Councillor Henderson, an old supporter of the West End Club, who described Association football as one of the most manly sports that it was possible for Englishmen to take part in, said the attendance there that evening proved that so far as Newcastle was concerned, football was not losing its influence amongst the people. (Applause.) Football was one of the best exercises that their youths could indulge in. He believed that the motive of the East End directorate in taking possession of the ground was to place before then the highest possible standard of football; and, therefore, they were deserving of the support of all lovers of Association football in Newcastle and district. (Hear, hear and applause.) He knew from the internal working of the West End club that the reason it went down was that it did not receive their support at the right time, and that was 'the beginning of the downward career which ended in entire failure'. If there was any good to result from that meeting the people of Newcastle would have to give their unanimous support to the directorate to enable them to maintain a satisfactory team. (Hear, hear.) In conclusion, Councillor Henderson said whoever had the management of the tea would have to see to it that the football field was not turned into a pugilistic arena, for this sort of thing had had the effect of disgusting many people who took an interest in the game.

The End Bits...

> *The Chairmen then invited anyone in the body of the hall who thought it advisable that the name of the club should be altered to move a resolution to that effect, which was moved, seconded and carried with only three dissentients. – In like manner three propositions were moved and seconded that the name of the club should be altered to the 'Newcastle United', 'Newcastle' and 'Newcastle City' respectively; and on a vote being taken the preponderance was in favour of the club being called the 'Newcastle United' Eventually the latter name was submitted to the meeting by the chairman as a substantive motion, when it was carried practically unanimously.*
>
> *The Chairman said immediate steps would be taken to have the named altered at once by placing the matter before the council of the English Football Association at their meeting on Monday night first. – After the transaction of other routine business, the meeting was brought to a close with the usual vote of thanks to the chairman."*
>
> The Newcastle Daily Chronicle. Saturday, December 10, 1892 [p7e]

So, there you have it, West End already Defunct, East End now no more, welcome to Newcastle United! It even earned a mention in the Sunderland Echo, or to be more precise the "Sunderland Daily Echo and Shipping Gazette":

> ### NEWCASTLE EAST END CLUB
> "At a meeting of the supporters of this club last night it was decided to change the name on the club to that of the Newcastle United"
>
> Sunderland Daily Echo. Saturday, December 10, 1892.

As in more or less testament to, *and recognition of*, the feelings that had been felt, *and eluded to previously*, regarding the risky nature of East End's move across the city and taking over West End's ground the Newcastle Daily Chronicle contained the following a couple of days after the meeting:

> "'Newcastle United' will now, subject to the approval of the English Association, be the name of East End club, and it is to be hoped that those followers of the game who wished for this and refused to support the club otherwise, will now do so. The meeting was pretty unanimous in the selection of the name on Friday last, and under the new designation, all will wish the directorate greater success than even they have had previously."
>
> The Newcastle Daily Chronicle. Tuesday, December 13, 1892.

Game Changer 2: Friday, December 23, 1892   *Newcastle United begins...*

This simple paragraph that appeared in the Newcastle Daily Chronicle today announces the 'true' beginning of the journey for Newcastle "United":

> "Newcastle United Football Club – Followers of the old East and West End clubs will be pleased to know that the English Association have agreed to the proposed change of name of the East End Club, and that henceforth it will be known as Newcastle United."
>
> The Newcastle Daily Chronicle, Friday December 23, 1892.

In its simplicity the gravity of the decision made by the Football Association could be lost. In agreeing with the representatives and fans of the club, *quite rightly too*, it may have been that the Association was presented with a *"fait accompli"*, for Newcastle East End was already calling itself "Newcastle United". The fans had readily adopted the new name since the meeting at Bath Lane, many opposition sides recognised the new name and several newspapers were already using it too. So, whether it was a fait accompli, or not, it was certainly a momentous decision on Tyneside.

Newcastle West End officially defunct, Newcastle East End officially renamed, the face of football in Newcastle and its surroundings districts had been changed forever, in what was only a matter of a few short months. So Yes, it may not have felt like it at the time, but the Football Association's sanctioning of the request is one of the most momentous decisions ever made (*for the region*) and it's a decision that we still rejoice in today.

The Conundrum — when was *Newcastle United's first game?*

So now to the vexing conundrum of when exactly was the first game played by "Newcastle United"? We have as our choices three very good candidates. These being:

1. **December 10 vs. Middlesbrough Ironopolis.** This is a good candidate and stems from the fact that this was the first game after the meeting at which the change of name from Newcastle East End to Newcastle United was voted upon and agreed by the club and its supporters. "Vox pop" as it were, surely this must be the first game as it is the club and the fans who are at the centre of the decision and tis they who will ensure the new names' adoption.

2. **December 24 game vs Middlesbrough.** In a many a circle this game is accredited with being the first game played by the 'new' Newcastle United, and it is easy to understand why. As always there is bureaucracy, and at times for very good reason, after all, without it clubs could be changing their names every other week. So, taking bureaucracy into account we arrive at the Football Association executive meeting, on Monday last, there the change of name request from the representatives of Newcastle East End had been accepted, and sanctioned, the club now, officially being called "Newcastle United". *Or was it?*

3. **December 31 vs Corinthians.** This leads us to our final candidate, which is equally as strong a candidate as the other two, if not more so. There is an old saying that "*you sometimes have to go away to see what's happening at home*". Is that the case here? The reason being is that we need to consider, *or at least consider*, the following report:

> "The English Association have sanctioned the change of name from East End to Newcastle United, and the club will assume their name on Saturday first when they play the Corinthians."

Scottish Referee, Monday December 26, 1892 [p4a].

The End — close of the season

So, that's it. Our Season Zero concludes with the following statement:

> "*Close of the Season – Football under the Association code terminated on Saturday. We would remind players that if they take part in unauthorised matches before September 1, they will render themselves ineligible to play in cup ties next season.*"

Now we can all relax and look forward to "Newcastle United 1893-94: Season 1", Newcastle United's first season in the Football Association League: Division 2.

About the Author

Born and bred in Newcastle and raised on a staple diet of stories of Hughie Gallacher from my Grandfather and Jackie Milburn from my Father there was never any doubt about where my football loyalties would lay. Going to St James's Park for the first time as a child and seeing Newcastle play a goalless draw with Everton, which if memory serves me correctly was an instantly forgettable game from a football point of view - but to me it was just amazing. I'd never seen so many people in the same place at the same time before, almost 30,000 - I was hooked straight away. Now, after more years than I care to remember, it's all about sharing the history of, to me, the greatest football club in the world with all you good people out there.

Also available from this Author:

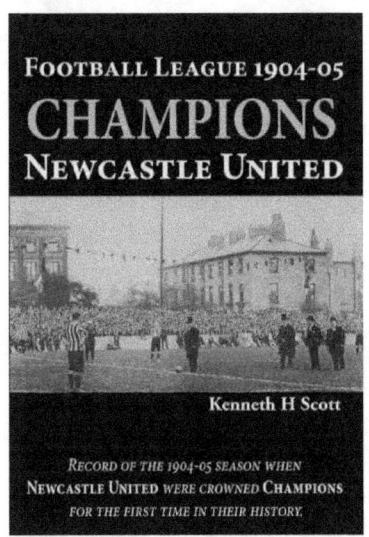

**Football League 1904-05
Champions Newcastle United**

Available in both Hardback and Paperback

ISBN: 978-0-9934201-4-6
ISBN: 978-0-9934201-3-9

**Newcastle United
Day by Day**

Available in both Hardback and Paperback

ISBN: 978-0-9934201-0-8
ISBN: 978-0-9934201-2-2

Newcastle United, Football League Champions - what a wonderful sound that is, and it was first heard at the end of the 1904-05 season. In a title race that went down to the very last game of the season Newcastle United were crowned Champions of the Football League and this book chronicles their passage through the Football League First Division, the 'top-tier' of English football, and the title. If you're a fan of Newcastle United then this is a "must read" book giving you the facts and figures for each of the steps it took to take the title, If you're a football fan in general then this book is for you too as it details game by game the 1904-05 season in all its glory...

Think of the great games, think of the great players, and even think of those players who, for whatever reason, only appeared on a single occasion (*as their contribution is equally valued*) this book has them all.

Plotting its way through the history of Newcastle United on a day-by-day basis this book delivers and highlights some of the interesting facts, figures anecdotes, and trivia that may have occurred on that day.

This book includes every debut, every first meeting against every opposition faced, each scoring debut, and much, much more...

Bibliography

Newcastle Daily Chronicle. (1892). *Chief Matches To-Day*, Saturday, September 3rd. [p7d]. Newcastle upon Tyne, England.
Athletic News and Cyclists' Journal. (1892). *Wearside Notes*, Monday, September 5th. [p7e]. Manchester, England.
Evening Chronicle. (1892). *Notes and Comments*, Monday, September 5th. [p2d]. Newcastle upon Tyne, England.
Glasgow Herald. (1892). *Newcastle East End v. Celtic*, Monday, September 5th. [p10d]. Glasgow, Scotland.
Newcastle Daily Chronicle. (1892). *Newcastle East End v. Celtic*, Monday, September 5th. [pp6f-7a]. Newcastle upon Tyne, England.
Scottish Referee. (1892). *The Celtic on Tour. Victorious at Middlesbro' and Newcastle*, Monday, September 5th. [p4b]. Glasgow, Scotland.
Town Moor. (1892). *East End v. Celtic*, The Athletic News and Cyclists' Journal. Monday, September 5th. [p7e]. Manchester, England.
Newcastle Daily Chronicle. (1892). *Football. East End v. Sunderland*, Thursday, September 8th. [p7e]. Newcastle upon Tyne, England.
Sportsman. (1892). *Football. East End v. Sunderland*, Thursday, September 8th. [p4e]. London, England.
Sunderland Daily Echo. (1892). *Yesterday's Football. Sunderland v. East End*, Thursday, September 8th. [p4e]. Sunderland, England.
Newcastle Daily Chronicle. (1892). *Newcastle East End v. Ironopolis*, Monday, September 12th. [p6f]. Newcastle upon Tyne, England.
Northern Echo. (1892). *Saturday's Football*, Monday, September 12th. [p4d]. Darlington, England.
Sporting Life. (1892). *Results of Saturday's Football Matches*, Monday, September 12th. [p4a]. London, England.
Town Moor. (1892). *Ironopolis at Newcastle*, The Athletic News and Cyclists' Journal. Monday, September 12th. [p7e]. Manchester, England.
Newcastle Daily Chronicle. (1892). *Chief Matches To-Day*, Saturday, September 17th. [p7e]. Newcastle upon Tyne, England.
Newcastle Daily Chronicle. (1892). *Ironopolis v. East End*, Monday, September 19th. [p6f]. Newcastle upon Tyne, England.
Northern Daily Telegraph. (1892). *Football. Saturday's Results*, Monday, September 19th. [p3f]. Blackburn, England.
North-Eastern Daily Gazette. (1892). *Football. Saturday's Play*, Monday, September 19th. [p3e]. Middlesbrough, England.
Yorkshire Herald. (1892). *Middlesbrough Ironopolis v. East End (Newcastle)*, Monday, September 19th. [p7e]. York, England.
Sheffield and Rotherham Independent. (1892). *Sheffield United v. Newcastle East End*, Saturday, September 24th. [p11c]. Sheffield, England.
Reynolds Newspaper. (1892). *Yesterday's Football*, Sunday, September 25th. London, England.
Birmingham Daily Post. (1892). *Sporting News, The Northern League*, Monday, September 26th. Birmingham, England.
Newcastle Daily Chronicle. (1892). *Sheffield United v. Newcastle East End*, Monday, September 26th. [p6f]. Newcastle upon Tyne, England.
Northern Echo. (1892). *Football. Sheffield United 5 Newcastle East End 1*, Monday, September 26th. [p4d]. Durham, England.
Northern Echo. (1892). *Football*, Monday, September 26th. Darlington, England.
Sheffield Daily Telegraph. (1892). *Northern League*, Monday, September 26th. [p7d]. Sheffield, England.
Sporting Life. (1892). *Sheffield United v. Newcastle East End*, Monday, September 26th. [p4c]. London, England.
Northern Echo. (1892). *Football*, Tuesday, September 27th. Darlington, England.
Newcastle Daily Chronicle. (1892). *Newcastle East End v. Middlesbrough*, Saturday, October 1st. [p7e]. Newcastle upon Tyne, England.
Evening Press. (1892). *Northern League. Middlesbrough v Newcastle East End*, Monday, October 3rd. [p4g]. Yorkshire, England.
Newcastle Daily Chronicle. (1892). *Newcastle East End v. Middlesbrough*, Monday, October 3rd. [p5f]. Newcastle upon Tyne, England.
Northern Echo. (1892). *East End v. Middlesbrough*, Monday, October 3rd. [p4e]. Darlington, England.
Sporting Life. (1892). *The Northern League*, Monday, October 3rd. [p4d]. London, England.
Newcastle Daily Chronicle. (1892). *Stockton v Newcastle East End*, Friday, October 7th. [p7e]. Newcastle upon Tyne, England.
Northern Daily Telegraph. (1892). *Football. Other Matches*, Friday, October 7th, 1892. [p3g]. Lancashire, England.
Northern Echo. (1892). *Stockton v. East End*, Friday, October 7th. [p2f]. Darlington, England.
Newcastle Daily Chronicle. (1892). *Chief Matches To-Morrow*, Saturday, October 8th. [p7d]. Newcastle upon Tyne, England.
Evening Press. (1892). *Football. Middlesbrough v. Newcastle East End*, Monday, October 10th. [p4g]. Yorkshire, England.
Newcastle Daily Chronicle. (1892). *Middlesbrough v Newcastle East End*, Monday, October 10th. [p6e]. Newcastle upon Tyne, England.
Sporting Life. (1892). *Northern League*, Monday, October 10th. [p4e]. London, England.
Town Moor. (1892). *Notes from The North*, The Athletic News and Cyclists' Journal. Monday, October 10th. [p6d]. Manchester, England.
Newcastle Daily Chronicle. (1892). *East End v South of Ayrshire*, Saturday, October 15th. [p7e]. Newcastle upon Tyne, England.
Newcastle Daily Chronicle. (1892). *Newcastle East End v. South of Ayrshire*, Monday, October 17th. [p6e]. Newcastle upon Tyne, England.
Sporting Life. (1892). *Results of Saturday's Football Matches*, Monday, October 17th. [p4a]. London, England.
T.T.Mac. (1892). *Newcastle and Middlesboro' Gossip*, The Scottish Referee. Monday, October 17th. [p4b]. Glasgow, Scotland.
Edinburgh Evening News. (1892). *Newcastle East End v. Heart of Midlothian*, Saturday, October 22nd. [p4f]. Edinburgh, Scotland.
Newcastle Daily Chronicle. (1892). *Chief Matches To-Day*, Saturday, October 22nd. [p7e]. Newcastle upon Tyne, England.
Sheffield Daily Telegraph. (1892). *Ardwick v. Newcastle United*, Sunday, October 23rd. [p6f]. Sheffield, England.
Edinburgh Evening News. (1892). *Football and Swimming Notes*, Monday, October 24th. [p4e]. Edinburgh, Scotland.
Newcastle Daily Chronicle. (1892). *East End v. Heart of Midlothian*, Monday, October 24th. [p6d]. Newcastle upon Tyne, England.
Sunderland Daily Echo. (1892). *The Northern Alliance*, Monday, October 24th. [p4b]. Sunderland, England.
T.T.Mac. (1892). *Newcastle and Middlesbrough Gossip*, The Scottish Referee. Monday, October 24th. [p4a]. Glasgow, Scotland.
Newcastle Daily Chronicle. (1892). *Chief Matches To-Day*, Saturday, October 29th. [p7e]. Newcastle upon Tyne, England.
Referee. (1892). *Football. Combination*, Sunday, October 30th. [p6c]. London, England.
Newcastle Daily Chronicle. (1892). *Newcastle East End v. Mossend Swifts*, Monday, October 31st. [p6e]. Newcastle upon Tyne, England.
T.T.Mac. (1892). *Over the Border. Newcastle and Middlesboro' Gossip*, The Scottish Referee. Monday, October 31st. [p4a]. Glasgow, Scotland.
Town Moor. (1892). *Notes from The North*, The Athletic News and Cyclists' Journal. Monday, October 31st. [p7d]. Manchester, England.
Newcastle Daily Chronicle. (1892). *East End v Sheffield United*, Monday, November 7th. [p6d]. Newcastle upon Tyne, England.
Sheffield and Rotherham Independent. (1892). *Newcastle East End v. Sheffield United*, Monday, November 7th. [p7g]. Sheffield, England.
Sporting Life. (1892). *Results of Saturday's Football Matches*, Monday, November 7th. [p4a]. London, England.
Town Moor. (1892). *East End v. Sheffield*, The Athletic News and Cyclists' Journal. Monday, November 7th. [p5e]. Manchester, England.
Newcastle Daily Chronicle. (1892). *Northern League*, Saturday, November 12th. [p7d]. Newcastle upon Tyne, England.
Newcastle Daily Chronicle. (1892). *Northern League. East End v. Darlington*, Monday, November 14th. [p6e]. Newcastle upon Tyne, England.

Newcastle United 1892-93: Season Zero

Northern Echo. (1892). *East End 5: Darlington 0*, The Northern Echo. Monday, November 14th. [p4d]. Darlington, England.
Town Moor. (1892). *East End Go Up*, The Athletic News and Cyclists' Journal. Monday, November 14th. [p6d]. Manchester, England.
Newcastle Daily Chronicle. (1892). *Chief Matches To-Morrow*, Friday, November 18th. [p7d]. Newcastle upon Tyne, England.
Athletic News and Cyclists' Journal. (1892). *Notes from the North*, Monday, November 21st. [p6a]. Manchester, England.
Newcastle Daily Chronicle. (1892). *Ironopolis v. Newcastle East End*, Monday, November 21st. [p6e]. Newcastle upon Tyne, England.
Northern Daily Telegraph. (1892). *Saturday's Results. Association.*, Monday, November 21st. [p3e]. Blackburn, England.
Northern Echo. (1892). *Saturday's Football*, Monday, November 21st. [p4e]. Darlington, England.
Sheffield Daily Telegraph. (1892). *Middlesbrough Ironopolis v Newcastle East End*, Monday, November 21st. [p7e]. Sheffield, England.
Sheffield and Rotherham Independent. (1892). *Middlesbro' Ironopolis v. East End*, Monday, November 21st. [p7d]. Sheffield, England.
Shields Daily Gazette. (1892). *Ironopolis v. Newcastle East End*, Monday, November 21st. [p3e]. South Shields, England.
Northern Echo. (1892). *To-Day's Football*, Saturday, November 26th. [p4e]. Darlington, England.
Birmingham Daily Post. (1892). *Saturday's Football, Northern League*, Monday, November 28th. [p5f]. Birmingham, England.
Newcastle Daily Chronicle. (1892). *East End (Newcastle) v. Darlington*, Monday, November 28th. [p6f]. Newcastle upon Tyne, England.
Northern Daily Telegraph. (1892). *Football. Saturday's Results. Association*, Monday, November 28th. [p3e]. Blackburn, England.
Northern Echo. (1892). *Saturday's Football. East End 7 : Darlington 0*, Monday, November 28th. [p4e]. Darlington, England.
Sheffield and Rotherham Independent. (1892). *Newcastle East End v. Darlington*, Monday, November 28th. [p7g]. Sheffield, England.
Sporting Life. (1892). *Results of Saturday's Football Matches*, Monday, November 28th. [p4a]. London, England.
Yorkshire Herald. (1892). *Northern League. Newcastle East End v. Darlington*, Monday, November 28th. [p6e]. York, England.
Newcastle Daily Chronicle. (1892). *Northern League: East End v. Stockton*, Thursday, December 1st. [p7d]. Newcastle upon Tyne, England.
Ipswich Journal. (1892). *The Week's Football*, Saturday, December 3rd. Ipswich, England.
Newcastle Daily Chronicle. (1892). *To-Day's Chief Matches*, Saturday, December 3rd. [p7e]. Newcastle upon Tyne, England.
Referee. (1892). *Northern League*, Sunday, December 4th. [p6b]. London, England.
Newcastle Daily Chronicle. (1892). *Northern League: East End v. Stockton*, Monday, December 5th. [p6c]. Newcastle upon Tyne, England.
Northern Daily Telegraph. (1892). *Football. Saturday's Results. Association*, Monday, December 5th. [p3e]. Blackburn, England.
Shields Daily Gazette and Shipping Telegraph. (1892). *East End v. Stockton*, Monday, December 5th. [p3e]. Newcastle upon Tyne, England.
Newcastle Daily Chronicle. (1892). *Football Notes: Association*, Tuesday, December 6th. [p7e]. Newcastle upon Tyne, England.
Newcastle Daily Chronicle. (1892). *Chief Matches To-Day*, Saturday, December 10th. [p7e]. Newcastle upon Tyne, England.
Forward. (1892). *Notes from the North*, The Athletic News and Cyclists' Journal. Monday, December 12th. [p7f]. Manchester, England.
London Evening Standard. (1892). *The Northern League*, London Evening Standard. Monday, December 12th. [p7f]. London, England.
Manchester Courier and Lancashire Advertiser. (1892). *Northern League*, Monday, December 12th. [p3c]. Manchester, England.
Newcastle Daily Chronicle. (1892). *East End v. Middlesbrough Ironopolis*, Monday, December 12th. [p7a]. Newcastle upon Tyne, England.
Northern Daily Telegraph. (1892). *Football. Saturday's Matches*, Monday, December 12th. [p3e]. Blackburn, England.
Northern Echo. (1892). *Newcastle East End v Ironopolis*, Monday, December 12th. [p4e]. Darlington, England.
Shields Daily Gazette and Shipping Telegraph. (1892). *East End v Ironopolis*, Monday, December 12th. [p3e]. Newcastle upon Tyne, England.
York Herald. (1892). *Northern League Newcastle East End v Ironopolis*, Monday, December 12th. [p8e]. York, England.
Newcastle Daily Chronicle. (1892). *Football Notes. Association*, Tuesday, December 13th. [p7e]. Newcastle upon Tyne, England.
Athletic News and Cyclists' Journal. (1892). *TEES SIDE*, Monday, December 19th. [p6a]. Manchester, England.
Newcastle Daily Chronicle. (1892). *Stockton v. Newcastle East End*, Monday, December 19th. [p6d]. Newcastle upon Tyne, England.
Northern Daily Mail. (1892). *Association. Northern League*, Monday, December 19th. [p4c]. West Hartlepool, England.
Northern Echo. (1892). *Stockton v. Newcastle East End*, Monday, December 19th. [p4d]. Darlington, England.
Sporting Life. (1892). *The Football Association*, Thursday, December 22nd. [p4d]. London, England.
Newcastle Daily Chronicle. (1892). *Football. Association*, Saturday, December 24th. [p7e]. Newcastle upon Tyne, England.
Newcastle Daily Chronicle. (1892). *Newcastle United v. Middlesbrough*, Monday, December 26th. [p6e]. Newcastle upon Tyne, England.
The Sportsman. (1892). *Saturday's Results*, Monday, December 26th. [p4e]. London, England.
T.T.Mac. (1892). *Newcastle and Middlesbro' gossip*, The Scottish Referee. Monday, December 26th. [p4a]. Glasgow, Scotland.
Sheffield and Rotherham Independent. (1892). *Sheffield Wednesday v. Newcastle East End*, Tuesday, December 27th. [p7g]. Sheffield, England.
Sheffield Daily Telegraph. (1892). *Sheffield Wednesday v. Newcastle East End*, Tuesday, December 27th. [p8c]. Sheffield, England.
Shields Daily Gazette. (1892). *Northern Alliance*, Friday, December 30th. [p3c]. South Shields, England.
Newcastle Daily Chronicle. (1892). *Chief Matches To-Day*, Saturday, December 31st. [p7e]. Newcastle upon Tyne, England.
Evening Chronicle. (1893). *Newcastle United v Everton*, Monday, January 2nd, 1893. [p4d]. Newcastle upon Tyne, England.
Liverpool Echo. (1893). *Today's Football. Everton v. Newcastle United*, Monday, January 2nd. [p4a]. Liverpool, England.
Newcastle Daily Chronicle. (1893). *Newcastle United v. Corinthians*, Monday, January 2nd. [p6f]. Newcastle upon Tyne, England.
Northern Echo. (1893). *Saturday's Football*, Monday, January 2nd. [p4e]. England.
Custos. (1893). *Football Notes. Association*, Newcastle Daily Journal. Tuesday, January 3rd. [p7b]. Newcastle upon Tyne, England.
Newcastle Daily Chronicle. (1893). *Newcastle United v. Everton*, Tuesday, January 3rd. [pp6-7]. Newcastle upon Tyne, England.
Newcastle Daily Journal. (1893). *Newcastle United v. Everton*, Tuesday, January 3rd. [p7d]. Newcastle upon Tyne, England.
Sheffield Daily Telegraph. (1893). *Newcastle United v. Everton*, Tuesday, January 3rd. [p8c]. Sheffield, England.
Sheffield and Rotherham Independent. (1893). *Newcastle United v. Everton*, Tuesday, January 3rd. [p8b]. Sheffield, England.
Glasgow Herald. (1893). *Newcastle United v. Glasgow Rangers*, Wednesday, January 4th. [p11d]. Glasgow, Scotland.
Newcastle Daily Chronicle. (1893). *Newcastle United v. Glasgow Rangers*, Wednesday, January 4th. [p7b]. Newcastle upon Tyne, England.
Newcastle Daily Chronicle. (1893). *To-Day's Chief Matches*, Saturday, January 7th. [p7e]. Newcastle upon Tyne, England.
Athletic News and Cyclists' Journal. (1893). *Notes from the North: Tyneside*, Monday, January 9th. [p6a]. Manchester, England.
Bolton Evening News. (1893). *The Football Field*, Monday, January 9th. [p2d]. Bolton, England.
Manchester Courier. (1893). *Newcastle United v. Bolton Wanderers*, Monday, January 9th. [p3g]. Manchester, England.
Newcastle Daily Chronicle. (1893). *Newcastle United v. Bolton Wanderers*, Monday, January 9th. [pp6-7]. Newcastle upon Tyne, England.

Bibliography

North-Eastern Daily Gazette. (1893). *Football: Northern League*, Monday, January 16th. [p4f]. Middlesbrough, England.
Newcastle Daily Chronicle. (1893). *Newcastle United v. Sheffield United*, Monday, January 16th. [p6e]. Newcastle upon Tyne, England.
Newcastle Daily Journal. (1893). *Newcastle United v. Sheffield United*, Monday, January 16th. [p7d]. Newcastle upon Tyne, England.
Northern Echo. (1893). *Newcastle United v. Sheffield United*, Monday, January 16th. [p4e]. Darlington, England.
Sheffield Daily Telegraph. (1893). *Newcastle United v. Sheffield United*, Monday, January 16th. [p7d]. Sheffield, England.
Sheffield and Rotherham Independent. (1893). *Newcastle United v. Sheffield United*, Monday, January 16th. [p7d]. Sheffield, England.
Sheffield Daily Telegraph. (1893). *Newcastle United v. Sheffield United*, Monday, January 16th. [p7d]. Sheffield, England.
Half-Back. (1893). *The Weeks Football*, The Ipswich Journal. Saturday, January 21st. [p3]. Ipswich, England.
Newcastle Daily Chronicle. (1893). *Newcastle United v. Middlesbrough*, Monday, January 23rd. [p6e]. Newcastle upon Tyne, England.
Newcastle Daily Journal. (1893). *Newcastle United v. Middlesbrough*, Monday, January 23rd. [p7e]. Newcastle upon Tyne, England.
Northern Echo. (1893). *English Cup Ties*, Monday, January 23rd. [p4d]. Darlington, England.
Newcastle Daily Chronicle. (1893). *Chief Matches To-Morrow*, Friday, January 27th. [p7e]. Newcastle upon Tyne, England.
Athletic News and Cyclists' Journal. (1893). *Notes from the North*, Monday, January 30th. [p7e]. Newcastle upon Tyne, England.
Newcastle Daily Chronicle. (1893). *Stockton v. Newcastle United*, Monday, January 30th. [p6e]. Newcastle upon Tyne, England.
Newcastle Daily Journal. (1893). *Stockton v. Newcastle United*, Monday, January 30th. [p7d]. Newcastle upon Tyne, England.
Northern Echo. (1893). *Stockton v. Newcastle United*, Monday, January 30th. [p4d]. Darlington, England.
Custos. (1893). *Football Notes*, The Newcastle Daily Journal. Tuesday, January 31st. [p7c]. Newcastle upon Tyne, England.
Newcastle Daily Chronicle. (1893). *Chief Matches To-Morrow*, Friday, February 3rd. [p7d]. Newcastle upon Tyne, England.
Newcastle Daily Chronicle. (1893). *Northern Alliance*, Monday, February 6th. [p6e]. Newcastle upon Tyne, England.
Newcastle Daily Chronicle. (1893). *Newcastle United v Stockton*, Monday, February 6th. [p6d]. Newcastle upon Tyne, England.
Northern Echo. (1893). *Newcastle United v. Stockton*, Monday, February 6th. [p4e]. Darlington, England.
Athletic News and Cyclists' Journal. (1893). *Notes from the North*, Monday, February 13th. [p7f]. Manchester, England.
Newcastle Daily Chronicle. (1893). *Northern League*, Monday, February 13th. [p6f]. Newcastle upon Tyne, England.
Northern Echo. (1893). *Saturday's Football*, Monday, February 13th. [p4d]. Darlington, England.
Shields Daily Gazette and Shipping Telegraph. (1893). *Northern League*, Monday, February 13th, 1893. [p3a]. South Shields, England.
Newcastle Daily Chronicle. (1893). *Chief Matches To-morrow*, Friday, February 17th. [p7d]. Newcastle upon Tyne, England.
Newcastle Daily Chronicle. (1893). *Newcastle United v Notts County*, Saturday, February 18th. [p7e]. Newcastle upon Tyne, England.
Newcastle Daily Chronicle. (1893). *Newcastle United v. Notts County*, Monday, February 20th. [p6e]. Newcastle upon Tyne, England.
Newcastle Daily Chronicle. (1893). *Football Notes. Association*, Monday, February 20th. [p6f]. Newcastle upon Tyne, England.
Newcastle Daily Journal. (1893). *Newcastle United v. Notts County*, Monday, February 20th. [p7d]. Newcastle upon Tyne, England.
Northern Echo. (1893). *Newcastle United 3: Notts County 2*, Monday, February 20th. [p4c]. Darlington, England.
Newcastle Daily Chronicle. (1893). *Football. Sunderland v. Newcastle United*, Thursday, February 23rd. [p7e]. Newcastle upon Tyne, England.
Newcastle Daily Chronicle. (1893). *Chief Matches To-day*, Saturday, February 25th. [p7e]. Newcastle upon Tyne, England.
Newcastle Daily Chronicle. (1893). *Newcastle United v Sunderland*, Monday, February 27th. [p6d]. Newcastle upon Tyne, England.
Northern Echo. (1893). *Newcastle United v. Sunderland*, Monday, February 27th. [p4c]. Darlington, England.
Sunderland Daily Echo and Shipping Gazette. (1893). *Sunderland v. Newcastle United*, Monday, February 27th. [p4a]. Sunderland, England.
Captain. (1893). *Football Notes. Association*, Newcastle Daily Chronicle. Tuesday, February 28th. [p7e]. Newcastle upon Tyne, England.
Newcastle Daily Chronicle. (1893). *Newcastle United v Stoke*, Saturday, March 4th. [p7e]. Newcastle upon Tyne, England.
Birmingham Daily Post. (1893). *Newcastle United v. Stoke*, Monday, March 6th. [p7f]. Birmingham, England.
Forward. (1893). *Notes from the North*, The Athletic News and Cyclists' Journal. Monday, March 6th. [p6a]. Manchester, England.
Newcastle Daily Chronicle. (1893). *Newcastle United v. Stoke*, Monday, March 6th. [p6e]. Newcastle upon Tyne, England.
Shields Daily Gazette. (1893). *Hebburn Argyle v. Newcastle United A*, Monday, March 6th. [p3c]. South Shields, England.
Sunderland Daily Echo. (1893). *The Northern Alliance*, Monday, March 6th. [p4a]. Sunderland, England.
Newcastle Daily Chronicle. (1893). *Chief Matches To-morrow*, Friday, March 10th. [p7d]. Newcastle upon Tyne, England.
Forward. (1893). *Newcastle United v. Annbank*, The Athletic News and Cyclists' Journal. Monday, March 13th. [p7a]. Manchester, England.
Newcastle Daily Chronicle. (1893). *Newcastle United v. Annbank*, Monday, March 13th. [p6d]. Newcastle upon Tyne, England.
Sunderland Daily Echo. (1893). *The Northern Alliance*, Monday, March 13th. [p4b]. Sunderland, England.
The Scotsman. (1893). *Newcastle United v. Annbank*, Monday, March 13th. [p7e]. Edinburgh, Scotland.
Derby Daily Telegraph. (1893). *Derby County v. Newcastle United*, Monday, March 20th. [p3g]. Derby, England.
Forward. (1893). *Newcastle v. Derby County*, The Athletic News and Cyclists' Journal. Monday, March 20th. [p6c]. Manchester, England.
Newcastle Daily Chronicle. (1893). *Newcastle United v. Derby County*, Monday, March 20th. [p6e]. Newcastle upon Tyne, England.
Newcastle Daily Journal. (1893). *Newcastle United v. Derby County*, Monday, March 20th. [p7d]. Newcastle upon Tyne, England.
Northern Echo. (1893). *Newcastle United v. Derby County*, Monday, March 20th. [p4b]. Darlington, England.
Sunderland Daily Echo. (1893). *The Northern Alliance*, Monday, March 20th. [p4a]. Sunderland, England.
Newcastle Daily Chronicle. (1893). *Newcastle United v Notts Forest*, Saturday, March 25th. [p7e]. Newcastle upon Tyne, England.
Newcastle Daily Chronicle. (1893). *Newcastle United v. Notts Forest*, Monday, March 27th. [p6f]. Newcastle upon Tyne, England.
Newcastle Daily Journal. (1893). *Newcastle United v. Notts Forest*, Monday, March 27th. [p7c]. Newcastle upon Tyne, England.
Nottingham Daily Express. (1893). *Notts Forest v. Newcastle United*, Monday, March 27th. [p7c]. Nottingham, England.
Town Moor. (1893). *Newcastle v. Notts Forest*, The Athletic News and Cyclists' Journal. Monday, March 27th. [p6b]. Manchester, England.
Daily Telegraph. (1893). *Other Association Games*, Monday, April 3rd. [p6e]. London, England.
Newcastle Daily Chronicle. (1893). *Newcastle United v. Casuals*, Monday, April 3rd. [p7b]. Newcastle upon Tyne, England.
Sporting Life. (1893). *Results of Saturday's Matches*, Monday, April 3rd. [p4c]. London, England.
Sunderland Daily Echo. (1893). *The Northern Alliance*, Monday, April 3rd. [p4b]. Sunderland, England.
Newcastle Daily Chronicle. (1893). *Football. Association*, Tuesday, April 4th. [p7d]. Newcastle upon Tyne, England.
Newcastle Daily Chronicle. (1893). *Stockton v. Newcastle United*, Tuesday, April 4th, 1893. [p4d]. Newcastle upon Tyne, England.

Newcastle United 1892-93: Season Zero

Northern Echo. (1893). *Stockton v. Newcastle United*, The Northern Echo. Tuesday, April 4th, 1893. [p4a]. Darlington, England.
Sunderland Daily Echo. (1893). *The Northern Alliance. Willington Athletic v. Sunderland A*, Tuesday, April 4th. [p4b]. Sunderland, England.
Newcastle Daily Chronicle. (1893). *Newcastle United v Liverpool*, Saturday, April 8th, 1893. [p7d]. Newcastle upon Tyne, England.
Liverpool Mercury. (1893). *Liverpool v. Newcastle United*, Monday, April 10th. [p7j]. Liverpool, England.
Manchester Courier and Lancashire Advertiser. (1893). *Newcastle United v. Liverpool*, Monday, April 10th. [p7d]. Manchester, England.
Newcastle Daily Chronicle. (1893). *Newcastle United v. Liverpool*, Monday, April 10th. [p7c]. Newcastle upon Tyne, England.
Newcastle Daily Journal. (1893). *Newcastle United v. Liverpool*, Monday, April 10th. [p4d]. Newcastle upon Tyne, England.
Sporting Life. (1893). *Newcastle-on-Tyne United v. Liverpool*, Monday, April 10th. [p3d]. London, England.
Sunderland Daily Echo. (1893). *The Northern Alliance*, Monday, April 10th. [p4b]. Sunderland, England.
Town Moor. (1893). *Newcastle United v. Liverpool*, The Athletic News and Cyclists' Journal. Monday, April 10th. [p6a]. Manchester, England.
Newcastle Daily Chronicle. (1893). *Sunderland v. Newcastle United*, Wednesday, April 12th. [p7d]. Newcastle upon Tyne, England.
Newcastle Daily Chronicle. (1893). *Football. Association*, Monday, April 13th. [p7e]. Newcastle upon Tyne, England.
Newcastle Daily Journal. (1893). *Newcastle United v. Sunderland*, Thursday, April 13th. [p7c]. Newcastle upon Tyne, England.
Sunderland Echo. (1893). *Sunderland v. Newcastle United*, Thursday, April 13th. [p4c]. Sunderland, England.
Athletic News and Cyclists' Journal. (1893). *Newcastle United Outclassed*, Monday, April 17th. [p6c]. Manchester, England.
Birmingham Daily Post. (1893). *Newcastle United v. West Bromwich Albion*, Monday, April 17th. [p7g]. Birmingham, England.
Liverpool Echo. (1893). *A New Player for the Everton Club*, Monday, April 17th. [p4b]. Liverpool, England.
Newcastle Daily Chronicle. (1893). *Newcastle United v. West Bromwich Albion*, Monday, April 17th. [p7a]. Newcastle upon Tyne, England.
Sunderland Daily Echo. (1893). *The Northern Alliance*, Monday, April 17th. [p4b]. Sunderland, England.
Liverpool Mercury. (1893). *Everton v. Newcastle United*, Tuesday, April 18th. [p7b]. Liverpool, England.
Newcastle Daily Chronicle. (1893). *Everton v. Newcastle United*, Tuesday, April 18th. [p7d]. Newcastle upon Tyne, England.
Newcastle Daily Journal. (1893). *Everton v. Newcastle United*, Tuesday, April 18th. [p7f]. Newcastle upon Tyne, England.
Northern Daily Telegraph. (1893). *Yesterday's Matches*, Tuesday, April 18th. [p3f]. Blackburn, England.
Newcastle Daily Chronicle. (1893). *Newcastle United v. Stockton*, Wednesday, April 19th. [p7d]. Newcastle upon Tyne, England.
Newcastle Daily Chronicle. (1893). *Newcastle United v. Accrington*, Saturday, April 22nd. [p7e]. Newcastle upon Tyne, England.
Athletic News and Cyclists' Journal. (1893). *Notes from the North. Tees-side*, Monday, April 24th, 1893. [p7c]. Manchester, England.
Manchester Courier and Lancashire Advertiser. (1893). *Sheffield United v. Accrington*, Monday, April 24th. [p3b]. Manchester, England.
Newcastle Daily Chronicle. (1893). *Newcastle United v. Accrington*, Monday, April 24th. [p7b]. Newcastle upon Tyne, England.
Newcastle Daily Chronicle. (1893). *Newcastle United v. Ironopolis*, Wednesday, April 26th. [p7d]. Newcastle upon Tyne, England.
Newcastle Daily Journal. (1893). *Newcastle United v. Ironopolis*, Thursday, April 27th. [p7c]. Newcastle upon Tyne, England.
Sunderland Daily Echo and Shipping Gazette. (1893). *Sunderland A*, Saturday, April 29th. [p3c]. Sunderland, England.
Athletic News and Cyclists' Journal. (1893). *Notes from the North. Tyneside*, Monday, May 1st, 1893. [p2f]. Manchester, England.
Newcastle Daily Chronicle. (1893). *Saturday's Football. Association*, Monday, May 1st, 1893. [p6f]. Newcastle upon Tyne, England.
Newcastle Daily Chronicle. (1893). *Newcastle United v. Preston North End*, Monday, May 1st, 1893. [p7a]. Newcastle upon Tyne, England.
Town Moor. (1893). *The Last Match*, The Athletic News and Cyclists' Journal. Monday, May 1st, 1893. [p2f]. Manchester, England.
Newcastle Daily Chronicle. (1893). *Close of the Season*, Tuesday, May 2nd, 1893. [p7d]. Newcastle upon Tyne, England.
Preston Herald. (1893). *Newcastle United v. Preston North End*, Wednesday, May 3rd. [p6d]. Preston, England.
Sunderland Daily Echo and Shipping Gazette. (1893). *Club Records. Southwick*, Wednesday, May 3rd. [p4c]. Sunderland, England.
Centre. (1893). *Northern Alliance*, Blyth Weekly News. Saturday, May 6th. [p5d]. Northumberland, England.

www.ingramcontent.com/pod-product-compliance
Lightning Source LLC
Chambersburg PA
CBHW070611010526
44118CB00012B/1485